CAPITAL PUNISHMENT AND THE BIBLE

Capital Punishment and the Bible

Gardner C. Hanks

Herald
Press

Scottdale, Pennsylvania
Waterloo, Ontario

Library of Congress Cataloging-in-Publication Data
Hanks, Gardner C., 1947-
Capital punishment and the Bible / Gardner C. Hanks.
    p. cm.
Includes bibliographical references and index.
ISBN 0-8361-9195-1 (pbk. : alk. paper)
1. Capital punishment—Biblical teaching. 2. Capital punishment—
Religious aspects—Christianity. I. Title.
BS680.C3 H36 2002
261.8′3366—dc21

                                                    2001006113

The paper used in this publication is recycled and meets the minimum
requirements of American National Standard for Information
Sciences—Permanence of Paper for Printed Library Materials, ANSI
Z39.48-1984.

Quotation on the dedication page is from a Van Morrison song title.
Bible text is from *New Revised Standard Version Bible,* copyright 1989 by
the Division of Christian Education of the National Council of the
Churches of Christ in the USA, and used by permission.

CAPITAL PUNISHMENT AND THE BIBLE
Copyright © 2002 by Herald Press, Scottdale, Pa. 15683
    Published simultaneously in Canada by
    Herald Press, Waterloo, Ont. N2L 6H7. All rights reserved
Library of Congress Control Number: 2001006113
International Standard Book Number: 0-8361-9195-1
Printed in the United States of America
Book and cover design by Jim Butti

11 10 09 08 07 06 05 04 03 02 10 9 8 7 6 5 4 3 2 1

To order or request information, please call 1-800-759-4447
(individuals); 1-800-245-7894 (trade). Website: www.mph.org

To my wife,
Suzie Hanks

"Have I told you lately
that I love you?"

Contents

Foreword

The act of the death penalty is swift and decisive; yet the conversations that surround it swirl with questions, emotions, and strong opinions. According to national polls, a majority of Christians are in favor of the death penalty. However, few of us have had to closely wrestle with the ethical implications of what the death penalty means in our lives.

Families who have lost loved ones in grievous ways often face daunting moral questions about the death penalty in ways most of us never have to address. If we argue hypothetically about the death penalty based on cost, deterrence, or the fairness of its application, we create the swirls that cause division among colleagues, churches, and families. Yet any of us would have a struggle of the soul if we were forced to confront the "other," the one accused of killing our loved one, and are asked by friends, co-workers, the media, and those in the legal system what we think about the death penalty.

I work with families who find their private grief played out in the public sector. With the shock and pain of losing someone to homicide, their questions are often sidelined due to the nature of the judicial system. Their loved ones have been killed because of politics, hatred, lust, revenge. Their questions are simple and raw: "Why? Why my son? My daughter? Was it a quick death? What were her last words?" Families discover how they have to live with questions.

Emotions exacerbated by mourning make it easy to cry out for justice, retribution, and revenge. One can understand the perspective of the victim's family—the pain, the profound loss. We become part of the crowd that gathers around the family, rallying to make certain that the offender is adequately punished. This is similar to a story of Jesus, who happens upon a madding crowd prepared to stone a woman. "Jesus," they yell, "this woman broke the law, which mandates her death. What do you think?"

Jesus' answer challenges the very core of our humanity. He does not argue against the law nor does he debate the injustice of condemning the woman but not both the man and the woman who committed the adulterous act. Rather, he focuses on the integrity of the human spirit. Jesus' challenge comes with the response, "Let the person who is without sin cast the first stone."

As I work with victims, I find that their deepest struggle is with their faith. It is commonly at this place in their grieving where I meet families for the first time. Well-meaning people (and I am one of them) express condolences and earnestly ask how the case against the accused is going. We do this partly out of curiosity, and partly out of our role as participants in the crowd rallying for justice. This conversation usually leads to the morally loaded subject regarding the death penalty. Victims should not feel responsible for answering such questions. Their loved one did not deserve the acts committed against them. The family should not be mourning, but living a joyful life, with their family intact.

Our intentions to reach out to the family are right, but our actions are often wrong. If we are to bear witness to survivors' sorrow, we need to sit with the pain and ambiguity that tragedy creates. Our role is to listen. Cry. Mourn. Laugh. Hug. Hold a hand. Sit. Eat. Be steady in the chaos. The anguish that survivors experience is an uncharted course, and their questions are very real.

Where do we find answers in the Bible? The Old Testament? The New? Is one more right than the other? The answers regarding the death penalty are complex, yet simple. Jesus was a Jewish rabbi. He was not forging a new religion but reminding people of their faith and heritage. Jesus' teachings come from the Torah, also called the Old Testament. But his life, as recorded in the New Testament, is an example that we are called to follow.

In this book, Gardner Hanks shows the complexities of the stories in the Bible. He expands the biblical verses into a living dialogue about the customs, laws, and practices of Jesus' time. This book goes beyond justifying the death penalty or making a proof-text case against the death penalty—what we often hear from pundits using the Bible as the basis for their arguments.

Reading this book gives me courage to reflect on questions that go beyond the politics of our society, the politics that demand blood for redemption. Hanks searches for something beyond the mastery of words or arguments, seeking the integrity of the spirit of Jesus. Victims should not be used as tokens for justice; they should be enveloped by a community of love that honors their pain and acknowledges their loss.

Jesus is a hard act to follow. But he never expected people to live and love to the extent that he did. He only asked us to love in the manner in which he loved. Jesus set the pattern for us to follow.

May this book be a guide for all of us grappling with the question of the law of our country and the law of our conscience.

—*Tammy Krause*
  Victim Liaison
  Soros Justice Fellow
  Institute for Justice and Peacebuilding,
      Eastern Mennonite University, Harrisonburg, Virginia

Preface

On most Wednesdays at noon, I join a number of friends at the Idaho State Capitol Building, to vigil against the death penalty. We stand quietly for an hour, to show that we oppose the state's use of capital punishment. A couple of banners announce what we are doing to passing motorists.

Most people driving by show no emotion whatsoever, doing their best to avoid eye contact. A few shout words of encouragement or give us the thumbs-up sign. A few others yell words of opposition, occasionally obscene.

This last group falls into two categories. The first are simply angry. Their comments range from, "Kill 'em all!" to the anachronistic "Fry 'em!" (Idaho uses lethal injection as its mode of execution, not the electric chair.) One even exclaimed, "I hate people! Kill every _____ one of 'em!" Occasionally they shout personal invective. Once a young child yelled from a passing car, "I'm for the death penalty! I hate you!" Another young woman, waiting at the stoplight, spent the entire time leaning out her window, screaming expletives of the filthiest kind. She had two small children with her.

While this kind of behavior is disturbing, it is hardly surprising. Capital punishment is a violently emotional subject, and it frequently brings out the worst in people, on both sides of the issue. Like all kinds of human sacrifice, one purpose of the death penalty is cathartic. It allows people who find their lives difficult and unpleasant to vent their anger. These are the kind of people who made up the mobs at public hangings a century ago. They are the kind of people who still show up—often drunk—outside a prison where an execution is taking place, to celebrate the death of a fellow human being as if it were a sporting event. This first group may simply be labeled the angry proponents of capital punishment.

It is a second group of proponents, however, who bother me most. These are the people who justify their support of capital punishment as a Christian practice. Almost invariably, they comment, "An eye for an eye." A Gallup Poll taken in February 2000 found that 46 percent of those who favored capital punishment used this rationale. The same poll found that an additional 3 percent said that capital punishment was the biblical remedy for serious crime.[1]

We have seen that opinion at our vigil, too. Recently, as a car sped by, a woman yelled simply, "Read your Bible!" However, when on occasion I have had the opportunity to speak to Christians who support capital punishment, they usually know little about the biblical perspective on the death penalty other than the eye-for-an-eye proof text.

The Bible actually has much to say about human sacrifice and capital punishment. The Old Testament, the Hebrew Scriptures preserved by the Israelites, allowed capital punishment but set strict limits on its use. Moreover, the use of capital punishment in the Hebrew Scriptures was a move away from a more arbitrary and violent system of criminal justice. The central event in the Christian Bible is an execution, seen by the early church as the final sacrifice. The early Christians believed that Jesus' death on the cross ended the need for further human and animal sacrifices.

In my first book, I briefly discussed the biblical perspectives on capital punishment.[2] The reaction has been surprising. A few reviewers rightly pointed out that the treatment of the biblical perspective had merely scratched the surface, and that some issues were treated in a cursory manner. However, I was intrigued by a number of reviews that were complimentary of the two chapters on the Bible and maintained that the Christian community had not satisfactorily examined such information.

For both of these reasons, I have written this book. On one hand, I hope to give a much fuller treatment of the Bible's approach to capital punishment. At the same time, I hope I will help Christian proponents of capital punishment take a second look at the death penalty, particularly if they take the Bible seriously as a guide for their lives and opinions. As in my first book, I use the masculine pronoun when speaking of persons on death row since over 98 percent of such inmates are men.

I write with a great deal of humility, however. I am neither a theologian nor a biblical scholar. Instead, I am a curious layman who has received a call to oppose the taking of human life by the state. In this, I am in much the same position as John Howard Yoder, who complained that the experts on biblical studies and the experts on ethics had not seriously addressed the social ethics of Jesus; hence Yoder, an expert in neither field, felt compelled to do so.[3]

Because I am an activist against the death penalty, I make no claim to objectivity, although I have done my best to avoid taking cheap shots or carrying an argument farther than the Bible warrants. I have also done my best to read as widely as I can in the subject area. I believe that the conclusions I have drawn about capital punishment have a solid base in orthodox biblical teachings.

The conclusions I have come to, however, are quite different from those of the majority of Christians for the past 1,700 years. Since the time of Emperor Constantine in the fourth century, most Christians have accepted participation in both capital punishment and warfare as civic duties somehow unrelated to their ethical obligations as individual Christians. This position was a departure from that of the early Christians, who abhorred and refused to practice bloodshed of any kind.

Under Constantine, the alliance of the church with the Roman Empire changed the fundamental teachings of the church on violence. In the fifth century, Augustine of Hippo provided the basic intellectual justification for Christian participation in state-sanctioned bloodshed. Ever since, most theologians have followed his lead. Not surprisingly, the majority of church members have also accepted state violence as a necessary evil.

However, there has always been uneasiness about the endorsement of such violence within church teachings. It was difficult to reconcile the great scriptural passages on love and forgiveness with the torture and killing practiced by many governments. Only the most arcane arguments and redefinition of terms appeared to justify the church's approval of such practices.[4]

Even with the full intellectual machinery of the church at its command, however, the argument for the acceptability of state violence never won over the entire body of Christ. A small minority of Christians, who almost always based their beliefs on the teachings of the Bible, continued to oppose Christian participation in both war and capital punishment. This minority has included—

• Some monks and nuns who left behind the violence of the world and lived in monasteries in the Middle Ages.[5]

• Waldenses (Waldensians, ca. 1170 and later), followers of Peter Waldo, who were virtually exterminated for their peaceful beliefs.[6]

• Peter Chelčický and the Czech Brethren, from the mid 1400s, forming the Society of the Bohemian Brethren, or Unitas Fratrum.[7]

• Most Anabaptists, who from 1525 represented the radical wing of the Reformation; and the German Baptist Brethren from 1708.[8]

• Quakers, who emerged in the 1650s, led by George Fox and stressing the "Inner Light."[9]

Now the faithful witness of the few has finally borne fruit. As scientific evidence mounted that capital punishment served no useful social purpose and that it was applied arbitrarily and capriciously, Christians began to take a second look. Slowly the teachings of the mainline churches began to change. In 1955, the Methodist Church made the first statement of opposition to the death penalty from any major Protestant denomination in America. Over the years, many other Protestant and Roman Catholic statements opposing capital punishment were approved.[10] While frequently referring to the Bible, these statements also often address secular reasons for opposing the death penalty.

Despite these statements, however, American Christians continue to support capital punishment at the same level or even at higher levels than the general population.[11] In my opinion, this is partly due to the fact that Christian opponents of the death penalty have not yet produced adequate studies of capital punishment in the light of biblical teachings. One survey found that support for capital punishment among white Christians who sustained regular devotional practices was lower than for those who did not.[12] This seems to indicate that church teachings based on the Bible can make a difference in the way Christians view the death penalty.

Moreover, after examining both secular and religious arguments against capital punishment, as a Christian I find the reasons based on the Bible to be the most comprehensive and compelling. Most of the secular arguments against capital punishment hold that the death penalty is an ineffective and unfair instrument of justice. On that track, one might assume that if the problems with imposing capital punishment could be alleviated, and if it could be shown that the death penalty actually deters crime, then it would be an acceptable practice.

Biblical arguments against the death penalty delve more deeply into the morality of violence than the secular arguments do. In the Bible, we are no longer working merely with human wisdom, but with the wisdom of God. The Bible brings us directly up against our limitations. We cannot predict what the future holds for any human being. We cannot replace life. We cannot trust that any government will always do the right thing. The Bible asks us to look beyond the problem of capital punishment to the broader problems of human existence. It leads us to ask hard questions: What is the value of human life? What is the nature of evil? Should we do evil in the hope that good may come of it? Can we balance one human life against another? How do we balance the relationship of the individual and society?

Thus, any book that fully examines the biblical views on capital punishment must necessarily be more than a listing and exegesis of biblical passages dealing with this subject. It must cast its net more broadly than simply looking at the classic death-penalty texts in the Bible. We must examine passages that discuss the origin of evil and the role of government in a fallen world. We must discover the general principles of the biblical writers and then try to apply these principles to social practices necessarily different from what they were when the Bible was written. Accordingly, I have done my best to put the biblical passages in the context of their times, and then to find the principles being taught. Once this has been done, I attempt to apply those principles to twenty-first-century America.

Since this is a book about applying the Bible to a specific social problem, it is appropriate for me to briefly discuss my view of biblical interpretation. I am an evangelical. I believe that the Bible is the single best source of information about God and his relationship with us and with our world. Yet I am not a literalist. I do not believe that every word of the Bible is based on what modern people would call facts, but I do believe that every word of the Bible reveals God's truth and must be taken seriously.

I do not agree with theologians who seem to believe that whole sections of the Bible—normally things they do not like—can be safely discounted as outdated vestiges of an ancient society. Each passage of the Bible, whether or not it is what modern Westerners would call historically reliable, reflects a belief so important historically that those who affirmed the canon of Scripture felt it must be included. Since God, through those who first recognized the canon, included a passage, it is important to try to find God's meaning for us in that text, whether it is history, poetry, or folklore.

The first question I ask of any biblical passage is, What did this mean to the people who first read or heard it? For example, a practice that we might find to be abhorrent in our culture may have seemed to be an act of great humanity at the time the passage was written. This is something an interpreter needs to know before applying the passage to the modern situation.

Based on what the biblical passage said to the people for whom it was originally written, we may be able to find a principle that can be applied in our different cultural environment. Then, by consistently living according to that principle, we can claim to be following biblical teachings, with God's help. As we do this, we need to remain open to the Spirit's ongoing guidance as discerned among God's people in response to the Jesus event.

Keeping this approach in mind, I have begun this book with a chapter on the context of the Hebrew Scriptures. In chapter 2, I examine the Mosaic Law within this context, bringing in interpretations made by ancient rabbis in the Talmud. Chapter 3 then looks at the stories of the behavior of the Hebrew God, Yahweh ("the LORD" in NRSV). I examine the concept of Yahweh's forgiveness in the Hebrew Scriptures with a special view toward how Yahweh treated murderers. In chapter 4, I finish the section on the Hebrew Scriptures with an attempt to apply the principles that have been found, using them in the modern context.

I begin the part of the book that covers the New Testament with the teachings of Jesus in chapter 5, looking especially at the near execution of the woman caught in adultery (John 8:2-11). In chapter 6, I examine the stories of executions in the New Testament, to see if they have lessons to teach us about capital punishment. In chapter 7, I try to see how Paul and other apostles viewed capital punishment in the light of the crucifixion and the persecution of the church. As an epilogue in chapter 8, we will examine how some of the earliest Christian theologians viewed the death penalty. Finally, I attempt to draw all of this together in a Conclusion.

I make no claim that this book is the final word on what the Bible has to say about capital punishment. Indeed, my hope is that it is the opening of a dialogue about Christianity and the death penalty. Nevertheless, I temper that hope with the desire that such a discussion will soon become obsolete in America.

There have been many signs of hope for the opponents of capital punishment in the United States recently, but the end of the death penalty in this country may be some years away. If that is the case, then Christians need to approach this issue with a good deal of self-examination and discernment. For serious Christians, discernment must always begin with the biblical perspective. In this way, we open ourselves up to the mind of Jesus Christ.

—*Gardner C. Hanks*
  Boise, Idaho

Acknowledgments

As a librarian, I am fully aware that no intellectual work is ever completely the work of an individual. Nor does an author ever write a book without sacrificing other parts of his life while he does so. First, I am indebted to many authors of the works I have cited in this book. Not only have their works provided much of the information I needed, but also in some cases they have led me down new paths that I would not otherwise have explored.

I have discussed this book with many people over the year or so in which it was written. In particular, I have discussed it with Tim Cooper, the head of the Boise Catholic Workers, as we stood at the vigil against the death penalty mentioned above. As a trained pastor, Tim was able to give me insights into many of the issues covered in this work. In addition to Tim, the entire group of activists at the vigil has been a constant source of inspiration and support for me. I would be remiss in not mentioning especially Henry Krewer and Jim Holden, whose retirements have been spent doing good works. Some day I hope to emulate them.

Linda Nafziger-Meiser, pastor of my home congregation, the Hyde Park Mennonite Fellowship in Boise, has provided encouragement and some translation of Greek words for me as the book was written. Larry Hauder, the conference pastor for the Pacific Northwest Mennonite Conference, encouraged (or even nagged!) me into writing my first book. For this volume, he simply cheered me on. Indeed, throughout the process of writing, I have received much encouragement from the Hyde Park Fellowship, and particularly from my fellow writer Leonard Nolt.

The members of my small group—Rob and Annette Hanson, Rick and Carole Skinner, John and Sandy Wargo, and Anna Zook—gave me encouragement and also, along with Karen Nolt, spent an evening helping me with the tedious, yet necessary, work of verifying biblical references.

For many years I have been inspired by my fellow death-row spiritual advisers here in Boise. These men, whose lives embody Christ's command to visit prisoners, have gently pushed me to expand my view of what it means to be a Christian. Although we do not agree on every point of biblical interpretation or theology, I think we all feel the sense of camaraderie that comes from doing the same sometimes difficult and frustrating job.

I mention specifically Jack Muldoon, Ed Good, Rick Bollman, Robert Garber, Henry Warren, and again Tim Cooper, who have acted as a support group for me and for each other. Nor would the group be complete without naming Harley Brueck, the former chaplain at the Idaho Maximum Security Institution, who did much to smooth the way for our work.

For the past five years, I have visited with Jim Wood, an inmate on Idaho's death row. He has provided me with remarkable insights into the culture that helps create murderers. Even more important, Jim has shown me that someone raised in this culture still craves the love and affection of God and his fellow human beings. My prayer times with Jim have been some of the most moving of my life, and he has particularly encouraged me with my writing.

The staffs of both the Albertsons Library at Boise State University and the Boise Public Library have been quite helpful. Boise Public Library's reference staff provided most of the interlibrary loans that I needed to write this book. At the Idaho State Library, where I am employed, Stephanie Kukay again provided me with exemplary reference services. She gave me a tremendous lift one day when she told me I had almost convinced her that I was right about the death penalty.

I cannot express enough the appreciation that I feel for Herald Press and particularly for my editor, Dave Garber, in taking another chance on a death-penalty book, after first publishing my book *Against the Death Penalty: Christian and Secular Arguments Against Capital Punishment.* Publishing books on controversial topics is a risky business, especially for a small press, but Herald Press has now stepped up to the plate twice. They make me proud to be the member of a denomination whose publishing house is willing to take chances to spread the gospel of peace.

Last, I must thank my family. My father and mother and brother gave me the basic foundation of love and many of the values incorporated in this book. Not till I began to work with prison inmates did I come to appreciate what a blessing a loving, nonviolent family is. My daughters, Karin and Kathryn, have missed many hours of my time, and at times had to put up with my grumpiness when the writing was going slowly.

Finally, I simply could not have written this book without the love and care of my wife, Suzie, to whom it is dedicated. She was the person who, more than any other, led me to Christ. She has been my loving companion for more than twenty-five years, providing me with a balance and stability that would not otherwise have been available to me. She is a loving critic for my ideas and always the first editor for my writing. Suzie has helped me be a better writer, but more importantly, she has helped me become a better person. Her love in the here and now has helped me to better understand God's eternal love, and for that I will be eternally grateful.

CAPITAL PUNISHMENT AND THE BIBLE

1
The Hebrew Scriptures in Context

For us to understand what the Scriptures have to teach us today, it is important to know what they meant to those who wrote them and those who first read or heard them. To read the Scriptures while ignoring their historical context may lead to significant misunderstandings about what God is saying to us through them. This is particularly true of the Hebrew Scriptures, which many Christians call the Old Testament.

Since the beginning of the Christian church, Christians have had difficulty in reconciling the seemingly endless stories of violence in the Hebrew Scriptures with Jesus' message of love and mercy. The second-century heretical writer Marcion even asserted that Christians should no longer include the Hebrew Scriptures as part of their scriptural canon. According to him, the god portrayed in the Hebrew Scriptures could not be the same God represented by Jesus.

John Howard Yoder suggests that a proper way to understand the Hebrew Scriptures is *not* to read them with a backward view from the New Testament. Instead, it is better first to interpret them in relationship to their own time. He states, "It is therefore more proper in reading the Old Testament story, to ask not how it is different from what came later, but rather from what went before, or what prevailed at the time, and how it moves toward what was to come later."[1] To understand the meaning of violence in the Hebrew Scriptures, according to Yoder, it is necessary to examine that violence in the "concrete historical anthropological" situation in which these texts were written.

There can be no doubt that the Hebrew Scriptures allowed capital punishment for many crimes. Modern Christian death-penalty proponents use this fact to justify their support of capital punishment in our own time. Often they do this by quoting Jesus' statement: "Until heaven and earth pass away, not one letter, not one stroke of a letter, will pass from the law until all is accomplished" (Matt. 5:18; cf. Luke 16:17).

Death-penalty proponents, however, are silent about other Mosaic laws clearly out of step with modern life. For example, according to Deuteronomy 22:28-29, the punishment for a man who rapes an unengaged woman is that he must make a payment to the victim's father and marry the victim. In our day, no one would claim that a rape victim should be forced to marry the rapist, yet this is what the highly patriarchal society of the Hebrew Scriptures demanded.[2]

To understand what the Scriptures have to tell us today, then, we must understand what they meant within the historical context in which they were written. In this chapter we will look at the historical situation in which the Hebrew Scriptures were created. From this context, we will then examine what the Hebrew Scriptures have to say about capital punishment and how this might be applied today.

From Shepherds to Farmers

Many of the stories and sayings of the Hebrew Scriptures had circulated through oral tradition for centuries before they were written down. The Torah reports that Moses wrote Yahweh's words and covenant law (e.g., Exod. 24:4; 34:28; Deut. 31:9, 22). Eventually the oldest connected texts of these Scriptures, including traditions of the Torah, were likely first written around 1100 B.C. This was a time of great change for the Hebrew people, notably including the increased use of writing. The fact that material from the oral tradition was now placed in written form shows that the Hebrews (Israelites) were becoming a settled, agricultural people.

The developed use of writing is one of the major indicators that a seminomadic society is becoming a civilization. Others signs are—

• Firmly organized states, with definite boundaries and systematic political institutions.

• Distinctions between social classes.

• Economic specialization.

• Conscious development of the arts and intellectual attitudes.[3]

These social changes gave society a greater level of economic stability and provided advantages for powerful subgroups within the community. But they came with a price. Social injustice—with growing disparities between the rich and the poor, men and women, and militaristic empires and conquered colonies—would result in much suffering.

In general, the Hebrew Scriptures take a critical stance toward these changes. For example, Cain, the first murderer, is a farmer who kills his brother, Abel, a shepherd. The murder occurs because the Hebrew God, Yahweh ("the LORD" in NRSV), rejects Cain's offering of farm products, but accepts Abel's nomadic sacrifice of lambs (Gen. 4:1-17). Yet the reason the LORD gives Cain is that "sin is lurking at the door" and he does not "do well," or he would be "accepted" (Gen. 4:7).

Similarly, the tower of Babel is erected in a city. Cities were the most visible products of the new civilized order. In the text, the inhabitants of the city boastfully describe its purpose:

> Come, let us build ourselves a city, and a tower with its top in the heavens, and let us make a name for ourselves; otherwise we shall be scattered abroad upon the face of the whole earth. (Gen. 11:4)

In wishing to make a name for themselves, the people of the

city were rejecting the name and the role that Yahweh had given them, and thus were rejecting Yahweh himself. For conservative pastoralists, the city represented a sacrilegious rejection of their God-given way of life.

Likewise, the Exodus was an escape from Egypt, a land of cities as well as slavery. The seminomadic social structure of the Hebrews was relatively flat and fluid. The primary economic group was the clan or tribe, rather than an economic class. Although there was a form of slavery, it was not as rigid as slavery would become in civilized societies. For example, Abram (later Abraham) could speak of making "a slave born in my house" his heir because of his lack of offspring (Gen. 15:3). For the nomads, city life was necessarily associated with the much harsher and more-rigid form of class slavery described in Exodus 1:8-22.

The Scriptures report that the Hebrews' demand for a king, the primary symbol of the civilized state, also represented a rejection of Yahweh. When the Hebrews demand that Samuel appoint a king for them, Yahweh tells Samuel, "Listen to the voice of the people in all that they say to you; for they have not rejected you, but they have rejected me from being king over them" (1 Sam. 8:7). Then Yahweh tells Samuel to warn the people of the dangers of living under a king and the state he would represent:

> These will be the ways of the king who will reign over you: he will take your sons and appoint them to his chariots and to be his horsemen, and to run before his chariots; and he will appoint for himself commanders of thousands and commanders of fifties, and some to plow his ground and to reap his harvest, and to make his implements of war and the equipment of his chariots. He will take your daughters to be perfumers and cooks and bakers. He will take the best of your fields and vineyards and olive orchards and give them to his courtiers. He will take one-tenth of your grain and of your vineyards and give it to his officers and his courtiers. He will take your male and female slaves, and the best of your cattle and donkeys, and put them to his work. He will take one-tenth of your flocks, and you

shall be his slaves. And in that day you will cry out because of your king, whom you have chosen for yourselves; but the LORD will not answer you in that day. (1 Sam. 8:11-18; cf. 10:25; Deut. 17:14-20)

The First Written Codes

The Hebrews were not unique in making the social change from a nomadic, pastoral society to a settled civilization. All over the ancient Near East, civilized states were being formed. The first cities were founded in Mesopotamia around 3500 B.C. Located in a fertile area between the Tigris and Euphrates rivers, the region provided both agricultural resources and rivers by which surplus produce could be transported for trade. With trade came a new kind of people, merchants who lived neither by following livestock nor by tilling the soil, but through the exchange of goods. It was probably this trading class that first developed writing. Commerce demanded a more-permanent form of social memory than could be provided by the oral tradition.

Commercial life also demanded more-uniform practices and customs than independent cities could provide. Over time, larger states developed, and with them came the first written legal codes, also initially developed in Mesopotamia. There is evidence that the earliest codes were designed to place some limits on the power of the strong over the weak. But they also reflect the needs of a society in which a self-help form of justice negotiated between families or clans no longer worked.

The first known code in Mesopotamia is that of Urukagina, written around 2300 B.C.[4] A second code is attributed to Ur-Nammu (ca. 2100 B.C.), but it may have been developed during the reign of his son, Shulgi.[5] The most famous code, the one most fully surviving, is that of Hammurabi, developed around 1700 B.C. This code is inscribed on an eight-foot-high slab of diorite found at Susa in 1901.

The Code of Hammurabi contains 282 laws, ranging from

regulations on slavery to criminal law, but its primary focus is on business and trade.[6] Later codes, including the Mosaic Law found in the Hebrew Scriptures, have some regulations in common with Hammurabi's Code. Hence, scholars think this code or others deriving from it had some influence on the Mosaic Law.

Like the Mosaic Law, the Code of Hammurabi contains a number of capital offenses. Both codes include the *lex talionis*, law of retaliation, naming penalties such as "an eye for an eye" (e.g., Exod. 21:23-25; Lev. 24:20; Deut. 19:18-21). This law allowed for equivalent injury as a punishment for injury sustained. Unlike the Mosaic Law, Hammurabi gives the death penalty for some crimes against property, particularly theft. The Mosaic Law, on the other hand, provides capital sentences for some religious offenses not included in the Code of Hammurabi.

The Conflict of Religions

The important role of religion in the Mosaic Law reflects the serious religious conflict that existed in Hebrew society. As the Hebrews settled into their new agricultural way of life, they were challenged to develop new knowledge and skills. It was natural for them to seek instruction from the land's indigenous inhabitants, the Canaanites. After all, the Canaanites had lived in an agricultural society for some time before the Hebrews conquered their territory.

From a religious point of view, turning to the Canaanites for instruction was dangerous. Intermixed with information about plowing, sowing grain, and harvesting, the Canaanites also included beliefs about their agricultural deities, particularly the Baals. According to Canaanite religion, these gods controlled the success of their crops.

Canaanite religion was a polytheistic fertility cult focused on the changing agricultural seasons. The gods were highly anthropomorphic and, like the Greek gods, displayed many less-desirable human traits. They were contentious, jealous, vindictive, lustful, and lazy, apparently having little to teach the Canaanites in the moral sphere.[7] Temple prostitutes of both genders were part of the cult.[8] Human sacrifice, particularly the sacrifice of children, was also occasionally practiced.[9]

By the time the Torah was written, the Hebrew religion was generally monotheistic, though the text still carries hints of an older polytheism.[10] Polytheism was an outgrowth of animistic religion, in which objects were imbued with spiritual power. As cities and states were formed, it was natural for each to develop local deities especially interested in the fortunes of the area. Nomadic peoples also maintained polytheistic religious systems. Outside of revelation, there appears to be no convincing explanation for the Hebrew's monotheistic worship of the single, almighty God Yahweh. From the time of the writing of their Scriptures, it was their clearest cultural distinction, and it provided them with a uniformity that has kept their culture alive throughout history.

Intolerance, however, is a natural danger of monotheistic religious systems. If there is one God, then there is one truth. This is the way the conservative worshipers of Yahweh approached the Canaanite gods. At its most violent, this approach justified the massacre of entire Canaanite cities in the name of purity, to protect the Israelites from corrupting their faith in Yahweh. In Deuteronomy, Yahweh commands:

> When the LORD your God brings you into the land that you are about to enter and occupy, and he clears away many nations before you—the Hittites, the Girgashites, the Amorites, the Canaanites, the Perizzites, the Hivites, and the Jebusites, seven nations mightier and more numerous than you—and when the LORD your God gives them over to you and you defeat them, then you must utterly destroy them. Make no covenant with them and show them no mercy. Do not intermarry with them, giving your daughters to their sons or taking their daughters for your sons, for that would turn away your children from following me, to serve other gods. Then the anger of the LORD would be kindled against you, and he would destroy you quickly.

But this is how you must deal with them: break down their altars, smash their pillars, hew down their sacred poles, and burn their idols with fire. For you are a people holy to the LORD your God; the LORD your God has chosen you out of all the peoples on earth to be his people, his treasured possession. (Deut. 7:1-6)

During the early days of the conquest of Canaan, it appears that the Hebrews followed this commandment, at least on some occasions. The fall of Jericho resulted in a total massacre. "Then they devoted to destruction by the edge of the sword all in the city, both men and women, young and old, oxen, sheep, and donkeys" (Josh. 6:21). The city of Ai suffered a similar fate, "The total of those who fell that day, both men and women, was twelve thousand—all the people of Ai. For Joshua did not draw back his hand, with which he stretched out the sword, until he had utterly destroyed all the inhabitants of Ai" (Josh. 8:25-26).

In addition, the towns of Makkedah, Libnah, Lachish, Eglon, Hebron, and Debir all were massacred (Josh. 10:28-39). Hazor was wiped out. "And they put to the sword all who were in it, utterly destroying them; there was no one left who breathed, and he burned Hazor with fire" (Josh. 11:11). Other unnamed towns were also massacred: "All the people they struck down with the edge of the sword, until they had destroyed them, and they did not leave any who breathed" (Josh. 11:14).

While modern standards rightly condemn this kind of genocidal warfare, the historical setting of the conquest of Canaan explains some of the violence. The Bible tells us that the Hebrews were not as numerous as the people they attacked, nor were they as sophisticated. At this point in their history, they remained a seminomadic people attacking an established civilization with walled cities. They had no standing army, and these advances were probably made on an ad hoc basis. With no homeland of their own, they had no systems in place to deal with prisoners of war or captured civilian populations. Leaving cities inhabited by their enemies in their rear would have placed the Israelites at constant risk, particularly, as we will see later, in the age of the blood feud.

Perhaps most importantly, they felt that their religion required a sacrifice for their successes. Primitive religions tend to view their gods as capricious and demanding, and that view was certainly shared to some extent by the early Hebrews.[11] Success called for some form of payment—a sacrifice. The Hebrew word *kherem,* meaning "devoted to destruction" (as in Josh. 6:18), implies that the massacres of these cities were considered a sacrifice to Yahweh for the success that the Hebrews had experienced.

Although to modern people the practice of *kherem* is excessively brutal, it was not exclusive to the Hebrews at that time.[12] The practice guarded warfare from being conducted merely to collect booty or to capture slaves. It may have had the functional purpose of warding off plague and other diseases that followed in the wake of war. As mentioned above, it also helped to preserve their faith in Yahweh from being corrupted (Deut. 7:1-6).

Yet such massacres were not the universal or even the usual practice. The Bible reports that the Gibeonites made a bargain with Joshua and became slaves (Josh. 9). This would seem to be the fate of many of the peoples eventually conquered by the Hebrews. The first chapter of Judges reports that the Israelite tribes did not drive out the inhabitants of Canaan, but instead enslaved them.

As is typical with conquered peoples who are more sophisticated than their conquerors, the ideas and religious practices of the Canaanites came to have major influences on the Hebrews. The conflict between the religious beliefs of the Hebrews and the Canaanites is one of the major themes of the Hebrew Scriptures, and Canaanite religious practices make repeated appearances throughout the history of the Israelites.

Given the intensity of the religious feelings of the Hebrews, it is not surprising that they would develop capital sentences for some religious transgressions. As we shall see later, however, the religious beliefs of the Hebrews would also restrict the use of capital punishment in these and other instances.

Patriarchy

The coming of civilization may also have signaled the beginning of highly patriarchal societies.[13] In the first description of creation in Genesis 1:27, women and men are created at the same time, giving them equal status before Yahweh. In the second story, the woman is created out of man, but has equal standing with him until the Fall (Gen. 2:22-24). Only at that point and as a consequence of the Fall, is Eve told that her husband would rule over her (Gen. 3:16).

From the evidence of primitive groups that still exist, it appears that there has always been some division of labor between men and women. It is probable that these distinctions in gender roles are based on the relative strength and size of men and women and the needs of nursing mothers and their children. Nevertheless, subsistence-level living tends to equalize social status: all members of society are needed for the group to survive. The women who gather roots near the campsite are just as important to the group's survival as the men who are hunting for meat miles away.

The level of equality may be shown in some of the social structures of primitive societies. Some societies were matrilineal: descent was passed through the mother rather than the father. Some societies were matrilocal, in which the man went to live with the wife's family, a situation perhaps suggested in Genesis 2:24: "Therefore a man leaves his father and his mother and clings to his wife, and they become one flesh."[14] Thus, it is likely that equality between the sexes was not an issue in primitive society.

By the time the Scriptures were being written, Hebrew society was becoming patriarchal, controlled largely by men. There are still narratives of women acting indepen-dently, such as the stories of Tamar (daughter-in-law of Judah), Rahab, Deborah, Jael, Ruth, and Abigail (Gen. 38; Judg. 4–5;

Ruth 1–4; 1 Sam. 25). But most of the Scripture passages portray women in the light of their fathers or husbands, or do not tell us much about women at all.

The patriarch of a Hebrew family had tremendous power over his wife and children. Paternal descent had both social and religious importance. It was of the utmost importance for a man to have heirs, and preferably male heirs. Any behavior that brought a child's paternity into question was considered to be dangerous to society and was dealt with severely. Disrespect of parents, particularly of the father, tore at the basic social fabric and could lead to the most severe punishment.

The Blood Feud

The primary instrument of justice in the seminomadic Hebrew culture was the family or clan. Individuals were so deeply imbedded within their family structure that the difference between an individual and his or her family group was completely blurred. Family groups provided protection for their members. Injury to one family member was considered to be an injury to the family as a whole. Similarly, the action of a family member was considered to be representative of the entire family. Disputes between individuals were therefore understood as disputes between families. This led to the social custom of the blood feud.

Emrys Peters has defined the blood feud as

> a set of relationships between two tribal [secondary] groups which are characterized by hostility whenever two or more of their members meet. These hostilities are of a sort that cannot be terminated; feud is not a matter of a group indulging in hostilities here at one moment and there the next, but a sequence of hostilities, which . . . know no beginning and are insoluble.[15]

Peters' definition points to the permanent nature of the blood feud. In addition to providing protection for group members, the feud establishes the relative social positions of the groups. Stronger groups can seek higher levels of revenge than weaker groups. That in turn means that the lives of individuals within weaker groups have correspondingly less value. When a member of a powerful group kills a member of a weaker group, he or his group may be required to pay blood money for the life that was taken. If a member of a weaker group injures or even insults a member of more-powerful group, the more-powerful group may take one or more lives in revenge.

Within the context of the society at large, the injured family sets the level of revenge required. This level will depend on the amount of revenge that they can reasonably take, given their relative strength; or in the case of strong groups, the level that they can take before other clans within the society will step in.

It is important to note here that revenge is not necessarily taken on the person who committed the injury. It is the family group that must pay. Any male family member could be killed in revenge, no matter how innocent he may be. Sometimes children were exempted, but not always.

In a number of places, the Hebrew Scriptures refer to the blood feud. After Cain murdered Abel and Yahweh cast him out of his family, Cain complained bitterly; without his family's protection, he feared that anyone would be able to murder him. Cain's concern was a real one. The outcast, not protected by his clan, lost all social status and protection in Hebrew society. Others could treat him however they wished. But Yahweh did not allow this in the case of Cain. The LORD stated, "Whoever kills Cain will suffer a sevenfold vengeance." With these words, Yahweh assured Cain that he would remain responsible for Cain's welfare. Yahweh told Cain's potential enemies that he would set a high level of revenge if Cain was murdered, and he gave Cain a special mark indicating that Cain was under his protection (Gen. 4:13-16).

The story of Lamech, following shortly after the story of Cain, shows the escalating level of violence possible in feuding societies. In revenge, Lamech murdered a young man who had wounded him. As the story opens, he is concerned that the young man's family will exact vengeance on him. He tells his wives, "If Cain is avenged sevenfold, truly Lamech seventy-sevenfold" (Gen. 4:23-24). The level of revenge that Lamech set for his life probably indicates the relative strength of the two families involved. Lamech felt that a murder was an appropriate level of revenge on the young man who had merely injured him. This shows that the young man was not of the same social status as Lamech, an important and powerful man, who could afford multiple wives.

Now that Lamech has taken his revenge, he sets a high level of retaliation if he is murdered in return. Seventy-seven of the murderer's male kin must die before Lamech's killing is adequately avenged. Again, this indicates the unequal status of the feuding families and unrestrained blood revenge.

The story of the rape of Dinah in Genesis 34 is also a story of a blood feud. Dinah is the daughter of Jacob and Leah. She is raped and kidnapped by a man named Shechem, a Hivite. Shechem's father, Hamor, is willing to make reparations and to conclude a marriage between his son and Dinah. Jacob's sons seem to go along with the arrangement, but they require that the men in Hamor's city be circumcised. After these Hivites have been circumcised and are still convalescing, Dinah's brothers kill all the males of Hamor's family.

Jacob is worried that the excessive level of revenge will cause other groups to retaliate against his family, but Dinah's brothers feel that the level of revenge is justified. They ask Jacob, "Should our sister be treated like a whore?"

This story is instructive for a number of reasons. It shows that homicide could be used as revenge for any kind of crime, not just for murder. It also shows that the social control of the family could not always regulate the behavior of the members in feud situations. Presumably Jacob, the family patriarch, had approved the marriage of his daughter and had accepted some form of payment for the honor of his family.

His sons, however, did not feel that it was enough to restore the family honor. On their own, therefore, they sought a higher level of revenge than Jacob felt was appropriate. In doing so, they opened their family to a much higher level of revenge in return.

It is significant that the story ends with Jacob taking his family out of that territory to avert further bloodshed. Only Yahweh's protection keeps them from being pursued (Gen. 35:1-5).

Another story of a blood feud involves David and Nabal in 1 Samuel 25. David is living as an outlaw, with a large gang of bandits. Nabal is a wealthy but foolish sheepherder, with many men working for him; in Hebrew, his name *Nabal* means "fool."[16] David sends some of his men to Nabal to give him a message that sounds much like extortion. David tells Nabal that his men have protected Nabal's men and have not robbed them. Therefore, Nabal should be willing to provide some food to David's men as a payment for his "protection." But instead of showing his gratitude for these services, Nabal insults David.

When David hears of the insult, he immediately prepares to attack Nabal, bringing two hundred men with him. He states, "God do so to David and more also, if by morning I leave so much as one male of all who belong to him" (1 Sam. 25:22). This threat to kill all of the males is the language of a blood feud. When Nabal's wife, Abigail, hears about what is happening, she brings David the food he had demanded. But the food is not enough to turn David away from seeking revenge. Instead, Abigail must appeal to the Mosaic injunction against taking vengeance outside of the Law.

Abigail therefore says, "Now then, my lord, as the LORD lives, and as you yourself live, since the LORD has restrained you from bloodguilt and from taking vengeance with your own hand, now let your enemies and those who seek to do evil to my lord be like Nabal" (1 Sam. 25:26). Thus it is only through Abigail's intervention that David is restrained from killing Nabal and all of his men.

Another possible example of a feud situation is mixed with elements of human sacrifice, in 2 Samuel 21:1-14. In this story, a famine appears in the land, and Yahweh informs David that the famine is the result of the bloodguilt of Saul, who killed a number of Gibeonites. Saul is already dead, so the Gibeonites ask for seven of his sons as the blood payment. David turns over two of Saul's sons and five of his grandsons; the Gibeonites murder them by impalement and leave their bodies to rot on a mountain. "After that, God heeded supplications for the land," and the famine ended.

By its very nature, the blood feud is unregulated violence. The level of violence will depend on many different factors. Joseph Ginat, who has studied blood feuds among modern seminomadic peoples, suggests several factors:

• The need of the offended group's leader to increase group cohesiveness through a demand for revenge.

• The social status of the groups involved.

• The presence of a mediator with suitable authority to help resolve the conflict.

• The willingness of the offending group to punish the offender.

• Especially important: the stage of integration of the feuding groups into a larger society that does not practice or approve of blood revenge.[17]

In a nomadic or seminomadic society, blood feuds would have a limited impact because of the mobile nature of the participants. In the story of the rape of Dinah, the blood feud is suspended by the departure of Jacob and his family.

The separation of Abram and Lot in Genesis 13:1-12 is a similar but more-peaceful story. When the countryside can no longer support both of their herds, there is dissension between the two family groups. So Abram and Lot agree to separate specifically to avoid conflict.

Abram tells Lot, "Let there be no strife between you and me, and between your herders and my herders; for we are kindred. Is not the whole land before you? Separate yourself from me. If you take the left hand, then I will go to the right; or if you take the right hand, then I will go to the left" (Gen. 13:8-9).

The departure of Jacob from Esau also has the undertone of separation to avoid possible feuding (Gen. 33).

As ancient people left their nomadic existence behind and began living in permanent settlements, the safety valve of mobility was removed. Students of modern feuding societies report that feuding among settled people is usually more intense and deadly than in nomadic cultures. According to Jacob Black-Michaud,

> Anyone who has read reasonably widely on the feud in the Mediterranean and Middle East will have been struck by an at-first unaccountable qualitative difference between the practice of feud in sedentary agricultural societies, on the one hand, and among nomadic pastoralists, on the other. In the [settled farming societies], feud seems on the whole to be more intensive, more frequent, more destructive, and less "rational," that is, less bent on achievement of overtly practical aims. Sedentary societies also appear to be much more prone to intragroup killing, and the penalties incurred by such an act are considerably more severe than among nomadic pastoralists.
>
> Feuding relations among the [nomadic pastoralists], however, tend to oppose groups, which, more often than not, have extremely good and perfectly obvious reasons founded in a realistic perception of ecological conditions to distrust each others' territorial ambitions. Nomadic pastoralists also accept compensation to bring about temporary truce with greater readiness than sedentary populations. . . . The general impression gained from the literature on agricultural village-based communities is that feud is often flippantly regarded as a kind of game which it is unsporting to interrupt.[18]

Let us build on Black-Michaud's observations. As the Hebrews began to enter a settled, agricultural lifestyle, the intensity of feuding likely increased. Feuding probably became a serious internal problem for some communities, but it also may have had another important negative effect on the larger society—it would have interfered with trade. The written criminal laws of the state were to some extent an attempt to regulate and limit feuding. As the next chapter shows, although the Mosaic Law seems excessively harsh by modern standards, it was in its own time an attempt to restrain violence.

Scapegoating and Human Sacrifice

Before turning to the law, we must examine one more important historical anthropological factor in Hebrew society. This factor was to have tremendous theological importance both in the religion of the Hebrews and the religion of the New Testament Christians. It was the practice of scapegoating and human sacrifice.

Human sacrifice and the blood feud both allowed what might be called substitutionary homicide. In both practices, a person could be killed, not for any particular crime one had committed, but as a substitute for the real menace. In the blood feud, a family member could be killed in the place of the person committing the original offense. In human sacrifice, the victim is killed as an appeasement for some unknown offense committed by the society at large.

Because most contemporary Christians have never participated in the ritualistic slaughter of animals within a sacrificial cult, we do not fully recognize the importance of scapegoating and human sacrifice in the Bible. We speak of Jesus' atonement for our sins on the cross; yet we do not understand as intensely as the first Christians that this atonement was in fact a case of human sacrifice. In taking our punishment for us, Jesus also was serving as a scapegoat for our wrongdoing. The scapegoat was an important part of the Hebrew ritualistic law and was related directly to the forgiveness of the community's sins. Scapegoating and human sacrifice are so intertwined in the Hebrew Scriptures that we will treat them together.

René Girard, a historian and literary critic, has developed an important theory of scapegoating as a primary source of religious ritual and violence. According to this theory, violence begins with imitation. Girard describes the process:

> If the appropriative gesture of an individual named *A* is rooted in the imitation of an individual named *B,* it means that both *A* and *B* must reach together for one and the same object. They become rivals for that object. If the tendency to imitate appropriation is on both sides, imitative rivalry must become reciprocal; it must become subject to the back-and-forth reinforcement that communication theorists call positive feedback.
>
> In other words, the individual who first acts as a model will experience an increase in his own appropriative urge when he finds himself thwarted by his imitator. And reciprocally, each becomes the imitator of his own imitator and the model of his own model. Each tries to push aside the obstacles that the other places in his path. Violence is generated by this process; or rather, violence is the process itself when two or more partners try to prevent one another from appropriating the object they all desire through physical and other means.[19]

Girard believes that as mimetic rivalry becomes more intense, it attracts other participants, eventually spreading to many members of the community. When this occurs, it leads to a crisis. The mimetic tension becomes too great and must find a release. To avoid an all-against-all situation, a ritual that mimics uncontrolled violence is developed. Girard states:

> Sacrifice is the resolution and conclusion of ritual because a collective murder or expulsion resolves the mimetic crisis that the ritual mimics. What kind of mechanism can this be? Judging from the evidence, direct and indirect, this resolution must belong to the realm of what is commonly called a scapegoat effect. . . . [This is] the strange process through which two or more people are reconciled at the expense of a third party [an identified scapegoat] who

appears guilty or responsible for whatever ails, disturbs, or frightens the scapegoaters. They feel relieved of their tensions and they coalesce into a more harmonious group. They now have a single purpose, which is to prevent the scapegoat from harming them, by expelling or destroying [that scapegoat].[20]

In scapegoating, an individual or group becomes the focus of this tension and identified as the scapegoat. Human scapegoats are not chosen at random. Typically, such scapegoats bear common characteristics. First, they are individuals not fully integrated into the particular scapegoating society. In most cases, they come from groups that have little or no status. Typical scapegoats are prisoners of war, children, unmarried adolescents, slaves, people with disabilities, criminals, racial and ethnic minorities, foreigners, and newcomers.

Because the scapegoat has a position outside or on the fringe of the mainstream society, there is little likelihood that revenge will be sought for killing or expelling that scapegoat. Thus, the sacrifice may allow the violent tension between groups and individuals to dissipate without the continuance of the cycle of revenge. As Girard expresses it, "The desire to commit an act of violence on those near us cannot be suppressed without conflict; we must divert that impulse, therefore, toward the sacrificial victim, the creature we can strike down without fear of reprisal, since he lacks a champion."[21]

While sacrificial victims are usually chosen from the weaker members of a society, the ritualization of sacrifice claims superhuman powers for them. Because they must bear responsibility for all of the ills of society, they clearly must have powers above the common person.

Girard postulates that the sacrifice generated by mimetic violence lies behind all forms of human sacrifice:

In primitive culture, the belief is extremely widespread that parricide, incest, bestiality, and other transgressions destructive of elementary forms of human kinship can bring about deadly epidemics. Contagious disease is not clearly distinguished, it seems, from acute internal discord. This type of transgression is punished with a view to forestalling possible disasters. If some epidemic breaks out first, logic demands that the reverse order be followed: some "culprit" must be discovered who caused the disease, and in order to restore its health, the community must take appropriate sanctions.[22]

Nevertheless, Girard's theory does not sufficiently recognize how deeply imbedded individuals are within their family groups in primitive society. Hence, this lack makes his theory too individualistic to describe the scapegoating phenomenon in relationship to the blood feud. In primitive societies, scapegoating may have had a more-important effect in bringing groups rather than individuals to a peaceful resolution of conflict. Moreover, mimetic responses may be too simplistic to describe how groups interact with each other as they move toward and through violence. Yet the basic tenor of Girard's theory may be used as a framework for looking at scapegoating and human sacrifice in the Bible.

Human sacrifice is a major, if often unrecognized, theme of the Bible. Beginning early in the book of Genesis and continuing through the crucifixion of Jesus Christ, the Bible again and again returns to this theme. By the time the Hebrew Scriptures were being written, literal human sacrifice was not a normal practice among the Hebrews. It appears to have been practiced more frequently by the Canaanites and other surrounding cultures.[23] Thus it was still a temptation for the Hebrews in times of cultural crises, such as an epidemic or a military threat from an invader. The Hebrew Scriptures denounce human sacrifice, but there is evidence that Israelites occasionally practiced it (see below).[24]

Human sacrifice is distinguished from common homicide by its social nature and by the ritual attached to it. Human sacrifice is a public act performed on behalf of the society as a whole, against a person assigned the role of the scapegoat.

The victims of human sacrifice are often given a special place of honor before the sacrifice is carried out. They may be provided with special clothes or food. The killing itself follows certain ritualistic procedures. The purpose of the sacrifice is religious. The sacrifice is made to the gods either as a gift to assure future favors or to appease their anger, caused by some failure of the group or of individuals within it.

Human sacrifice is therefore always a means to an end; its purpose is either to avoid a feared catastrophe or to stop one already occurring. According to Edward Westermark,

> The custom of human sacrifice admits that the life of one is taken to save the lives of many, or that an inferior individual is put to death for the purpose of preventing the death of someone who has the higher right to live. . . . Very frequently the victims are prisoners of war, or other aliens, or slaves or criminals, that is, persons whose lives are held in little regard.[25]

In many cultures, human sacrifice was used to punish certain crimes seen not merely as a violation of human standards, but also as acts of sacrilege. Nigel Davis asserts,

> In general terms, throughout the history of mankind, sacrifice, vengeance, and penal justice were not separate notions, but different facets of the same process, needed alike to protect the state from the wrath of the gods.[26]

The prohibition of human sacrifice is an important theme of the Hebrew Scriptures. Yahweh sets strict limitations on the kind of sacrifices that can be made to him. He differentiates his people from others by commanding them to replace human sacrifice with the sacrifice of animals. When Yahweh withdraws his protection from the Israelites, he repeatedly cites their continuing practice of human sacrifice as one of the reasons.

In the story of Noah, human sacrifice is connected to forbidden food.[27] After the flood, Yahweh makes a new covenant with Noah, one that provides for an expansion of the human diet to include animal flesh:

> Every moving thing that lives shall be food for you; and just as I gave you the green plants, I give you everything. Only, you shall not eat flesh with its life, that is, its blood. For your own lifeblood I will surely require a reckoning: from every animal I will require it and from human beings, each one for the blood of another, I will require a reckoning for human life.
> Whoever sheds the blood of a human,
> by a human shall that person's blood be shed;
> for in his own image
> God made humankind. (Gen. 9:3-6)

Until this covenant with Noah, humans only had permission to eat vegetables and fruits. Now they are given permission to eat animal flesh as well, but Yahweh places limits on how animal flesh could be used. In particular, Noah and his descendants are not allowed to eat the blood of the animals. They are not to merely kill and devour the animal. In draining the blood of the animal, humans enter the realm of ritualistic sacrifice. These laws given to Noah are counted as binding on all humanity (cf. Acts 15:20; 21:25).

When Genesis 9 discusses the killing of humans, then, it is in this context of sacrifice as well as of homicide in general. Humans are not to sacrifice other human beings because in doing so, they sacrifice the image of God. To sacrifice a human being is to show disrespect to Yahweh's image (Gen. 9:6). The penalty for violating this prohibition is death (cf. Lev. 20:2-5).

Even when the passage is applied to other forms of homicide beyond human sacrifice, we must recognize the blood feud in these lines: "Whoever sheds the blood of a human, by a human shall that person's blood be shed." Hence, this is not an endorsement of the modern death penalty, as some death-penalty proponents claim.[28] Noah was clearly a seminomadic figure and did not live in a state that would provide the machinery of capital punishment.

In the light of the blood feud, this passage does two

things. First, it simply describes the likely consequences of murder. If a person kills another, the victim's family will seek revenge, and the murderer is likely to be murdered in retaliation. The passage speaks of a single person as the avenger. Hence, it describes the role of the *go'el*, the avenger of blood, a murder victim's close kinsman who carries responsibility for avenging the killing.[29] In this sense, the passage is merely descriptive of the actual situation, not necessarily prescriptive of what should happen.

Second, like other parts of the Hebrew Scriptures, this passage places a limit on the blood feud. In limiting the responsibility for vengeance to the *go'el*, it restricts other members of the family from seeking vengeance. It thereby reduces the possibility of a widening circle of violence. It also limits revenge to the murderer himself, not to other members of his family.

If there is any imperative in the passage, it is simply that only the murderer (and not other members of his family group) may be killed in revenge. Thus, the passage is a prohibition of substitutionary killing, in which one person is killed for the crime of another. As shown later, the Mosaic Law further emphasizes this second meaning of the passage.

The story of Abraham also carries an important message about human sacrifice. After Abram makes his covenant with Yahweh, thus becoming Abraham, there are a series of stories in which Yahweh reveals how Abraham's life and values must differ from the people around him. The first difference is that Abraham and all his male descendents are to be circumcised, thus giving them a physical symbol of their difference from other people (Gen. 17:9-14). The second difference is the contrast between Abraham's hospitality to strangers and the vicious reception of strangers exhibited by the people of Sodom and Gomorrah (Gen. 18:1—19:11). Then comes the story of Abraham's near sacrifice of Isaac, which addresses the issue of human sacrifice (Gen. 22:1-19).

Yahweh calls Abraham to sacrifice his son Isaac. The

demand for sacrifice is especially significant, because Isaac is Abraham's heir, through whom Yahweh is to fulfill his promise that Abraham will become a great nation. The sacrifice required, then, is not just of a beloved son, but also of Abraham's promised legacy. Just as Abraham is about to make the sacrifice, Yahweh provides a ram as a substitute victim. Again, Abraham is set apart from his neighbors. He is to substitute animals for human sacrificial victims. In this story, one imperative for the descendants of Abraham is clear. They are not to participate in human sacrifice; instead, they are to practice animal sacrifice.

Despite this prohibition, human sacrifice would continue to be an issue for the Hebrews. In the story of Jephthah in Judges 11, a human sacrifice is made in celebration of a victory in battle. Jephthah himself reminds us that the early Israelites were a mixed lot. Not only did the group consist of people who had escaped from Egypt, but also Egyptians who joined them as they left Egypt (Exod. 12:38), nomadic people who joined them in the wilderness, and Canaanites who joined them as they conquered Palestine.[30]

According to Judges 11, Jephthah is the son of a prostitute, which means that he is an outcast. His mother is likely a Canaanite, since the Mosaic Law prohibits any Hebrew woman from having sex with anyone other than her husband. Jephthah becomes an outlaw but then is called by Yahweh to become a judge, a charismatic leader for the Hebrews with a special mission to save them from their enemies. Before a battle with the Ammonites, Jephthah vows to make a sacrifice if the battle is successful. The vow itself may reflect his Canaanite background. He promises Yahweh, "Whoever comes out of the doors of my house to meet me, when I return victorious from the Ammonites, shall be the Lord's, to be offered up by me as a burnt offering" (Judg. 11:30-31).

After the victory, his only child, a daughter, comes out "to meet him with timbrels and dancing." Although he is reluctant, the daughter insists that he carry out his vow. After a period of preparation, she is sacrificed (Judg. 11:34-40).

In many ways, Jephthah's sacrifice is typical of human sacrifice. A vow is made at a time of emergency—in this case an impending battle against a stronger and more-sophisticated foe. The sacrificial victim is an unmarried girl, with no protectors outside her own family. The victim is portrayed as having some special insight into her situation. In this case, she is pictured as wise beyond her years. It is important to the sacrifice that she is perceived as a willing victim. She is given time to prepare for the ordeal, which implies the ritualism with which it is carried out.

Even into the time of nationhood, human sacrifice continued to be a problem for the Israelites. One reason given for the destruction of the Northern Kingdom of Israel was that "they made their sons and their daughters pass through fire" (2 Kings 17:17). The prophet Micah asks rhetorically, "Shall I give my firstborn for my transgression, the fruit of my body for the sin of my soul?" Then he denies that this is what Yahweh wants from his people (Mic. 6:7-8). Some of the people sent to replace the exiled Israelites are also accused of human sacrifice. "The Sepharvites burned their children in the fire to Adrammelech and Anammelech, the gods of Sepharvaim" (2 Kings 17:31).

Two Judean kings, Ahaz and Mannaseh, are condemned for practicing human sacrifice. Second Kings 16:3 reports that Ahaz "even made his son pass through fire, according to the abominable practices of the nations whom the LORD drove out before the people of Israel." Manasseh "made his son pass through fire," in addition to other offenses against the commands of Yahweh (2 Kings 21:6).

Jeremiah accuses the people of Judah of human sacrifice:

> And they go on building the high place of Topheth, which is in the valley of the son of Hinnom, to burn their sons and their daughters in the fire—which I [Yahweh] did not command, nor did it come into my mind. (Jer. 7:31)

Psalm 106 counts human sacrifice as part of Judah's history:

> They sacrificed their sons and their daughters to the
> demons;
> they poured out innocent blood,
>   the blood of their sons and daughters,
> whom they sacrificed to the idols of Canaan;
>   and the land was polluted with blood. (Ps. 106:37-38)

Finally, when the good king Josiah ruled, one of his achievements was that "he defiled Topheth, which is in the valley of Ben-hinnom, so that no one would make a son or a daughter pass through fire as an offering to Molech" (2 Kings 23:10).

All of this shows that human sacrifice, used to curry favor with the gods, continued to be a problem for the Hebrews at least until the time of the Babylonian exile. Over a period of several centuries, however, the law created alternatives to both sacrifice and the blood feud. In the next chapter, we will see the variety of ways in which the law turned the Israelites away from these forms of violence.

2
The Mosaic Law

As shown in the last chapter, the Hebrew Scriptures were written at a time of great social change, not just in Palestine, but also in all of the Near East. Moving from a seminomadic existence into a settled, agriculture-based civilization with a centralized government, the Hebrew people faced numerous difficult challenges. Many of the cultural practices functional in a seminomadic society created problems in their more-settled situation. With their emphasis on trade and the production of goods, the newly established civilizations had to regulate the behavior of their citizens to a much greater degree than nomadic existence had required.

These civilizations, on the other hand, also had some advantages in facing the new challenges. The movement of peoples had allowed new ideas to germinate and be disseminated. The sharing of ideas with other cultures led to increasingly complex intellectual and religious systems. Economic specialization was one result of this complexity. The crafts and the arts blossomed; for the first time, some individuals were able to support themselves through manufacture and trade rather than herding or agriculture. Writing allowed for greater and more-accurate communication of facts and ideas as well as longer-lasting records of decisions and agreements. It would also prove to be an invaluable tool for change.

All of these changes came together in the early written law codes. The Hebrew code, usually called the Mosaic Law because it is attributed to Moses, was developed over several centuries and is one of the great accomplishments of the human race. While it probably was influenced to a degree by earlier legal codes, it also made remarkable departures from them. Unlike the Code of Hammurabi, for example, the Mosaic Law combined both secular and religious regulations. The breadth and depth of its laws are truly remarkable compared to other codes of its time. But it went beyond that. The law was a teaching device. It educated and regulated, frequently supplying religious justification for its rules.

Indeed, unlike other early written codes, the writers of the Mosaic Law embedded it in a story: the founding of the Hebrew people. The law of Moses is given as a part of that story. Law supports story, just as narrative bolsters law. From a Jewish or Christian point of view, one without the other makes no sense. The story and the code are integral parts of a cohesive whole: the story tells what Yahweh did for the Hebrews, and the law describes their covenanted response to Yahweh's gift. Yahweh created the Hebrew people by setting them free from the Egyptians; the Hebrews acknowledged their role as the people of Yahweh through their acceptance of the law that would regulate their lives and religion.[1]

For this reason, all violations of the law, even those that a modern society would consider as secular offenses, were understood to be offenses against Yahweh because they broke the covenanted relationship. Thus, an offense against the family was an offense against Yahweh, who in the covenant had given the family its importance. Violence against a human being was violence against Yahweh, who had created that person in his own image and who was in a covenant relationship with each individual. This might be in the covenant mediated through Moses (Exod. 19–24), or at least in the covenant with Noah and all his descendants (Gen. 9).

Although scholars believe that the totality of the Mosaic Law was developed over a long period of time, they also believe the absolute law, or apodictic law, of the Ten Commandments probably dates back to the time of the

Exodus. The apodictic laws are unique to the Hebrews. They are stated in the imperative and are in the second person singular, indicating that they are directed toward each individual member of the community.[2] They are broadly stated and do not include specific consequences of their violation.

The bulk of the Mosaic Law consists of conditional laws (as in Exod. 21–23). These laws are stated using conditional clauses: "If something happens, such will be the legal consequence." This is also the typical pattern of other ancient codes. It can be argued that the conditional laws were an attempt to "fill in the blanks" of the apodictic code of the Ten Commandments. The absolute laws provided general principles, and the conditional laws specified how the principle was to be applied in given situations.

Capital Crimes in the Hebrew Scriptures

The Mosaic Law applies capital sentences for certain crimes:

- Trespassing on sacred territory (Exod. 19:12; Num. 1:51; 18:7).
- Homicide (Exod. 21:12; Lev. 24:17; Num. 35:16-34).
- Assault on one's mother or father (Exod. 21:15).
- Kidnapping (Exod. 21:16; Deut. 24:7).
- Cursing one's parents (Exod. 21:17; Lev. 20:9).
- Failure to restrain an ox known to be dangerous, if it results in the death of a human being (Exod. 21:29).
- Sorcery or witchcraft (Exod. 22:18, applying only to women; Lev. 20:27, applying to both genders).
- Bestiality (Exod. 22:19; Lev. 20:15-16).
- Sacrificing to gods other than Yahweh (Exod. 22:20).
- Profaning or working on the Sabbath (Exod. 31:14-15).
- Human sacrifice (Lev. 20:2-5).
- Adultery—both the man and the woman are put to death (Lev. 20:10; Deut. 22:22).

- Incest—son with father's wife; father-in-law with daughter-in-law; son-in-law with mother-in-law (Lev. 20:11-12, 14).
- Male homosexual conduct (Lev. 20:13).
- Prostitution on the part of a priest's daughter (Lev. 21:9).
- Blasphemy (Lev. 24:16).
- False prophecy (Deut. 13:1-5; 18:20).
- Enticing people to worship false gods (Deut. 13:1-11).
- Idolatry (Deut. 17:2-5).
- Disobeying judicial decisions of the priests (Deut. 17:8-13).
- False witness in a capital case (Deut. 19:18-19).
- Rebelliousness on the part of a son (Deut. 21:18-21).
- Failure to build a parapet on a roof, if someone falls and is killed (Deut. 22:8).
- Fornication (adultery) by an unmarried (engaged?) woman with one not her fiancé, discovered after marriage (Deut. 22:13-21).
- Sexual relations between an engaged woman and a man not her fiancé—both to be stoned to death (Duet. 22:23-24).
- Rape of an engaged woman (Deut. 22:25).

Family Laws

Although the list of capital crimes seems excessive by modern standards, each of these crimes was considered to be an attack on the very fabric of the Hebrew culture. For example, the laws that make it a capital offense to show disrespect or to injure one's parents reflect the overwhelming importance of the family in Israelite society. Families provided individuals with everything they had. Like modern families, they brought their members into the world and oversaw their growth into adulthood. But the ancient family was much more than that.

The family's status determined the individual's status. The family's vocation would become the vocation for all the family members. The family protected its members from danger—thus in some respects acting as a police force for its members. It was also like an insurance company; it took care of its members when they were sick, and took care of widows and orphans after a father died. The family provided social security for those who were too old or disabled to work.

The family was so important that the Ten Commandments spoke directly to its stability: "Honor your father and your mother, as the LORD your God commanded you, so that your days may be long and that it may go well with you in the land that the LORD your God is giving you" (Deut. 5:16; Exod. 20:12). The promise at the end of the commandment reflects the importance of the family to the Hebrew culture. A functional family helped assure long life and well-being for its members.

Patriarchs had almost unlimited authority over their families. Their position in the community affected the status for the entire family. The patriarch's status would determine the economic resources available to the family and how those resources could be expanded through the marriage of the children. Mothers were given respect not just because of their role as mothers, but because they were the father's wife, the father's chief "possession," and an important economic resource for the family.[3]

When a patriarch died, the eldest son was normally granted his position, thus gaining the same kind of authority over the family that the father had. In this context, a show of disrespect on the part of a son toward his parents was an unnatural act, usurping the patriarch's role. If the patriarch could not control his children, it endangered the family's position in the community because he would lose face and thereby lose status. The entire family, which extended far beyond the modern nuclear family, might suffer serious negative consequences from the child's rebelliousness. As Proverbs 17:25 puts it, "Foolish children are a grief to their father and bitterness to her who bore them."

Moreover, the *son* who was rebellious toward his parents could not be trusted to succeed the father. His foolishness and impulsiveness in a position of such power would be dangerous to the family. It was incumbent on the community to protect the natural order of the family. Thus, a child who struck his parents, or who cursed his parents, or who was generally rebellious toward his parents—that child could be put to death. One of the proverbs says this graphically:

> The eye that mocks a father
>   and scorns to obey a mother
> will be pecked out by the ravens of the valley
>   and eaten by the vultures. (Prov. 30:17)

In the case of cursing one's parents, this was not just a matter of angry words. A curse in the Hebrew culture had power. It was akin to witchcraft or sorcery. To curse someone was to ask powerful spiritual forces to harm the person. In the eyes of Hebrew culture, the crime of "cursing one's parents" was a real effort to hurt them.

Sexual Crimes

Sexual crimes were also considered to be an attack on the very basis of Hebrew culture. A family's survival depended on its ability to reproduce legitimate children. The father's duty was to leave behind children who would continue his family's line. In early Hebrew theology, the continued existence of the family appears to be the only kind of human immortality recognized. For a man to leave no surviving heirs behind destroyed his only hope of continued existence beyond death.[4]

Adultery and fornication threatened the Hebrew family structure. It is significant that the prohibition of adultery immediately follows the prohibition of murder in the Ten Commandments. For the Israelites, a woman who had sexual intercourse outside of marriage was permanently polluted (though Deut. 22:28-29 calls for marriage of an unengaged woman with her sexual partner). With their prescientific understanding of reproduction and their high rate of infant mortality, the Hebrews believed much more deeply than modern people do that a successful pregnancy was dependent on the good will of God.

Moreover, if a woman had sexual intercourse outside of marriage, it brought into question the legitimacy of all her children. It had the potential of tainting her children in Yahweh's eyes forever.[5] Adultery was considered so serious a crime that it was repeatedly used as a metaphor for Israel's unfaithfulness to Yahweh, breaking the covenant (cf. Hosea). Adultery was an unfaithfulness that threatened the very existence of the Israelites.

A child's paternity was an essential factor in his or her life. Illegitimate children faced a bleak future. They were not admitted to the assembly of the people even to the tenth generation, and thus were not counted as part of the Hebrew people (Deut. 23:2). They had no family to protect them or to take care of them if they were sick or disabled. Abject poverty and slavery were their likely destiny. For a woman to risk bringing such a child into the world, then, was a very serious offense—virtually the equivalent of killing her children.

Furthermore, if a woman brought a child into the world that was not her husband's, she increased the danger that the husband would assume he had an heir when he did not. This threatened the family line and the man's chance at immortality through his children; it was a serious offense against her husband and his entire family.

The marriage of a man and a woman in Hebrew society was the bringing together of two families, not just two individuals. Marriage was a form of alliance between the two families. The families continued their interest in the marriage partners not just out of love for them, but because they represented the family as a whole. For a woman to break faith with her husband was not just an insult to him, but to his whole family. Adultery could certainly lead to a blood feud between the families. That is one reason why, in the case of adultery involving a wife or an engaged woman, the man as well as the woman would be put to death (Deut. 22:22-24).

The man was impinging on the rights of another man and the rights of his family.

In the case of earlier fornication discovered on the marriage bed, only the woman was put to death (her sexual partner was apparently not identified; Deut. 22:13-21). This guarded against the woman passing off a child conceived before the marriage as that of her husband, resulting in the husband and his family believing they had an heir when they did not. When the woman committing fornication was the daughter of a priest, the crime had an added religious dimension. Because her father was a priest, the woman's crime was suggestive of Canaanite temple prostitution (Lev. 21:9).

In the case of rape of an engaged woman, the rapist was to be sentenced to death, since he had threatened the family line of another man (Deut. 22:25-27). But if the woman was not attached, the rapist was forced to take her as his wife and to pay the woman's family for her (Deut. 22:28-29). He was also prohibited from ever divorcing her. In this case, he had destroyed the woman's value to her family, since as a non-virgin, she had little chance of attracting a marriage partner who would enhance the family's position.

Like adultery, incest also threatened the stability of the family. A son who had intercourse with his father's wife (whether or not the woman was his mother) directly challenged the rights of his father. It was a usurpation of the father's role in the family and destroyed the basis of family life.[6] Other forms of incest mentioned in Leviticus are cross-family relationships—the father-in-law with his daughter-in-law, and the son-in-law with his mother-in-law. In each case, the incestuous relationship posed a threat to the alliance between the families, not to mention the possible intrafamily complications. Such relationships became the concern of the community-at-large since they threatened the peace between families.[7]

Male acts of homosexuality and bestiality are primarily considered to be sexual in modern society. In the Hebrew society, however, they had an important religious meaning.

Homosexual temple prostitution was a part of the Canaanite fertility ritual. Bestiality was also practiced as a religious rite in which a worshiper united with a god in the form of an animal.[8] Although homosexuality and bestiality may have been punished because they were abnormal behaviors, the severity of the punishment imposed probably indicates their religious significance.

Religious Crimes

We have already discussed the serious conflict that existed in Hebrew society between the religion of Yahweh and the Canaanite religions. The death penalty—for sorcery, witchcraft, violating the Sabbath, blasphemy, idolatry, false prophecy, male homosexuality, and bestiality—reflects the seriousness of this conflict.

Sorcery and witchcraft were attempts to use gods other than Yahweh to achieve human ends. The use of witchcraft was often associated with placing curses on a person's enemies, thus invoking spiritual powers to do physical harm. In Numbers 22–24, Balak asks the sorcerer Balaam to curse the Hebrew people as they move toward Canaan. Yahweh prevents this, and Balaam blesses the Hebrews instead and prophesies their success. As stated above, the ancients took curses seriously. If Balaam had been able to curse the Hebrews, this would have been a sign that Yahweh's attitude had become negative toward them.

Another case of witchcraft occurs in the story of Saul, when he uses a medium to summon up the spirit of his dead mentor, Samuel, so he can ask Samuel's advice. Saul's use of the medium shows his lack of faith in Yahweh, whose favor he had lost. Samuel, however, can only repeat that Saul has lost Yahweh's favor, and that Saul is doomed (1 Sam. 28:3-21).

Blasphemy is more than just "taking the LORD's name in vain." It is the crime of misusing the name of Yahweh, or of ascribing to him actions or attributes that are not his, or of equating oneself with Yahweh. It is a violation of the third commandment: "You shall not make wrongful use of the name of the LORD your God" (Exod. 20:7; Deut. 5:11). Names were much more important in Hebrew culture than in modern society. A person's name was believed to exert some control over the person himself. To know a person's name, therefore, was to have some power over that individual.

Yahweh gives new names to people after he has made covenants with them. Abram becomes Abraham, the meaning of the name changing from "exalted ancestor" to "ancestor of multitudes." His wife Sarai becomes Sarah (Gen. 17).[9] Similarly, Jacob becomes Israel after his wrestling match with God (Gen. 32:22-32).

To give Moses and the Israelites courage, Yahweh reveals his name to Moses. In the Hebrew way of thinking, this gives Moses and the Israelites a degree of control over Yahweh. The third commandment, however, places a strict limit on this control. The Hebrews know the name of their God, but a condition of this knowledge is that they are not to misuse the name. The Hebrews may expect Yahweh's support, but only so long as they do not speak or act in a way that brings discredit to Yahweh. To speak untruths about Yahweh or the actions of Yahweh, therefore, removes his support from the community; that is a serious crime.

Closely tied to blasphemy is false prophecy. Prophecy, of course, was not simply telling the future. It was speaking the prophetic word to the community for Yahweh. Because the Hebrews often failed to live up to their covenant with Yahweh, prophets frequently brought messages that the community did not want to hear.

On the other hand, there were professional prophets, often paid by the government, who gave messages to the community, either in the name of Yahweh or in the name of other gods, and thereby supported the government's position. The government used these prophets to build support for the "party line." Yahweh condemns these prophets, who did not speak Yahweh's truth to the people. The law equates their misuse of prophecy with blasphemy, a misuse of the name of Yahweh, since they prophesied in his name.

This condemnation occurs in Deuteronomy but not in earlier books of the Pentateuch. Hence, it may reflect the problem of false prophecy that resulted from the use of court prophets by the monarchy. These prophets invariably prophesied in a manner favorable to the king.

Idolatry was *the* major religious problem for the Hebrews. It violated both the first and second of the Ten Commandments. Idolatry looked to other gods for the nation's salvation, thus putting other gods before Yahweh. And it represented these gods in manmade images. The Hebrew religion was demanding because it gave humankind no control over God. Yahweh could not be fully understood, let alone coerced or manipulated.

The Canaanite religions, on the other hand, purported to offer the Hebrews the ability to control the gods who presumably affected their destiny. They tried to do this through the use of idols and various rituals, including sacred prostitution, which included both heterosexual and homosexual acts, bestiality, and the sacrifice of children. There were many among the Hebrews who felt that the Canaanite gods offered them more control over their lives than Yahweh did. These people easily fell into idolatry and enticed others into it as well.

Conversely, the Yahwist cult believed that the Lord had a special relationship with the Hebrews: he would show his love for them, but often in ways that were mysterious. They believed that it was not possible for humans to manipulate or control Yahweh. For them, idolatry was a symbol of the Hebrews' lack of faith in Yahweh's love and concern for them. The practice of idolatry could result in Yahweh's temporary withdrawal of his favor and protection. By the time of the monarchy, the problem was a serious one that struck at the heart of the Hebrew religion and culture. The use of the death penalty to curtail the practice shows that idolatry was regarded as a major threat to the Hebrew way of life.

The Sabbath day was one of the important symbols of the special relationship between Yahweh and his people. It was closely tied to the creation story and represented Yahweh's completion of his creative act (Gen. 2:1-3). The Sabbath pointed back to a time when the world was created perfectly and looked forward to a time when Yahweh would redeem his creation. To the writers of Deuteronomy, it also had the moral purpose of reminding people to treat slaves with consideration. The Sabbath gave all people a day of rest, and slaves were specifically included (Deut. 5:14).

Indeed, the Sabbath was meant to remind the Hebrews of their own enslavement in Egypt and of how Yahweh freed them from their own hard labor. "Remember that you were a slave in the land of Egypt, and the LORD your God brought you out from there with a mighty hand and an outstretched arm; therefore the LORD your God commanded you to keep the Sabbath day" (Deut. 5:15).

The Sabbath was thus an important sign of the Hebrews' religious identity. A passage in the Apocrypha, 1 Maccabees 2:29-38, reports an incident in which one group of Jews refused to fight on the Sabbath day and were therefore slaughtered. Foreign overlords also tried to break down the Jewish religion by forcing Jews to profane the Sabbath.[10] Given the importance of the symbol and the intensity of conflict with Canaanite and other religions, violating the Sabbath was considered to be a dangerous form of apostasy.

The intensity of feeling about breaking the Sabbath can be felt in the Gospel narratives of the religious leaders' reaction to Jesus' violations of Sabbath rest in order to heal the sick. The imposition of capital punishment for violating the Sabbath shows how the Hebrews felt that foreign religious practices menaced their way of life and had to be resisted to the death.

Trespassing on sacred territory, like the violation of the Sabbath, was an affront to Yahweh and to the holy rituals used to worship him. The importance of these laws can be seen in the New Testament story when Paul is nearly killed on the spot because he is accused of bringing Gentiles into the temple (Acts 21:27-30). Violation of holy ground profaned the sacredness of Yahweh represented by the temple. It was therefore punishable by death.

The priests, too, had to be respected. Failure to obey their judicial decisions not only threatened anarchy, but also was a direct affront to Yahweh, who had given his decision through them. Such disrespect threatened the cultural existence of the Hebrew people; it would be akin to modern sedition.

Violent Crime

Of all the capital crimes in the Hebrew Scriptures, only three—murder, kidnapping, and rape—would be considered serious crimes in modern society. Of these three, the ideas about rape (discussed above) were also quite different from modern ideas. Kidnapping was an especially heinous crime because of the common possibility of slavery. Kidnapping might occur not only for ransom, but also to provide slaves. Selling one's own people into slavery violated their rights as Hebrews; it also denied the action of Yahweh in setting them free. For the Hebrews, kidnapping carried all of the horror that it does for modern people and also had this additional religious dimension.

Murder, of course, is the ultimate denial of a person's rights because it wipes away the most fundamental right of all—the right to life. There has never been a society in which murder was not considered to be a serious offense.[11] In a culture that practiced the blood feud, reaction to a murder could be a prolonged and uncontrolled cycle of violence. A murder, then, was not just a personal crime; in addition, it was a crime against the community as a whole.

As already stated, in Hebrew society murder carried additional religious weight: to kill a human being was also to destroy the image of Yahweh—indeed, the only image of Yahweh that was allowed. An attack on a human was thus a direct attack on Yahweh himself, since the human form represented him.

Human beings were considered to be so important that

even some forms of negligence causing the loss of human life could be punished by death. Not securing an ox known to be dangerous, or not adequately fencing a roof—either could be punished by death if such negligence caused someone's death. However, there does seem to be some allowance for a blood payment in lieu of the death penalty for crimes of negligence (Exod. 21:29-30).

While the list of capital crimes in the Hebrew Scriptures is extensive, no crimes against property were to be punished by death. This is quite different from other ancient codes. The Code of Hammurabi, for example, punished with death the following crimes not mentioned in the Mosaic Law as calling for death:[12]

- Stealing the property of the temple or court (Law 6).
- Making a purchase from a slave or the son of another man without witnesses or a contract (considered theft; Law 7).
- Inability to pay a fine for theft (Law 8).
- Receiving stolen goods (Laws 9-11).
- Helping slaves escape; receiving escaped slaves (Laws 16, 19).[13]
- Breaking and entering (Law 21).
- Robbery (Law 22).
- Taking advantage of a fire to steal (Law 25).
- Failure to pay a military substitute (Law 26).
- Withdrawing a military substitute (Law 33).
- Stealing from or harming a military officer (unclear; Law 34).
- Cheating customers in a tavern (apparently applies only to women tavern keepers; Law 108).
- Allowing conspirators to meet in one's tavern (Law 109).
- Priestesses opening a tavern or entering to drink (Law 110).
- A merchant detaining for debt a freeborn man who dies from mistreatment; the merchant's son is put to death (Law 116).

- A wife bringing forth an unproved bill of divorce for abandonment or neglect (Law 143).
- Building an unsafe house that results in the death of its owner (Law 229). If the owner's son is killed, the builder's son is put to death (Law 230).

Considering the list of crimes in the Code of Hammurabi that do not appear in the Mosaic Law, one must draw the conclusion that human beings in Hebrew society were considered to be more important than property. In Mesopotamia, the opposite was true in many cases. This insight that human life is of greater value than property was an important step forward for early civilizations—an insight so revolutionary that it would take three thousand years before it became widespread and was applied to humankind as a whole. As late as the nineteenth century, adults and even children would continue to be executed for theft, even in Christian countries that presumably honored the Mosaic Law.

In abolishing capital punishment for property crimes, the Hebrews showed remarkable insight—certainly something that can truly be called inspired.

The Mosaic Law and the Blood Feud

Chapter 1 discussed the blood feud as a social institution. As the Hebrew people moved into permanent settlements from their seminomadic condition, the blood feud became a serious issue. Without the safety valve of mobility, feuding became more deadly and uncontrolled. As with other cultures moving from nomadic lifestyles to settled societies, the establishment of a written code to regulate personal and family behavior created an important tool to de-escalate the violence of feuding.

In this section we will examine some of the law's provisions to reduce violence. These provisions were important because they also came to protect anyone accused of a capital crime under the code. They not only moved the Hebrews away from the blood feud, but also from the precipitous imposition of the judicial death penalty under the law.

The End of the Blood Feud

Deuteronomy 24:16 states, "Parents shall not be put to death for their children, nor shall children be put to death for their parents; only for their own crimes may persons be put to death" (cf. Jer. 31:29-30; Ezek. 18). With these words, the Hebrew Scriptures put an end to the legality of the blood feud. The addition of this specific statement condemning the blood feud in Deuteronomy, written five to six hundred years after the earliest parts of the Torah were written, shows the tenacity of the feuding custom. Feuding undoubtedly continued in primitive rural parts of Palestine through the time of Christ, as indeed it continues even today in more remote parts of the Mediterranean basin.[14] However, earlier parts of the law had already placed limits on the practice of feuding.

The Cities of Refuge

The establishment of cities of refuge was an initial step away from the blood feud. Cities of refuge were established throughout the nation, so people who had accidentally killed someone else could be safe from deadly reprisals. The cities are described in Numbers 35:9-15. The passage distinguishes between two kinds of killings. The first is intentional, characterized by the use of weapons, apparent premeditation, and evidence of prior animosity. In this case, the avenger of blood may kill the murderer whenever they meet.

As stated in chapter 1, the avenger of blood was also a modification in the practice of the blood feud that made it less capricious and deadly. The avenger of blood was the victim's *go'el*, his redeemer, a close family member. The responsibility for avenging the death fell to the avenger of blood. This provision allowed only a single person to seek revenge for a murder, and then only on the actual murderer. The acceptance of the avenger of blood as the instrument of jus-

tice indicates that this passage was written before the full cur-
tailment of the blood feud as a provision for justice.

The second kind of killing distinguished by the law was
unintentional. In such killing, there was no prior animosity,
no premeditation, and all the appearances of an accident.
When these conditions were present, the killer could escape
to a city of refuge. Yahweh commanded that six cities of
refuge be designated, evenly spread around the country.
When a killing that appeared to be unintentional occurred,
the law required that the congregation judge between the
killer and the avenger of blood. If the congregation found
that the killing was an accident, the killer was sent to a city of
refuge, where he must remain until the death of the high
priest.

If the killer left the city at any time before this, the avenger
of blood had the right to kill him without incurring bloodguilt himself. No ransom could be paid in place of being banished to the city of refuge. The punishment was absolute; rich
and poor bore an equal punishment. However, after the
death of the high priest, the killer could return home, and the
killing could not be avenged without the avenger of blood
drawing bloodguilt upon himself.

Joshua 20 repeats information about the cities of refuge
and states that a killer may apply to the elders of the city for
refuge. If the elders accept his story, they take him into the
city and give him a place to stay. Joshua 20:7-8 lists the six
cities: Kadesh, Shechem, Hebron, Bezer, Ramoth, and Golan.
Joshua 21 identifies the six cities as places allotted to the tribe
of the Levites, giving them a special priestly and religious
status (21:13, 21, 27, 32, 38; 21:36 lists Bezer as a Levite city in
21:36 without calling it a city of refuge).

Two of the cities of refuge, Hebron and Shechem, are mentioned as such again in 1 Chronicles 6:57, 67, among cities of
the Levites. This absence of further mention probably indicates that the cities of refuge were an interim step in the cur-
tailment of the blood feud, rather than a permanent fixture in
the administration of justice. Still, they had the important

effect of requiring a hearing from impartial judges before bloodguilt could be avenged. In slowing down the process of vengeance, and in requiring that the intention of the killer be analyzed, the cities of refuge were an important step away from the blood feud. Another step was the imposition of limits on the level of retaliation that people could take.

The Lex Talionis

The *lex talionis* (law of retaliation) is a provision of ancient law that allows equal injury as the punishment for an injury inflicted (e.g., Exod. 21:23-25; Lev. 24:17-20; Deut. 19:18-21). While "an eye for an eye" is the most frequently used biblical argument for capital punishment, the lex talionis actually limited the level of revenge for injuries or death to equivalent damage. It thereby was a step away from unrestrained violence, in the style of Lamech (Gen. 4:24).

We find the idea of mutilation barbaric. Nevertheless, an eye for an eye, or a tooth for a tooth, when first imposed, was a restriction on violence rather than an endorsement of it. Under the earlier blood-feud justice, the family of the injured party determined the level of reprisal. The loss of an eye could be revenged by a cash payment, mutilation, or by homicide.

The retribution sought would depend, among other things, on the relative social status of the family groups involved. Such social discrimination appears regularly in the Code of Hammurabi. An injury perpetrated by a person from a lower-status group on a person with higher status would usually result in a higher level of revenge. Conversely, injury to a lower-status person by one from a higher level normally resulted in a lower level of retaliation—often simply the payment of blood money.

The lex talionis equalized the levels of revenge between groups by setting upper limits on the revenge allowed. For conflict between Hebrew citizens, this limit was set at equivalent injury. If an eye was lost, then an eye and no more than an eye could be sought in revenge. The avenger was not allowed to do greater injury. Similarly, for a life the avenger could take one life, but no more than one life. Such a system removed the status-defining purpose of feuding. The levels of vengeance would be equal, regardless of the status of the groups involved.

The lex talionis passage appears three times in the Torah, each within a different context. Exodus 21:23-25 is part of a longer section of laws concerning violence and setting limits on revenge. It is immediately followed by laws that concern injury to slaves.

As would be expected in this early text, slaves are not allowed to seek equivalent revenge against Hebrew citizens. Instead, they are set free. The meaning to the Hebrews is clear. Slaves are given human status. Masters are responsible for treating them humanely and under the law will be held accountable if they do not. If a master mutilates a slave, then the master does not deserve to own the slave, and the slave thereby gains a level of equality with the master. He is given his freedom. Even though slaves are not given completely equal status, the law does set limits on how higher-status persons may treat persons of significantly lower status.

In Leviticus 24:13-22, the lex talionis appears in a passage about blasphemy. Blasphemy is condemned and specified as a capital crime, and then the law is applied to both Hebrews and resident aliens. For committing blasphemy, aliens will be put to death, just as citizens will be. Then the passage states the formula of lex talionis. It ends with a statement that the law will be the same for the resident alien and for the citizen. In moving through the lex talionis, the message of the passage applies to both parties. At the beginning, the reader is told that aliens will be expected to follow the Hebrew religious law. But at the end, this uniformity is turned around; Yahweh tells the Hebrews to treat aliens with equality under the law because Yahweh is their God.

Again, the law equalizes the status of different groups. Just because a person is a stranger, without the protection of family or friends, does not mean that he can be treated differently than those who have familial protection. A stranger who harms a Hebrew will receive the same injury that a Hebrew would. Just because he is an alien does not mean that a greater level of punishment can be sought. Moreover, a crime against a stranger must be treated the same as a crime against a Hebrew. Before God and the law, there is equality between citizens and sojourners.

The last lex talionis passage appears in Deuteronomy 19:18-21. The text discusses the matter of presenting false testimony in a trial. The punishment for the false witness is the equivalent injury that the perjured testimony would demand. Thus, if the alleged offense would result in a fine, the false witness would pay a fine. If it is a capital charge, the perjurer forfeits his life. The passage ends with stern words: "Show no pity: life for life, eye for eye, tooth for tooth, hand for hand, foot for foot."

More detail on the requirements for witnesses in capital cases will be given later. At this point it is enough to say that the law stepped between the parties of a blood feud, using outside judges who weighed the evidence from both sides, to determine the level of culpability and punishment. The feuding parties were no longer allowed to evaluate the evidence on their own and then act according to their one-sided perception of the truth. Those who inflamed a situation with false words were to receive harsh punishments, whose level would depend on the potential damage they caused.

The Hebrews had apparently made some progress against the blood feud by the time Deuteronomy was written. In this last appearance, the lex talionis is used against someone who attempts to mislead a court into killing his enemy. This assumes a trial setting, so at least the one giving false testimony was not trying to kill the enemy himself.

The Abolition of Blood Payment for Murder

The prohibition of blood money in lieu of death as the

penalty for murder was another indication that the law was an attempt to equalize the level of punishment for criminal conduct. The prohibition occurs in Numbers 35:31: "Moreover you shall accept no ransom for the life of the murderer who is subject to the death penalty; a murderer must be put to death."[15] This provision may appear to be the strongest biblical endorsement of capital punishment. Nevertheless, in the ancient Hebrew society it would have had the effect of equalizing punishment and thereby making it less likely that blood-feud killings would occur.

As stated above, the blood feud gave an advantage to the more-powerful family groups. Their strength allowed them to seek more-severe retaliation for injuries to their members, and to discourage weaker families from seeking comparable retribution. In many cases, the powerful clans could simply buy off retribution by paying blood money. Under this law, however, members of the powerful family could no longer buy their way out of a murder. The death penalty would apply equally to all.

That this provision was directly aimed at curtailing blood feuds is seen in the passage that follows. The text demands that a person who has fled to a city of refuge also cannot be ransomed. They must stay there until the death of the high priest. The following reason is given for not accepting ransom in the cases of bloodshed:

> You shall not pollute the land in which you live; for blood pollutes the land, and no expiation can be made for the land, for the blood that is shed in it, *except by the blood of the one who shed it.* You shall not defile the land in which you live, in which I also dwell; for I the LORD dwell among the Israelites. (Num. 35:33, emphasis added)

Here the end of the blood feud is tied directly to the worship of Yahweh. Bloodshed among Yahweh's people pollutes Yahweh's land. When a murder occurs, only the life of the murderer, not the lives of other members of the murderer's family, can be used to pay for the murder. Feuding is therefore an insult to Yahweh since it makes no distinction between the guilty and the innocent. Under Yahweh's law, only the murderer could make the payment, and the payment had to be made with his life, not with money. The feud's purpose of establishing the relative status of families is thereby destroyed.

So we can see that the law set up a number of social mechanisms to counter the blood feud. The cities of refuge forced the Hebrews to look more closely at a killing to see if it truly required the life of the perpetrator as a payment. The lex talionis limited the level of revenge and thereby took away the feud's purpose of setting social status for feuding groups. The elimination of the payment of blood money required from both the wealthy and the poor the same payment for murder—life for life. These three measures, then, undercut much of the social foundation for feuding.

The Creation of a Court System

It would not have been possible to destroy the blood feud as the primary mechanism of justice without replacing it with something else. The Mosaic Law not only forbade the practice of the blood feud; it also set up an alternative institution through which injured parties could seek justice. During the days of the blood feud, mediators from uninvolved families were employed to negotiate settlements. The use of judges probably grew out of this practice. Exodus 18:13-27 indicates that Moses had already appointed judges even before the Hebrews entered Canaan. Moses' father-in-law, Jethro, suggested the system. The judges dealt with minor cases, while harder cases were passed on to Moses.

Deuteronomy 1:16-17 contains Moses' charge to the judges:

> Give the members of your community a fair hearing, and
> judge rightly between one person and another, whether cit-
> izen or resident alien. You must not be partial in judging:
> hear out the small and the great alike; you shall not be

intimidated by anyone, for the judgment is God's. Any case that is too hard for you, bring to me, and I will hear it.

The provisions for the cities of refuge show that some form of court was used to determine an accused killer's eligibility for this recourse. The assembly or the elders of the city determined whether the story of an accidental homicide was plausible, and the avenger of blood was required to abide by their decision.

Exodus 21:22 gives an example of how the judges worked in one case of injury. When a pregnant woman miscarried as a result of injury caused by people fighting, the parties responsible were required to pay a fine to the husband. The husband could ask for any amount he wanted, but the judges made the final determination of what the fine would be. This is a case where a blood feud may have resulted in homicide under the old system. The loss of progeny was a major injury that could call for a violent act of revenge.

The new system limited the level of revenge, replacing blood revenge with a fine, enforced for the injured party by the community as a whole, through the court. The injured party could ask for any level of fine he wished, but the court made the final decision about the level of restitution required. The court, not the injured party, set the punishment, though the injured party did have a say in the proceedings.

As they are about to enter Canaan, Yahweh tells the Hebrews to appoint judges for each town. He warns the judges not to distort justice or take bribes, for he wants his land to be known as a place of justice (Deut. 16:18-20).

The judges' role in working through corporate blood-guilt is demonstrated in Deuteronomy 21:1-9. If a body is found in the open country between towns, the judges measure the distance between the body and the surrounding communities. The town that is closest to the body must provide a heifer for a sacrifice. Over the sacrifice, the officials of the town take an oath that they neither committed nor witnessed the murder. By this action, they are absolved of guilt for the crime.

Again, under the blood-feud system, if a citizen of one community was murdered near another community, it could be assumed that citizens of the nearby town were involved in the murder. This could begin a feud between the two towns, resulting in continuing bloodshed. The judicial system provided a method for stopping such a cycle of violence before it started.

Witness Requirements

In order to provide a sufficient level of revenge to assuage the injured family, the courts were allowed to impose the death penalty in some cases. However, the law set three rules of evidence that made it difficult for them to do so. The first requirement was that there had to be a minimum of two eyewitnesses to the crime before a death sentence could be imposed. Numbers 35:30 states, "If anyone kills another, the murderer shall be put to death on the evidence of witnesses; but no one shall be put to death on the testimony of a single witness."

Although Numbers 35:30 applies only to murder, Deuteronomy 17:6 applies the same witness requirement to accusations of idolatry. Deuteronomy 19:15 extends the provision to all crimes and calls for two or even three eyewitnesses: "A single witness shall not suffice to convict a person of any crime or wrongdoing in connection with any offense that may be committed. Only on the evidence of two or three witnesses shall a charge be sustained."

The requirement that there be at least two eyewitnesses is a high level of proof, particularly when only adult males were eligible to be witnesses.[16] Most murders and other capital crimes were committed in secrecy, either with the perpetrator acting alone or with accomplices who, as we shall see later, probably would not be allowed to be witnesses in a capital case. In other words, the level of proof required by the Mosaic Law passed "beyond a reasonable doubt" to virtually "absolute certainty."

Another requirement made it difficult to obtain a conviction in a capital case—the penalty for a false witness. This has already been referred to above in the section on the lex talionis. In a capital case, the penalty for a false witness was death (Deut. 19:16-21). The severity of the penalty was undoubtedly an attempt to give higher credibility to the courts, as a new institution of justice. Several other ancient codes, including that of Hammurabi and the Twelve Tables of the Romans, had similar provisions.[17]

Since providing testimony in the court was a rigorous experience, it is doubtful that disinterested parties would provide false testimony. The testimony of the victim's friends, if allowed at all, would be suspect and likely to receive rigorous cross-examination from the judges. Thus, most witnesses who would testify under this law would be careful to simply report what they had seen or heard without inference or embellishments.

The final provision for witnesses was that they had to participate in the execution that their testimony brought about. Deuteronomy 17:7 states in the case of idolatry, "The hands of the witnesses shall be the first raised against the person to execute the death penalty, and afterward the hands of all the people" (cf. Acts 7:58). Passages of the Mishnah show that in all capital crimes, witnesses were required to participate in the execution (M. Sanhedrin 6.4; 7.3).

In ancient Israel, there was a direct connection between being a witness in a capital case and the infliction of the death penalty. A witness could not testify and then let a professional executioner do the dirty work of the execution. Even in a time when such violence may have been more acceptable, some people would not have wanted to participate in the actual killing of another human being. They therefore would not come forward to testify.

In the Mosaic Law, these three provisions for witnesses would have made it difficult to obtain a conviction in a capital case. This high standard may have been the result of the Israelites' evolving understanding of Yahweh's prohibition of human sacrifice.

The Law and Human Sacrifice

As seen in chapter 1, human sacrifice continued to be an issue for the Israelites at least up to the time of the Babylonian exile. Just as the law ended the practice of the blood feud, it also demanded an end to human sacrifice and provided the death penalty for violating this prohibition. The prohibition is found in Leviticus 20:2-5:

> Any of the people of Israel, or of the aliens who reside in Israel, who give any of their offspring to Molech shall be put to death; the people of the land shall stone them to death. I myself will set my face against them, and will cut them off from the people, because they have given their offspring to Molech, defiling my sanctuary and profaning my holy name. And if the people of the land should ever close their eyes to them, when they give of their offspring to Molech, and do not put them to death, I myself will set my face against them and against their family, and will cut them off from among their people, them and all who follow them in prostituting themselves to Molech.

As the court system provided an alternative system of justice to the blood feud, the Mosaic Law created an alternative to human sacrifice in the highly ritualistic sacrifice of animals in the temple. The story of Abraham and Isaac provides a narrative justification for this change, showing that Yahweh required animal sacrifice rather than human sacrifice from the first patriarch of the people.

At the time of the conquest of Canaan, however, the Hebrews did practice human sacrifice. The *kherem* ("devoted to destruction"), the massacre of entire settlements, was a form of human sacrifice in gratitude to Yahweh for giving the Israelites victory over their enemies. The story of Jephthah's sacrifice of his daughter also indicates that human sacrifice was still occasionally practiced by some Hebrews during the conquest.

The belief that wrongdoers caused community catastrophes is seen in the story of Phinehas killing an Israelite man and a Midianite woman to stop a plague (Num. 25). The story has a feel of human sacrifice since a couple—one a foreign woman—is killed in order to end a community disaster.

Joshua 7 tells a similar story. After the fall of Jericho, Achan disobeys Yahweh and takes some of the items devoted to Yahweh, items *kherem,* to be destroyed (Josh. 6:18-21; 7:10-26). As a result, the Israelites lose the first battle of Ai. Achan is found to be guilty of sin by lot rather than by trial. He is then stoned to death, and this sacrifice enables the Hebrews to successfully attack Ai.

As late as the writing of Jonah, human sacrifice continued to be practiced. By casting lots, the sailors of the ship on which Jonah is trying to escape from Yahweh discover that he is the cause of the storm that is threatening their lives. When the lot falls on Jonah, he becomes a willing sacrificial victim and tells them to cast him into the sea to stop the storm (Jon. 1:1-12).

Human sacrifice was thus seen as a way of balancing the universe. If someone had offended a god, a sacrifice was required to restore the balance. Payment or offerings to atone for crime, in other words, were considered to be a form of sacrifice, of moral balancing. If the offense was severe enough, then even a human life might be required. In the case of crime where the perpetrator was known, the life of the criminal would be forfeit. But when no one knew the cause of the catastrophe, a human with little value to the community could be sacrificed to atone for the unknown sin.

The Mosaic Law does little to stop the sacrifice of proven criminals for their own crimes, although it does set a high standard of proof. On the other hand, it does stop the practice of sacrificing humans to atone for unknown crimes and provides an alternative ritual to take its place. Leviticus 16 describes the national day of sacrifice known as the Day of Atonement. On this day, an elaborate ritual involving animal sacrifice is performed.

First, the high priest sacrifices a bull to atone for his own sins and the sins of his household. After he has purged his own sins, he is purified to offer sacrifices for the sins of the people. Next he sacrifices a goat to purify the temple from the sins of the community. Then he takes another goat (the scapegoat), confesses the sins of the people, and lays his hands on its head. This goat is taken into the wilderness and released. The sins of the people are carried away with the goat into a barren region, and they are no longer held accountable for them.

In the practice of the scapegoat, Yahweh does not require equivalent injury when the perpetrator of a crime is not known. The goat carries away the sin, regardless of who committed it, and Yahweh thereby forgives the sin. The moral balance is restored not through the payment of equivalent injury, but by the grace of Yahweh.

For the Hebrew perspective, the law took a step away from violence by providing animal sacrifice as a substitute for human sacrifice. For Christians, this is an important foreshadowing of the New Testament, in which God's Son will play the role of the scapegoat (the Lamb of God) and carry away the sin not just of the community, but of the whole world (John 1:29).

The Talmud Interpreting the Torah

The extent to which Jewish law placed limits on the death penalty is shown in the Talmud. Its discussions are based on the Mishnah, a collection of oral interpretations of the law from prominent Jewish teachers of about 200 B.C. to about A.D. 200. The Mishnah received its written form late in the second century. The Palestinian (Jerusalem) Talmud was given its written form late in the fourth century. The Babylonian Talmud (four times as long!) received its final form in the late fifth and early sixth centuries.

Although many of the Talmudic teachers lived after the time of Christ, it is generally agreed that their interpretations of the law represent traditions that reach backward for centuries.[18] These collections of teachings provide a variety of opinions rather than a single interpretation of the law. In some cases, the interpretations may even be contradictory.

For example, in Mishnah Sanhedrin 6:2, Rabbi Judah says of a man about to be executed, "If he knew that he had been subjected to perjury, he says, 'Let my death be atonement for all my sins, except for this particular sin (of which I have been convicted by false testimony)!'" To which other rabbis reportedly reply, "If so, then everyone is going to say that, so as to clear themselves."[19]

The Mishnah, the earliest part of the Talmud, contains many provisions concerning capital punishment. It was written around A.D. 200, after the temple was destroyed and many Jews were dispersed from Palestine. Jacob Neusner believes that the writers of the Mishnah were describing an ideal reality that contrasted with their own disoriented situation. Its attention to detail brought some order to the disorder of their world.[20]

The Mishnah describes in great detail the system of witnesses. Beginning with property cases, Sanhedrin 3:4 excludes all relatives from being witnesses or judges in a criminal case. Fathers and brothers, uncles from both sides of the family, uncles by marriage, fathers-in-law, sons, and sons-in-law, and anyone who stands to inherit from the defendant—all these are not allowed to be witnesses. Anyone related to the defendant may not be a witness. The text excludes both friends and enemies.[21] Also, men of questionable character—gamblers, usurers, and those who do business in produce during the Sabbath Year—cannot be witnesses.[22]

The evidence of codefendants cannot be used against each other, based on the previous witness exemptions. Sanhedrin 9:3-4 states, "A murderer who was mixed up with others—all of them are exempt [from execution]." Rabbi Judah says that they all should be put in prison.[23] This appears to mean that in the case of codefendants in a murder, none are put to death, perhaps because it is difficult to determine who is most responsible for the death.

However, there were several contrary opinions about this.[24]

In capital cases, witnesses are carefully admonished. According to the Sanhedrin 4:5, they are told,

> Perhaps it is your intention to give testimony (1) on the basis of supposition, (2) hearsay, or (3) of what one witness has told another, or you may be thinking, "We heard it from a reliable person," or you may not know that in the end we are going to interrogate you with appropriate interrogation and examination. You should know that the laws governing a trial for property cases are different from the laws governing a trial for capital cases. In the case of a trial for property cases, a person pays money and achieves atonement for himself. In capital cases the accused's blood and the blood of all those destined to be born from him who was wrongfully convicted are held against him who testifies falsely to the end of time.
>
> For so we find in the case of Cain, who slew his brother, as it is said, "The bloods of your brother cry (Gen. 4:10). It does not say "The blood of your brother," but "The bloods of your brother"—his blood and the blood of all those who were destined to be born from him. . . . Therefore man was created alone . . . to teach you that whoever destroys a single Israelite soul is deemed by Scripture as if he destroyed the whole world. And whoever saves a single Israelite soul is deemed by Scripture as if he had saved a whole world.[25]

In capital cases, there were to be twenty-three judges.[26] The judges had to be priests, Levites, or Israelites eligible to marry into the priesthood—those most knowledgeable about the law.[27] The judges were given specific instructions for questioning the witnesses about the time and place of the crime. Rabbi Jose (or Yose) held that the witnesses should be asked if they warned the defendant of the consequences of his act.[28] He believed, "Under no circumstances is one put to death unless both witnesses against him have given warning to him."[29] The judges were admonished to be tough cross-examiners: "The more they expand the interrogation, the more one is to be praised."[30]

There appears to be two levels of questioning. An examination, which may be preliminary to the trial, allows a greater level of contradiction between witnesses. At this stage, witnesses may admit their ignorance of an important question. However, at the interrogation stage, apparently a rigorous cross-examination, such an admission voids the testimony. In the case of either examination or interrogation, however, if the testimony of two witnesses is contradictory, the testimony of both is thrown out.[31]

The Mishnah also gives some rules regarding when evidence becomes contradictory, although this is one place where there is some disagreement. The testimony stands if the witnesses are off from each other by one day. It is voided if they are off by two or more days. Similarly, if the testimony is off by one hour, it stands. Some felt that it was voided if it was off by two hours, but Rabbi Judah disagreed. However, all appear to agree that the testimony is voided if the disagreement about the time would mean that the crime occurred when the sun was in a significantly different position in the sky.[32]

Once the testimony is heard, the judges begin to analyze it and make the decision of innocence or guilt. This is done in public. Unlike trials over property rights during which arguments for guilt and innocence can occur at the same time, in capital cases, the judges must hear the reasons for acquittal first.[33] This gives the arguments for acquittal a place of prominence. Learned men who are not among the judges but who wish to argue for conviction are not allowed to speak. Yet learned ones who wish to speak for acquittal are given permission to make their arguments. They are even allowed to sit with the judges. The defendant is also allowed to argue in his own defense.[34]

When a vote is taken on innocence or guilt, if the defendant is found innocent, he is allowed to go free, and the judgment cannot be reversed.[35] However, if the vote finds the defendant guilty, the judges go off in pairs and discuss the case further throughout the night. During this time, they do not eat much, and they drink no wine.[36]

When they return the next day, those who argued for or voted for acquittal the day before may not change their votes or argue for conviction. Those who argued for conviction, however, may now argue for innocence if they have changed their minds, and they may also change their votes to help declare the defendant innocent. In other words, the second day's vote can only be changed from guilty to innocent.

The vote to condemn must be made by at least a two-vote majority. However, if a single judge cannot come to an opinion (even if the vote is overwhelmingly for conviction or acquittal), they add to the number of judges, two-by-two, up to seventy-one judges. At any time in the process, if there is a vote by a simple majority of the judges for acquittal, with no judge stating that he has no opinion, the defendant is freed. If they get to a vote of thirty-six for guilt and thirty-five for innocence, they argue until one of the judges who voted for conviction comes over to the side for acquittal, and the defendant is freed.[37]

Even if the defendant is condemned, however, the process is not over. Although the execution is held immediately, there are a number of ways in which it can be stopped. As the condemned is being led out, a man stands at the door with flags in his hand. If a judge decides that he has a new argument for acquittal, the man waves the flags, and a horseman is dispatched to stop the execution. Up to five times, the condemned person also can bring up new evidence for acquittal. As they proceed to the place of execution, a herald shouts out the reason for the execution and asks any witnesses for acquittal to come forward.[38]

Just before the execution, the condemned man is allowed to confess, or once again to proclaim his innocence. However, as stated above, there was some argument about whether to allow the condemned man to claim his innocence at this point.

The process is clearly stacked in favor of an acquittal. Those who can be witnesses are severely limited. Further evidence of innocence is allowed after the witnesses are heard, but no additional evidence of guilt is accepted. Judges are not permitted to change from an innocent vote to one for conviction. The Mishnah makes what appears to be a consensual statement of the rabbis' reluctance to impose death sentences: "A Sanhedrin which imposes the death penalty once in seven years is called murderous."

This declaration is followed by three dissenting voices. According to Rabbi Eleazar ben Arariah, a Sanhedrin that imposes [the death penalty] once in seventy years is murderous. Rabbis Tarfon and Aqiba say, "If we were on the Sanhedrin, no one would ever be put to death." Rabban Simeon ben Gamaliel replies, "So they would multiply the number of murderers in Israel."[39]

The Mishnah did not outlaw the death penalty. Indeed, it gives extensive instructions for carrying out stonings, burnings, decapitations, and strangulations, describing in detail explicit roles for the witnesses.[40] However, the comprehensive restrictions placed on the witnesses and judges in capital trials would have made it extremely difficult to impose death sentences if the restrictions were strictly applied. To the extent that the Mishnah reflects the traditions of those most familiar with the Hebrew Scriptures, it points to an extremely careful application of death-penalty statutes—a conscientious application unique at that time in history.

In addition to these provisions of the Mishnah, the modern Talmudic scholar Adin Steinhaltz has found other restrictions on witnesses and capital procedures in the Talmud. According to Steinhaltz, the court operated under a standing instruction to avoid inflicting a death sentence if possible. As a result, any judge who might not be impartial toward the defendant was removed. No one could be a judge who had witnessed the crime, because personal resentment might lead him to be too hard on the defendant. Childless men and aged persons were disqualified because they might forget "the sorrow of raising children."[41]

Any witness ever accused of a crime was not eligible to testify. Written testimony was not accepted, since the person writing it would not be available for cross-examination. Examination and cross-examination was rigorous. Confessions were not admitted as evidence because this might cause the criminal to harm himself, which is prohibited. This eliminated the possibility of using forced confessions as evidence.[42]

As one example, Steinhaltz cites the Talmud's "fierce urge to arrive at the absolute truth," which eliminated the use of circumstantial evidence:

> If witnesses see a man, sword in hand, pursuing someone, both enter a building, the pursuer emerges alone with a bloodstained weapon and the other is found dead inside, the pursuer cannot be convicted on the basis of this eyewitness evidence. Witnesses can only attest to what they have seen with their own eyes, and neither conjectures, theories, nor hearsay evidence will be accepted by the court. Evidence concerning a crime is valid only when the witnesses actually saw the crime occur.[43]

Steinhaltz also cites the Talmud's demands that the offender must have fully understood what he was doing, and that the offense was punishable by death. The Talmud does not accept as evidence of premeditation apparent planning and preparation on the part of the accused. Instead, according to the Talmud, the accused must have been warned that what they were doing is a crime punishable by death. Even further, defendants had to indicate that they understood the warning and were ignoring it.[44] If the accused persons chose to commit the crime in spite of this warning, only then could they be executed.

According to Steinhaltz, the procedures and rules of evidence made it so difficult to convict criminals under the Jewish written and oral law that special administrative procedures and courts were set up to protect society in times of danger. These courts had much less stringent requirements, but it was understood that they were not following the Hebrew law, either written or oral.

The provisions of the Talmud show how the most knowledgeable authorities interpreted the Hebrew Scriptures. For them, the death penalty was possible, but it could only be applied under extremely rigid restrictions. This interpretation points to the general message of the Scriptures, which is not of revenge but of redemption. We now turn to this important redemptive message and how it reflects on capital punishment.

3
Yahweh's Grace and Forgiveness

Because of the many stories of violence in the Hebrew Scriptures, readers often forget that the real message of these writings is not of Yahweh's vengeance, but of his grace and forgiveness. Again and again the Hebrew people renege on their covenant with Yahweh. Again and again they suffer from the withdrawal of Yahweh's protection. But Yahweh always receives them back when they repent. Throughout the Hebrew Scriptures, one of the recurring refrains is that Yahweh's "steadfast love endures forever" (e.g., 2 Chron. 7:3; Jer. 33:11). The Hebrew Scriptures are the story of his steadfast love despite the failure of those whom he loves.

An Overview of the Hebrew Scriptures

Genesis begins with the creation of the world. Yahweh creates a good world and populates it with creatures with which he is well pleased. The crowning achievement is the creation of human beings. But then something goes wrong. Rather than returning Yahweh's love, the human beings wish to take charge of the world themselves. They challenge Yahweh. They want to decide for themselves what is right and wrong, rather than accepting Yahweh's world as he created it (Gen. 3).[1]

As a result, they lose the paradise that Yahweh created for them, and death enters the picture. Yet Yahweh allows them to live in the new and fallen world that they have created for themselves. From there on, matters get worse. At the beginning, Yahweh has the sole power over life and death. Humans are allowed to eat plants, but not animals (Gen. 1:29-30). Now the humans appropriate some of that life-and-death power for themselves. In the story of Cain, we see the first murder. Cain kills his brother. Yahweh says that Abel's blood cries out from the earth for vindication—from the very earth that Yahweh created (4:10). The story of degradation continues. The human race continues their desire to "be like god" (3:5) by marrying their daughters to the "sons of God" (6:4).[2]

Finally, the human race becomes so vile that Yahweh can no longer stand them. A terrible flood kills nearly everyone. But Yahweh has not given up. He saves a remnant, Noah and his family (Gen. 6–10). First appearing here, the recurring theme of the faithful remnant is important to both Jews and Christians (cf. 1 Pet. 3:20). The Flood ends with a covenant. Yahweh promises that he will never again destroy the earth. He allows humankind to eat meat, but prohibits human bloodshed (Gen. 9).

Noah and his family, however, prove to be no better at being Yahweh's people than the other descendants of Adam and Eve. Noah's son Ham shows disrespect to his father after Noah gets drunk, and he receives his father's curse for it (Gen. 9:20-27). The people of Babel build a city and start erecting a tower to the heavens so they can make a name for themselves, rather than keeping the name Yahweh has given them. Because of this, human speech becomes muddled, and understanding between peoples becomes more difficult (Gen. 11:1-9).

Then Yahweh begins a new phase of his relationship with the human race. From all the people, he chooses one man from which to create a people of God. That man is Abraham, who shows a remarkable faithfulness to Yahweh (Gen. 12). With Abraham and his descendants, Yahweh makes a new covenant. The physical sign of the covenant is circumcision, but the spiritual sign is faithfulness. Because of Abraham's faithfulness, Yahweh promises that his children will be as numerous as the stars in the sky and the sand in the sea, and that they will be given their own land (Gen. 15; 17; 22). Abraham's descendants, while hardly morally exemplary, maintain their faith in Yahweh, and finally through a series of adventures reach Egypt (Gen. 37–50).

There they run into trouble. Although originally invited in by a friendly ruler, after several generations they become slaves in the land (Exod. 1). Yahweh is the one who rescues them from their plight, showing once again that he is always with them even in the worst of times. Through his servant Moses, Yahweh leads his people out of the Egypt and into the land that he had promised to Abraham long before. At Sinai Yahweh gives Moses and his followers the law, the religious and moral symbol of their special covenant with God. The law and their adherence to it will identify them as Yahweh's people, "a priestly kingdom and a holy nation," with the task of eventually leading other people back to Yahweh (Exod. 2–24; 19:6).

But the Israelites do not remain faithful to Yahweh. At first they even fear to enter the Promised Land (Num. 13–14). Although they finally do enter Canaan and successfully subdue the native population, they are constantly tempted to follow the indigenous gods—gods seemingly more suited to their new agricultural lifestyle (Josh.; Judg. 1–3). Time and again, they turn away from Yahweh with disastrous results. Each time they repent, and Yahweh finds a way to rescue them from their self-created catastrophe.

In the early years, Yahweh does this by raising up judges, charismatic leaders. The book of Judges follows a repeated pattern:

- Faithfulness for a brief period.
- Unfaithfulness bringing disaster.
- Repentance, forgiveness, and salvation.
- A brief period of faithfulness before the cycle begins again.[3]

The selection of the judges shows Yahweh's power to use even the most unlikely persons as leaders. All are flawed, and at least two—Jephthah and Samson—are dangerous criminals (Judg. 11–16).

The instability of the period of the judges leads the Israelites to seek a permanent solution to their problems. They ask Samuel, who combines the roles of a judge, priest, and prophet, to appoint a king for them. Samuel feels that the creation of a monarchy means abandoning the way of Yahweh. But after consulting with Yahweh, he reluctantly agrees (1 Sam. 8). Yet the king is to be accountable to Yahweh and must work within the context of the law (10:25; cf. Deut. 17:14-20). The first king is Saul, a deeply flawed man who eventually goes insane under the pressures of the kingship (1 Sam. 9–31).

Following Saul, King David becomes the model king of the Israelites (1 Sam. 16—2 Sam. 24; 1 Kings 1–2). Though morally imperfect, David is able to unite the tribal confederation of the Hebrews into a nation. For his faithfulness, Yahweh promises David, "Your house and your kingdom shall be made sure forever before me; your throne shall be established forever" (2 Sam. 7:16).

Under David's son Solomon, the unified kingdom of Israel reaches its highest pinnacle of power (1 Kings 1–11). Solomon builds the first great temple for the worship of Yahweh, and the nation appears to have a bright future. But underneath this bright exterior, there is darkness. Solomon makes alliances with other nations through his many marriages. He allows his wives to bring their own gods as idols into the land and to worship them. The king himself takes part in such worship! Because of this unfaithfulness, the nation loses its unity.

Israel holds together during Solomon's lifetime, but upon his death, the nation is split by rebellion. The Northern Kingdom of Israel sets up the usurper Jeroboam I as its king, while Solomon's foolish son Rehoboam continues to rule over the Southern Kingdom of Judah (1 Kings 12). Both kingdoms become less and less faithful, except for a few brief periods when relatively good kings reign. The Northern Kingdom is wracked by dissension, and many of its kings begin and end their reigns with rebellions and assassinations. The Southern Kingdom's history is more stable, as the monarchy remains with the descendants of David (1–2 Kings).

Both kingdoms are pawns of powerful but ever-changing neighboring empires. Their kings play dangerous political games as they try to maintain their countries' independence through alliances and double-dealing. Often the political maneuvering involves idolatry, as political alliances seduce the Israelites into accepting the gods of their allies. Meanwhile, both nations develop the class system that marks early civilizations. More and more of the people become poverty stricken, while the small ruling class grows ever richer.

Into this situation comes a remarkable group, the Hebrew prophets, such as Elijah and Elisha (1 Kings 17—2 Kings 13), Hosea, Amos, Isaiah, Jeremiah, Ezekiel, and others. Ranging widely in background and interests, each bravely denounces the abuses of the kings and demands a return to the worship of Yahweh. They call for the social justice that would mark the people's faithfulness to Yahweh and his covenant with them at Sinai (Exod. 19–24).

But the words of the prophets fall mostly on deaf ears, and Yahweh withdraws his protection from his people. As a result, the Northern Kingdom falls to Assyria (722 B.C.; 2 Kings 16–17). Later, Judah falls to Babylon, and the temple is destroyed (587/6 B.C.; 2 Kings 24–25). In both cases, the ruling classes and many others are forced out of the country, becoming exiles in foreign lands.

Nevertheless, Yahweh still does not leave his people. The Babylonian exile, in particular, gives the Israelites a new understanding of their God. While many people in such circumstances would simply assume that their god was not powerful enough to protect them, the exiled Hebrews came to a startlingly different conclusion. Unlike other gods who were tied to a specific territory, Yahweh is the God of the entire world, they believed (Isa. 40).

Though the Babylonians defeated the Israelites in battle, it was only because Yahweh had allowed them to do so, not because he was impotent in the face of the Babylonian gods (e.g., Ezek. 6). The exile came to be seen as a chastisement of their nation, rather than as a defeat of Yahweh. With this, the hope of returning to their homeland became a cohesive force that held them together. Finally, after nearly fifty years of exile, the people of Judah were allowed to go home (Ezra; Neh.).

The people who returned, however, had a new understanding of their nationhood. Although they loved their land, they knew that their identity had more to do with their God than with where they lived. Judaism had been born. This resulted in two contradictory trends.[4] The first was a much-higher degree of ethnocentrism. At the restored temple, Ezra bitterly denounced mixed marriages with non-Jewish wives. The Jewish men who had married foreigners agreed to reject both their wives and their children (Ezra 9–10).

At the same time, the understanding of Yahweh as the God of all people brought a new sense of universalism to the life of the Jews. God had chosen them not just for their own benefit, but also as an example for the rest of the world to follow. The prophet Isaiah states this thought in some of the world's greatest poetry:

> In days to come
>   the mountain of the LORD's house
> shall be established as the highest of the mountains,
>   and shall be raised above the hills;
> all the nations shall stream to it.
>   Many people shall come and say,
> "Come, let us go up to the mountain of the LORD,
>   to the house of the god of Jacob;
> that he may teach us his ways
>   and that we may walk in his paths."
> For out of Zion shall go forth instruction,
>   and the word of the LORD from Jerusalem.
> He shall judge between the nations,

and shall arbitrate for many peoples;
they shall beat their swords into plowshares,
    and their spears into pruning hooks;
nation shall not lift up sword against nation,
    neither shall they learn war any more. (Isa. 2:2-4)

The steadfastness of Yahweh's love is the major theme of the Hebrew Scriptures. The stories of the unfaithfulness of the human race in general and the Hebrew people in particular make it clear that Yahweh's steadfast love has nothing to do with the merit of those toward whom it is directed. Yahweh is often disgusted and angry about the behavior of his people, but despite this, he continues to love them.

This does not mean that there is no price to be paid for evil deeds. The Israelites and the whole human race reap what they sow, but always there is a limit to the punishment inflicted. There is no final punishment that leaves them without hope. In the words of the prophet Ezekiel,

> As I live says the LORD God, I have no pleasure in the death of the wicked, but that the wicked turn from their ways and live; turn back, turn back from your evil ways, for why will you die, O House of Israel? And you, mortal, say to your people, The righteousness of the righ-teous shall not save them when they transgress; and as for the wickedness of the wicked, it shall not make them stumble when they turn from their wickedness; and the righteous shall not be able to live by their righteousness when they sin. Though I say to the righteous that they shall surely live, yet if they trust in their righteousness and commit iniquity, none of their righteous deeds shall be remembered; but in the iniquity that they have committed they shall die. Again, though I say to the wicked, "You shall surely die," yet if they turn from their sin and do what is lawful and right— if the wicked restore the pledge, give back what they have taken by robbery, and walk in the statutes of life, committing no iniquity—they shall surely live, they shall not die. None of the sins that they have committed shall be remembered against them; they have done what is lawful and right, they shall surely live. (Ezek. 33:11-16)

The prophet's message is clear. All of us, whether the world counts us among the righteous or among the wicked, need Yahweh's grace in order to live. We will suffer from our misdeeds and the misdeeds of others, but Yahweh will continue to love us. For Jews and Christians, our faith in God's continuing and steadfast love, despite what appears to be evidence to the contrary, lifts us above our guilt and suffering. Yahweh's love gives us confidence to continue on, just as knowledge of his love helped the Jews of the Babylonian exile to focus on their expected return to Judea.

The Hebrew Scriptures teach that we can do nothing to make Yahweh stop loving us. God's love is not dependent on our goodness or our ability to follow the law. This is shown in the repeated failures of the Israelites to remain faithful, and Yahweh's repeated forgiveness of their transgressions. The true story of the Hebrew Scriptures, then, is one of forgiveness, not vengeance.

Does Yahweh's forgiveness extend through the community as a whole, to the individuals within it? The stories of the patriarchs, judges, and kings indicate that it does. As already stated, the human leaders portrayed in the Hebrew Scriptures are all deeply flawed. They are frequently dishonest, cowardly, violent, and even sociopathic. Yet Yahweh finds ways to use their talents despite their deep imperfections.

But does Yahweh's ability to see beyond the sinfulness of his children extend to those who have taken human life? Or does his ruling to seek "life for life" represent his own behavior? To answer this question, we will look at how Yahweh treats the three most important murderers in the Hebrew Scriptures.

Three Murderers in the Hebrew Scriptures

Cain

As already seen, the story of the first murder in Genesis 4:1-17 is rich in meaning far beyond a simple tale of violence. Cain the farmer is a representative of the new agricultural order. His brother Abel is a shepherd, representative of the traditional nomadic life of the Hebrews. Yahweh accepts Abel's sacrifice of lambs but rejects Cain's sacrifice of agricultural products. Yahweh gives no specific reason for rejecting Cain's sacrifice (cf. Exod. 33:19). Yet he does say that Cain would be accepted if he will "do well," and that he must master "sin," which "is lurking at the door" like a predatory animal (Gen. 4:7).

The story is also symbolic of the struggle between the new agricultural economy and the traditional nomadic life.[5] The farmers undoubtedly wanted to restrict the nomadic wandering of the shepherds through planted fields; the shepherds felt that this was an imposition on their traditional way of living. The conservative writer of the story obviously sides with the shepherds. The murder of Abel may even be understood as an allegory of the destruction of the nomadic life by the forces of farming.

This economic meaning of the story adds to the seriousness of Cain's crime. Abel may not have been murdered out of simple jealousy, but for Cain's economic benefit, perhaps for a land claim. The murder itself is calculated and obviously premeditated. Cain lures Abel into a field, and there, when Abel does not expect it, Cain strikes him down.[6] Cain then tries to cover up the crime by lying to Yahweh when he is asked directly about his brother's whereabouts.

However, Yahweh does not demand "life for life" from Cain. Instead, Cain's punishment is banishment. Yahweh tells him, "You will be a fugitive and a wanderer on the earth" (Gen. 4:12). Though the punishment is not a death sentence, it is certainly serious. As an outcast, Cain loses the protection of his family.[7] He will be at the mercy of anyone who wishes to kill him. Cain clearly states his fear: "My punishment is greater than I can bear! Today you have driven me from the soil, and I shall be hidden from your face. I shall be a fugitive and a wanderer on the earth, and anyone who meets me may kill me" (4:13-14).

So Yahweh takes a further step. While not lifting the banishment, he states that he will continue to protect Cain. Yahweh sets a high level of revenge on anyone who would kill him. If Cain is murdered, the LORD himself will be Cain's *go'el*, his redeemer and his avenger of blood. Then he gives Cain a special mark to show that he is under Yahweh's protection. The story ends, not with Cain's execution, but with the birth of his son Enoch, and Cain's founding of the first city, another indication of the economic changes that underlie the story.

Moses

Cain murdered Abel because of jealousy and possibly for economic gain. Moses represents the political murderer. The story is told in Exodus 2:11-22. Moses, a Hebrew who was adopted by an Egyptian aristocrat (a daughter of Pharaoh), begins to identify with his people, who are slaves. We can imagine that the young man, while maintaining some contact with his birth family, has begun to feel sympathy for his people. His sympathy then turns into anger at Egyptians, who oppress them.

One day, as he watches the Hebrews working, he is overcome with righteous indignation when an Egyptian overseer beats a Hebrew slave. He is calm enough to look around, guarding against being observed, and then he murders the Egyptian. Moses' act of looking around shows that the murder was premeditated. It is not a crime committed simply on impulse, but something that he thinks through. He hides the body to cover up his crime.

Moses' murder of the Egyptian was a political act. He saw injustice and took the law into his own hands. Bishop Godfrey Ashby describes the murder:

> His actions, however, are those of a privileged and protected individual who suddenly realizes how the other half lives. His actions are those of a raw and untried champion of civil rights. He tackles the oppression of his newly discovered people head on, by violent action, by taking the law into his own hands. His motives are understandably misunderstood by another Hebrew, and his crusading zeal

changes to furtive fear and ignominious flight out of Egypt. . . .
[The writer intends] to depict Moses, not as a hero from cradle to grave, but as a meddling unstable agitator to be transformed into a persevering leader. The text nowhere states that Moses was acting, at this stage, under Yahweh's orders. In fact, neither Moses nor the Hebrews have any idea at this stage of who Yahweh is or of what he can do. Moses begins his career as a failed political agitator, his bravado turned into fear at the first sign of opposition.[8]

Some might argue that since Moses killed an enemy of the Israelites, Yahweh would not have viewed this as a murder. However, at this point in the Hebrew Scriptures, the killing occurs under the covenant with Noah, not under the law of Moses. Under the covenant with Noah, no ethnic distinction is made between murder victims. Moreover, the story does not commend Moses for his violent act, and nowhere in the Bible is this murder commended or treated as an act of war. As Bishop Ashby observes, the act is portrayed as a rash act by a privileged young man who is used to getting his own way.

From the Egyptian point of view, the act was clearly a murder. The overseer was a representative of the Pharaoh, and as such was a symbol of Pharaoh's authority. The murder was thus an act of rebellion or even terrorism. The text says, "When Pharaoh heard of it, he sought to kill Moses" (Exod. 2:15).

But Yahweh does not allow Moses to receive the punishment that the Egyptians believe he deserves. Yahweh does not demand that Moses' blood be shed for the blood he has shed, as the covenant with Noah seems to require. Instead, Moses receives banishment, the same punishment meted out to Cain. He is forced to leave all he knows behind. No longer the pampered adoptive son of the Egyptian aristocracy, Moses joins a group of primitive nomads in Midian and earns his living through the difficult work of herding sheep. Like the banished Cain, Moses' exile also includes his marriage and the birth of his son.

Eventually, Yahweh is able to turn this violent and impulsive young man into the greatest of all Hebrew leaders. Out of the disaster of the murder, Yahweh creates new life and a new possibility for his people.

David

Perhaps the most notorious and cowardly murder that occurs in the Hebrew Scriptures is David's murder of Uriah. The story is told in 2 Samuel 11–12. David has grown from a young national hero to become the mature king of the Israelites. Through bloody warfare and political intrigue, he has consolidated his hold on power. Indeed, he has become powerful enough that he no longer needs to lead his army in the field.

One day, after the army has gone out to war, David is walking on his roof and notices a woman bathing. He is immediately infatuated with her. Even though she is Bathsheba, the wife of one of his officers, Uriah, he brings her to the palace and has sex with her. There is no clear indication that the sex is consensual. One can certainly speculate that, because of David's power and prestige, Bathsheba may have felt she had no choice but to acquiesce.[9] In any case, she later discovers she is pregnant.

At first David tries to hide his sin by bringing Uriah home from the army, so that the child will appear to be his. But Uriah, loyal soldier that he is, refuses to have intercourse with his wife as long as his comrades are in the field.[10] David sends him back to the army with a note to his commander, Joab.

The message tells Joab to arrange for the death of Uriah. Obeying David's command, Joab places Uriah in the front line and at the fiercest point of battle. His comrades are then pulled back, assuring that he will be killed. The plan goes just as David wishes. The betrayed Uriah dies in the battle. On hearing the news, David's reply to Joab is chillingly callous: "Do not let this matter trouble you, for the sword devours now one and now another" (2 Sam. 11:25).

To cover up his sin, he then takes Bathsheba as his wife.

Yahweh has seen all that has happened, and through palace intrigues, it is probable that a number of others know what is going on. Yahweh sends the prophet Nathan to David. The prophet accuses him of the crime, described clearly as a murder: "You have struck down Uriah the Hittite with the sword, and have taken his wife to be your wife, and have killed him with the sword of the Ammonites" (1 Sam. 12:9). The crime is aggravated by the second capital crime of adultery, or even the rape of a married woman.

Although Yahweh is angry about David's sin, David's life is not demanded in return. David's punishment is that he will have an unsettled reign. He will experience rebellion and will not have peace. And the child that is the result of the sin will die (1 Sam. 12:10-14).

Symbolically, David's punishment is similar to the one given to both Cain and Moses. The prosperous life that they know disappears, and they experience a loss of family. As king, David cannot be banished in the traditional way. His banishment is one of the loss of peace and the loss of his child. David's life will never be the same again, but his life is not forfeit. Like the story of Cain, the story of David's murder of Uriah ends with new life, the life of David's son Solomon, who would rule the unified kingdom of Israel at its greatest time of power and prosperity.

In the Hebrew Scriptures, the pattern of recurring forgiveness softens their support of the death penalty. With Yahweh, there is always openness to repentance and forgiveness. Punishment is never his final word. The prophets repeatedly compare Israel's unfaithfulness to adultery, and Isaiah compares the Israelites to rebellious children (Isa. 1:2-4). According to the law, both are capital crimes. Yahweh has every right to destroy the nation for its sins. Yet there appears to be no crime Israel can commit that will lessen Yahweh's commitment to his people. They are always welcome to come home to him when they repent.

Similarly, Yahweh's treatment of individual murderers

also weakens the scriptural support for capital punishment. Cain, Moses and David are given second chances. As with other kinds of sinners in the Hebrew Scriptures, Yahweh is able to use murderers to carry out his plan. In addition, there seems to be considerable ambivalence throughout the Hebrew Scriptures about applying the death sentence for other capital crimes. Samson, for instance, is disrespectful toward his parents. With his erratic and violent nature, one might wonder if he abused them physically (Judg. 14:1-4). Yet he is celebrated as a champion of Yahweh.

The prophet Hosea does not demand the execution of an adulteress, but redeems her and marries her, all under Yahweh's orders (Hos. 1:2-8; 3:1-3). The worst of the idolatrous kings, Ahaz and Manasseh, sacrifice their own children; yet they are not punished with death (2 Kings 16; 2 Chron. 28). Second Chronicles reports that Manasseh eventually repents of his evil (2 Kings 21:1-18; 2 Chron. 33:1-20; cf. Prayer of Manasseh, in the Apocrypha). All these examples show that Yahweh does not, in fact, demand death sentence for sinners, even when they deserve it.

Executions in the Hebrew Scriptures

Despite the high level of violence in many stories in the Hebrew Scriptures, there are surprisingly few accounts of executions. Moreover, the distinction between human sacrifice and capital punishment in the Hebrew Scriptures is often tenuous. For example, Joshua 7 describes the stoning of Achan for looting the city of Jericho for personal gain, in direct violation of Yahweh's order. The story, however, relates like one of human sacrifice rather than of pure capital punishment. Achan's sin results in the loss of the first battle of Ai, a national catastrophe. He is found out by lot rather than by trial. As a story of human sacrifice, this incident has little to teach us about the acceptability of modern capital punishment.

There are, however, a number of stories that appear to

describe instances where the death penalty was applied after some kind of trial and without reference to national catastrophes. Leviticus 24:10-23 depicts the execution of a man who blasphemes. The man is of mixed race (Hebrew-Egyptian), which might indicate a sacrificial death, and there is a ritual laying on of hands associated with the killing. But there is no mention of a community crisis in the story, and there appears to have been some kind of trial. Perhaps the story illustrates a step between a human sacrifice and a judicial execution.

Numbers 15:32-36 describes what appears to be a trial and execution of a man who is found breaking the Sabbath. The charge seems to have been brought by witnesses, and he is not killed immediately. Although the trial is not described in detail, the man is brought before Moses, who pronounces a death sentence on him, based on the law.

In 1 Kings 21:1-16 there is the story of Naboth, who owned land coveted by King Ahab. When Naboth refuses to give up his ancestral property to the king, Ahab's wife, Jezebel, arranges for Naboth to be charged with blasphemy and treason. After what appears to be a trial, Naboth is stoned to death. Jezebel, though an enemy of the Yahwist religion, knows enough about the law to make sure that she has two false witnesses against Naboth. The story is one of several instances in the Hebrew Scriptures when political considerations override the protections of the law.

A similar story occurs in 2 Chronicles 24:20-22, about the execution of Zechariah, whose prophecies anger King Joash. The king commands that he be stoned. The method of Zechariah's execution seems to indicate that it was preceded by some kind of trial to justify the killing. The story ends with the murder of Joash in retaliation for the execution of the prophet. Like the execution of Naboth, the killing of Zechariah appears to have been done for political purposes rather than for any real violation of the law on Zechariah's part.

There are also a number of near executions in the books that describe the Babylonian exile. Nebuchadnezzar orders

Shadrach, Meshach, and Abednego to be burned alive for refusing to worship him as a god (Dan. 3). Daniel is thrown into the lions' den for refusing to give up praying to Yahweh (Dan. 6). In Esther, the king's minister Haman plots the hanging of Mordicai, Esther's uncle, but instead is hung himself (Esther 5:9—7:10).

The fullest description of a trial appears in the story of Susanna, an addition to the book of Daniel (chap. 13 in the Greek version), as told in the Apocrypha. In this drama, Susanna is tried for adultery based on the evidence of two unscrupulous religious leaders, "elders." Her children and all of her family accompany her to the trial; thus her family of origin is meeting its obligation of protecting her rights. The leaders testify against her because she has rebuffed their sexual advances. Based on their testimony, Susanna is condemned, but then Daniel calls for a more-thorough investigation of the charges.

Daniel separates the two false witnesses for cross-examination. He questions both witnesses rigorously and catches them when they disagree on details of the crime. One says the alleged adultery took place under a mastic tree, and the other says it was under an evergreen oak. According to the law of Moses, both witnesses are then put to death. The story is remarkable for the level of detail and for its agreement with the witness provisions of the Mishnah.

The earliest stories of executions in the Hebrew Scriptures do not leave any questions about the justice of the verdicts or of the final dispositions of the cases. The later Scriptures, however, present stories of how the death-penalty process can be corrupted. In the cases of Naboth and Susanna, the requisite two eyewitnesses are present, but they are false. In both cases, the corruption comes from powerful individuals who either wish to benefit from the death of the defendant or who have a personal grudge against the accused. There is less detail about the execution of Zechariah, but it is obvious that his death is brought about because of his criticism of the king.

We would not expect that the stories of attempted executions of Jews during the exile would feature trials under the Hebrew Law. Such accounts no doubt are portraits of attempted injustice toward Jews. However, these stories once again show capital punishment being used as a political tool, with powerful political leaders setting up the Jewish heroes for death sentences by manipulating public opinion and creating new laws especially to trap the Jews.

The tone of these stories shows that the later writers had more questions about the use of death as a penalty than the earlier writers.[11] Presumably, these questions were raised by the application of capital punishment in Israelite society. Laws meant to protect the innocent were not always followed. Political considerations had come into play. Some witnesses were given more prestige than others. All of these factors corrupted the law, which was meant to protect the innocent as well as to punish the guilty.

This pattern of increased questioning is important for two reasons. It undoubtedly led to attempts to tighten up the legal processes by which the law was applied. The oral law eventually recorded in the Talmud is the result of this process. For more-radical rabbis, it led to questioning the whole concept of capital punishment. They wondered whether any human legal system, even one given by Yahweh himself, could be free enough from human error and human malevolence to assure that no innocent person would ever be executed.

A young street preacher named Jesus appears to have shared these doubts. He finally created a new and impossible standard for those who wish to participate in executions. But before we turn to the New Testament, we will try to apply the teachings about capital punishment found in the Hebrew Scriptures to the use of the death penalty in twenty-first-century America.

4
Applying Hebrew Scriptures to the Debate

As stated in chapter 1, it would be a mistake to try to apply the teachings of the Hebrew Scriptures directly to today's society. The cultures of the ancient Hebrews and the modern world are simply too different to transfer elements of the ancient teachings directly to our modern situation without interpretation. For instance, even the most ardent death-penalty proponents would not wish to reinstate capital punishment for disrespectful children. Nor is it conceivable in our pluralistic American society that the death penalty would be levied for religious crimes, such as blasphemy or idolatry.

If we are to apply the teachings of the Hebrew Scriptures to the modern practice of capital punishment, it must be done *indirectly*. We can study to determine the meaning of these Scriptures in their original culture. Then we need to apply that meaning to our own culture. We must derive principles from the Scripture passages we have discussed, and then try to apply those principles in our modern context. Based on the reading of the Hebrew Scriptures we have made, we can derive a number of principles about their view of capital punishment.

Principles from the Hebrew Scriptures

1. The essential story is one of love and forgiveness.

The Hebrew Scriptures are first and foremost a history of

Yahweh's interactions with his people. While there is violence and vengeance within the story, it is primarily a love story. It tells of a God who so loves his people that it is inconceivable that he would ever stop. His love is steadfast in the face of their unfaithfulness. It is forgiving in the face of their sin. We must read individual passages of the Hebrew Scriptures within this overarching framework.

2. Justice in the Hebrew Scriptures is restorative.

The purpose of punishment is not merely to get revenge for the victims. It is also to restore the offender and to repair the damage done to society. Since the story of Yahweh and Israel is one of forgiveness and redemption, the purpose of punishment in the Hebrew Scriptures is always restorative. Yahweh's wrath is a two-edged sword. It punishes, but it also redeems.

The Hebrew people repeatedly sin, for which they are punished. However, the punishment is not meant to destroy them, but to bring them to repentance. Since the story of the Hebrew Scriptures is essentially the story of Yahweh's relationship to his people, we see Yahweh's redemptive wrath primarily within the political (peoplehood) realm rather than the individual sphere. But the recurring application of restorative justice in the story of Yahweh's relationship to specific leaders, makes it clear that the principle applies to individuals as well as to the people as a whole.

Restorative justice does not just apply to the sinner, however. It also applies to all of society. A society that has been damaged by a violent crime has to some degree been torn apart. Punishment of the offender is just part of the reparation. The society itself needs to be repaired. This restoration begins with the victims and their needs. Yahweh is deeply concerned for the poor of Israel, the victims of injustice by the wealthy. He demands that the powerful atone for their sins by taking care of those whom they have damaged.

In demanding restitution for the victims, Yahweh is essentially asking the Hebrews to re-create their society into the community he had envisioned from the beginning. If those who are powerful do not take selfish advantage of their resources, but instead use their power to ennoble the weak, then society will be better for all. People will be at peace with their neighbors, and both justice and mercy will be an integral part of the social structure. Such a response would be a return to the kind of society Yahweh originally created.

3. The death penalty is allowed only when the alternative would be worse.

The death penalty is allowed in the Hebrew Scriptures only for crimes that tear the fabric of society apart. It is instituted primarily as an alternative to the blood feud, which led to unacceptable levels of unregulated violence as the seminomadic Hebrews settled into agricultural communities. Capital punishment provided a more systematic form of justice through a court system that allowed specific levels of revenge relatively equivalent to the injury done. To a large degree, as envisioned in the law, this system equalized the position of the rich and the poor.

The other primary reason for using the death penalty was for religious deviations. To the modern mind, these crimes seem more like moral imperfections than legal issues. Yet the Hebrews recognized that their worship of Yahweh provided their primary source of cultural cohesion in a time of social crisis. Violations of this cohesiveness threatened the community, much in the same way that treason and sedition are seen to threaten a nation's existence in time of war. From the Hebrew point of view, if they had allowed religious freedom as they struggled for a national existence, their national identity would have been destroyed.

4. Capital punishment, if used, must be applied fairly and without prejudice.

The law's refusal to accept blood money as a substitute for the death penalty for murder meant that the punishment had to apply equally to the rich and the poor, the citizen and the alien. Similarly, the *lex talionis* (law of retaliation), which limited revenge to an equivalent injury as the punishment for an injury, meant that all were to stand equal before the law.

5. Capital punishment may not be used unless there is absolute certainty of guilt.

The Hebrew Scriptures called for two or three unimpeachable eyewitnesses who would face the death penalty themselves if they testified falsely. This provision created a requirement for a high level of certainty before a death sentence could be imposed. The standards of the Mishnah on implementing these general requirements made it virtually impossible for a guilty person to be sentenced to death.

6. Capital punishment may not be used unless the court examines mitigating circumstances and spares any perpetrator not fully culpable for the crime.

The cities of refuge showed that Yahweh was not interested in vengeance for the sake of getting even. The texts recognize that killings can occur accidentally, without anyone's intent. To determine whether this had happened, the courts were required to examine the motivation and the culpability of the killer.

7. Capital punishment should not be a form of human sacrifice, executing individuals for reasons other than their own crime.

Capital punishment in the Hebrew Scriptures is only used when it can be shown that the criminal has committed a particular capital crime. There had to be a direct connection between the person charged and the crime. In this sense, the execution was seen as restoring the moral balance of the universe. On the other hand, the Hebrew Scriptures outlawed the practice of human sacrifice—the use of community-sanctioned homicide—as a method of either avoiding or terminating a community crisis.

Applying These Seven Principles Today

The principles outlined above serve as a bridge between the ancient culture of the Hebrews and our own time. If we can agree that these principles lay behind the individual provisions of the law, then it is reasonable to assume that these principles, general in nature, may be applied in a different cultural context.

Hence, we can ask, Does the current practice of capital punishment in the United States follow the general principles, or moral standards, set by the Hebrew Scriptures? If we can answer yes to this question, then we can base a religious argument for our use of capital punishment on the teachings of the Hebrew Scriptures.

If the answer is no, then whether the Hebrew Scriptures support some form of capital punishment is moot, since our practice does not conform to the standards set by Yahweh for the Israelites. Instead, it might be argued that our use of the death penalty is actually a pagan practice rather than a Jewish or Christian one. With this in mind, we now turn to the application of these seven principles to the use of the death penalty in the United States.

1. The essential story is one of love and forgiveness.

Whatever else might be said about contemporary capital punishment, it cannot be claimed that it represents a loving or a forgiving act. Even at its most humane, the death penalty represents a form of psychological torture. The criminal waiting on death row is reminded daily of what is coming. On most American death rows, the inmates are given virtually nothing to do and are locked down in their individual cells for twenty-three hours a day or more. Their visiting privileges are restricted, and they have limited contact with other inmates. Many will be in this situation for ten years or more before their execution.

Moreover, the system will create special times of tension for the inmate. Because of the technicalities of the appeals process, many inmates receive premature execution dates between the time one appeal is lost and another is filed. Although it is known that no execution will take place, the inmate is read a death warrant and is treated as if the execution will go forward. He may be moved to a death cell and undergo special treatment, such as being shackled whenever he is moved.

The ritualistic nature of the execution itself only adds to the cruelty. The typical execution is scheduled a month in advance. When the schedule is set, the inmate is read the death warrant. Throughout the intervening period, defense attorneys are working desperately to stop the execution. Often during this stage, brief stays are granted and then just as quickly lifted. The inmate is torn between hope and despair.

During the last few hours before the execution, a number of ritualistic last steps are taken. Depending on the form of execution, the inmate's body may need to be prepared. If he is to be electrocuted, for example, his head and other parts of his body will be shaved. He may also be given special clothes. Members of his family may visit him for the last time. He will receive his last meal, usually one of his own choosing. At the execution itself, legal procedures may require that the inmate be read a notification of his execution. He will be asked for his last words, and then he will wait while the procedures for the actual execution are carried out.

Even if a capital sentence could be carried out swiftly and with no ritual, it would hardly be an act of forgiveness or love. The length of time spent waiting for execution, and the ritual of the execution itself—these are forms of psychological torture. Human-rights groups consider conditions on American death rows to be a major human-rights violation. Those conditions have been the subject of litigation in international courts.[1] The cruel conditions and procedures of applying capital punishment in the United States make it highly questionable that it can be made to agree with the first principle derived from the Hebrew Scriptures, to act with love and forgiveness.

The forms of execution in the USA include lethal injection,

electrocution, lethal gas, hanging, and the firing squad. In general, lethal injection is considered to be the most humane. Yet there has been resistance on the part of some states to move to this less-painful form of execution. Some state officials have openly declared that they *want* the death penalty applied in a cruel and painful manner.[2]

The behavior of pro-death-penalty crowds at executions also shows that the American form of capital punishment does not meet the first principle derived from the Hebrew Scriptures. Often drunk, members of the pro-death-penalty throng cheer the killing of a fellow human being as if it were a football game. At the execution of Keith Wells by lethal injection in Idaho, the crowd counted down to the time of execution (10-9-8-7 . . .) and then shouted in unison, "Drip, drip, drip." One sign read, "Let's get to the point!" and depicted a bloody needle.[3] At the execution of Willi Otey in Nebraska and at other executions of African-Americans, pro-death-penalty crowds yelled blatantly racist remarks, sometimes aiming their comments directly at African-Americans in the anti-death-penalty demonstrations.[4]

The comments of officials who wish to retain painful forms of executions and the behavior of pro-capital-punishment crowds do not qualify as forgiving or loving. They indicate that for many of its proponents, the death penalty is simply a matter of revenge, often actually becoming a celebration of blood lust and death. For these people, there is no pretense of improving society; they want vengeance and entertainment, pure and simple. Again, this proves that capital punishment as practiced in the United States does not follow the first principle derived from the Hebrew Scriptures, acting with love and forgiveness.

2. Justice in the Hebrew Scriptures is restorative.

According to this principle from the Hebrew Scriptures, the purpose of punishment is not merely to give revenge to the victims. It is also to restore the offender and to repair the damage done to society.

Since the offender is killed, the death penalty obviously does not restore him to society. Some do claim, and it may be true in some cases, that the fear of death does bring some criminals to more carefully consider the meaning of their lives and behavior and to change their behavior. However, even when this occurs, the death penalty is not waived. The case of Karla Faye Tucker is a prime example. As a young woman of twenty-three and while under the influence of illegal drugs, Ms. Tucker was involved in a particularly brutal murder in which a woman was killed with a hammer, in 1983.

However, it was almost universally agreed that Ms. Tucker was later rehabilitated through her religious conversion while awaiting execution. Her behavior in prison was exemplary, and Pat Robertson and Jerry Falwell, prominent conservative clergymen generally supportive of the death penalty, asked that her sentence be commuted. However, she was executed in 1998 as if there had been no change in her life.[5] Clearly, here was a case where restorative justice was thwarted by the death penalty. There have been many similar cases.

The other side of restorative justice affects families of the victims. Though many family members continue to seek the death penalty for the murderer of their loved one, closure will not come easily or quickly. Because of the lengthy process in carrying out a sentence, victim families often put their lives on hold for years as they wait for the final determination of the case. During this period, court hearings will revisit the case many times. Over and over, the most brutal details of the crime will be brought up in court and in the media, reopening wounds each time. Even if victim families want to put the case behind them, it is difficult to do so because of morbid interest by the press when the story resurfaces.

The court system also makes it difficult for the victim families to have any real understanding of the crime. Often they are not informed of the procedures or of how decisions will be made. Victim families' primary relationship with the prosecutors is to provide useful witnesses in making the case for a death sentence. Because they may help the prosecution in seeking the death penalty, the defense attorneys will do everything they possibly can to keep victim families away from the defendant. They will not be allowed to talk to the defendant about why and how the crime occurred. Such information might be extremely useful to them as they try to understand what happened.

While the offender may in fact be remorseful about the crime he committed, the victim family members' separation from the defendant may keep them from knowing this. After all, the only time they see him is in the formal courtroom setting, in which a confession of remorse would seem self-serving and staged.[6]

Some victim family members, awaiting the execution for anywhere from five to twenty years or more, focus most of their attention on the crime and the criminal. Others try to move on, which may cause conflict between family members. In many cases the sentence is overturned, leaving some victim family members bitterly disappointed years after the initial sentencing.

A life sentence, on the other hand, brings a much-quicker determination of the killer's fate, since a life sentence leaves significantly fewer appellate issues. Usually the killer disappears into the prison system, and the victim family members never hear about him again. While this form of punishment does not solve some of the other problems created by the court system, it does result in a much-faster and less-painful disposition of the case for the victim's family.

3. The death penalty is allowed only when the alternative would be worse.

As already stated, the death penalty in the Hebrew Scriptures was used primarily as an alternative to the blood feud and to enforce the religious homogeneity that they felt was necessary for the survival of their nation. As the Hebrews settled into villages, the blood feud became more deadly and uncontrolled. Because the court system was replacing a system whose sole focus was on revenge, the punishments the court imposed had to provide a sufficient feeling of revenge so that families would not seek vengeance on their own. Still, the court system was an attempt to replace the feud with a more-systematic and less-deadly form of social control.

Pluralistic modern society does not demand religious homogeneity. Modern people have found that different belief systems can exist together in peace. Certain religious practices, of course, push the limits of toleration, but in general, these are dealt with through legislative and legal systems, normally with minimal violence. The closest modern equivalent to capital religious crimes would probably be laws against sedition and treason. During peacetime, most nations of the world do not punish these crimes with death because they are normally not seen as a significant threat to national survival.

Although there were prisons when the Hebrew Scriptures were written, the concept of incarceration was new, and prisons were limited in size and designed for brief detention rather than long-term incarceration.[7] There was little scientific understanding of human behavior. Psychological and pharmaceutical methods of controlling aberrant behavior were unknown.

All these conditions have now changed. The court system has become so well established that families rarely seek revenge on their own; when they do, it is counted as a criminal act. The prison system has become large enough to house considerable numbers of violent offenders. Modern psychology, sociology, and medicine provide many more tools for controlling violent behavior and rehabilitating offenders. These changes open viable alternatives to the death penalty that were not available to the Hebrews. The option of life sentences to replace capital punishment is attractive to many people. Support for the death penalty usually declines when a true life-without-parole sentence is offered as an alternative.[8]

Pope John Paul II recognized this and gave it as one reason for the change in the Roman Catholic Church's position on the death penalty: "Modern society has the means of protecting itself, without definitely denying criminals the chance to reform. I renew the appeal I made most recently at Christmas for a consensus to end the death penalty, which is both cruel and unnecessary."[9]

Most nations agree with the pope's assessment. Of the 195 nations in the world, 108 of them (55 percent) no longer impose capital punishment.[10] Mexico effectively abolished the death penalty in 1937. Canada rejected the death penalty in 1976. International organizations, such as the United Nations, Organization of American States, and the European Union (EU) offer their members the opportunity to enter into international treaties by which they agree to abolish the death penalty.

The EU, composed of 15 countries, has abolished the death penalty. The Council of Europe with 43 countries, a steppingstone to membership in the EU, requires members to enter into a treaty to effectively abolish the death penalty.[11] Most nations definitely believe that there are now effective alternatives to the use of capital punishment as a means for achieving a safe and just society.

4. Capital punishment, if used, must be applied fairly and without prejudice.

Fairness in applying the death penalty in America has long been questioned. In 1997 the American Bar Association called for a moratorium on executions in the United States until a fairer system could be devised.[12] In 1999 the Nebraska legislature voted to place a moratorium on executions in that state because of perceived bias in its application. The governor, however, vetoed the bill.[13] In 2000, George Ryan, the governor of Illinois, placed a moratorium on executions in that state after thirteen men were released from death row because they were proved to be innocent.[14]

It has been generally recognized that capital punishment

is used more frequently on defendants who are poor. Part of this undoubtedly comes from the nature of the criminal justice system itself. Most lawyers and judges come from the middle and upper classes. All are well educated. So it is natural that they will react more favorably to a defendant who comes from the more-affluent classes and is better educated. Such a defendant is also more likely to know his rights than someone less in tune with the values of the system. He is less likely to be intimidated into giving a confession or other information that can be used against him.

The affluent defendant will also be able to take a more-active role in his defense. If convicted, he will be better able to articulate reasons for a plea bargain or for leniency. His attorney may see him as a better risk for the time and energy to be put into the case. Because the prosecutor also will recognize this defendant as a person like himself, he will be more likely to regard the defendant as a good candidate for rehabilitation. The same is true of the judge.

Most importantly, however, the affluent defendant will be able to hire his own attorney. While modern society no longer allows the payment of blood money in place of the death penalty, the affluent defendant can usually buy his way out of a death sentence by hiring an attorney to work on his case. An attorney hired by the defendant will normally be able to spend more time on the case than the indigent defendant's public defender. He will have more resources available to investigate and litigate the case. Often he will be a more experienced and knowledgeable attorney, better known to the prosecutor and the judge.

In such a case, the prosecutor may recognize that the defense attorney is able to put up a stronger defense that will demand more time and resources of the prosecutor's office. Hence, the prosecutor may be more willing to plead the charge down, thereby removing the death penalty as a possibility.

Most public defenders and court-appointed attorneys are hardworking and diligent lawyers. Yet many have less experience than attorneys in private practice who do not accept court-appointed cases.[15] Because public defenders are employed by the government, they are pressured to keep costs down. Their budgets often limit the kind of defense that they can mount for a defendant. In some cases, public defenders are hired as lowest-cost contractors when the service is put out to bid by a local government.

Such public defenders may bid on the contract as a part of their business, while also still having private clients. Protracted capital cases take time away from cases they handle for private clients, and thereby cost them money. When this occurs, they may short-circuit the capital trial by pleading the defendant guilty without negotiating to avoid a capital sentence. They do this even though they know that the defendant may receive the death penalty.[16]

The system itself makes it difficult for a poor defendant to receive the same level of legal protection as a better-off defendant. In some cases, the problem is much greater. There have also been instances where public defenders were simply incompetent. In a 1994 article in the *Yale Law Journal*, Stephen Bright cited a number of cases in which public defenders slept through parts of the trial or appeared in court under the influence of alcohol or drugs. In some of these cases, the defendant was later executed.[17]

A choice of two possible provisions would assure that the poor receive the same level of legal service as the wealthy in capital cases. As a first choice, every capital defendant needs to have the protection of a well-qualified attorney with a virtually unlimited budget. Or in a second option, all capital defendants would need to be defended by public defenders. The cost of the first solution would be astronomical. On the second, it is doubtful that legislators would ever force affluent defendants to risk their lives with overworked, inexperienced public defenders. Yet without this level of fairness, the use of capital punishment does not meet the fairness standard set by the Hebrew Scriptures.

The problem of the inequality of legal services created by

economic status is further complicated by racial prejudice. Consistently, since the reinstatement of the death penalty in the USA in 1976, about 40 percent of death-row inmates have been African-Americans.[18] This represents almost four times the percentage of African-Americans in the population. Death-penalty proponents have pointed out that since African-Americans commit more than 40 percent of the murders in the United States, the percentage of death-row inmates simply reflects their higher crime rate.

The high murder rate among African-Americans, however, can be attributed directly to the high poverty rate among this group.[19] Their poverty rate is related to the long history of prejudice against African-Americans, growing out of the practice of slavery. Racial prejudice is thus a direct cause of the higher murder rate among African-Americans. Therefore, it is also to blame for the higher number of African-Americans on America's death rows.

Beyond the effect of poverty, racial prejudice against African-American defendants also has a direct role to play in many death sentences. A statistical study of Philadelphia murder cases found that being African-American was counted as a more-important "aggravating factor" in a murder case than whether the murder was done by inflicting multiple stab wounds, happened as part of another felony, or caused great harm, fear, or pain. In other words, an African-American defendant was more likely to be sentenced to death for a murder that did not involve any of these other factors than a white defendant whose crime involved one of these factors.[20]

Race was particularly important in the cases of midrange aggravation. A notorious serial killer was likely to receive the death penalty regardless of his race. For a homicide committed in the heat of the moment with no inflammatory factors, neither African-Americans nor other defendants were likely to receive a death sentence. However, when there were some aggravating factors that made it more difficult for prosecutors and juries to decide whether to impose capital punishment, African-Americans were more likely to receive a death sentence. In one midrange aggravation, African-American defendants were five times more likely to receive a death sentence than their counterparts of other races.[21]

Racial prejudice is also shown when an examination of the race of the victims is made. In the 1980s David Baldus conducted studies showing that a murderer, regardless of his race, was more likely to receive a death sentence when the victim was white.[22] This discrepancy occurs chiefly because of decisions made by prosecutors and judges, most of whom are white and therefore can identify more easily with the family of a white victim.[23]

Baldus postulated a number of ways in which this affects the prosecutor's decisions.[24] White people tend to be more prominent in the community than African-Americans, and therefore there often will be more publicity and more pressure to seek the death penalty. Because of the high cost of capital litigation, the prosecutor may simply believe that it is not worth the price of seeking the death penalty when the victim is poor and little valued by the community, as would be the case with many African-American murder victims.

In a study of death-penalty cases in the Chattahoochee Judicial District of Georgia, Stephen Bright found that prosecutors often met with the families of white victims to discuss whether to seek the death penalty. But prosecutors did not meet with African-American victim families and frequently did not even tell them how the case was resolved. As a result, although 65 percent of the homicides in the district were of African-American victims, only 15 percent of the capital cases involved African-American victims.[25]

The U.S. Supreme Court has acknowledged that racial prejudice affects the implementation of the death penalty in the United States. In *McCleskey v. Kemp*, 481 U.S. 279 (1987), the majority opinion upheld the death sentence of an African-American man and stated that racial disparities were "an inevitable part of our criminal justice system."

However, the high court held that in order for racism to be considered as an appellate issue in a capital case, the defense had to prove that the prosecutor, judge, or jury considered the race of the defendant in applying the death sentence in that particular case. It was not enough to show that there was a pattern of racism in their behavior. Instead, the defense had to somehow show psychologically that this pattern affected the specific trial. This is, of course, a virtually impossible thing to prove, since it would require that the prosecutor, jury members, and judge acknowledge their racist behavior.

Much more could be said about how racism influences capital sentencing. It is well-known that prosecutors seek to exclude African-Americans from juries involving African-American defendants.[26] In some cases, police officers and judges have made blatantly racist remarks while investigating or trying capital cases involving African-American defendants.[27] Nevertheless, even if this obvious racism could be eliminated, the racism of American culture will still affect capital sentencing. Former U.S. Supreme Court Associate Justice Harry A. Blackmun stated this unequivocally: "Even under the most sophisticated death-penalty statutes, race continues to play a major role in determining who shall live and who shall die."[28]

Even proponents of capital punishment acknowledge that race plays a role in capital sentencing. When asked whether he would advise an African-American in a capital case that race would be a factor, Assistant Attorney General Edward Dennis said, "I think that I would certainly have to take into account that members of the jury or the prosecution might be swayed to view the crime as being more serious, perhaps, if there was some racial aspect to it."[29] He made this statement while he was testifying against the Racial Justice Act, which would have provided more protection for African-American defendants in capital cases.

Unfairness in applying the death penalty has begun to

strike a nerve with many Americans. Conservative religious broadcaster Pat Robertson has declared that he would support a moratorium on executions because capital punishment in the United States is administered in a way that is unfair to minorities and the poor.[30]

All of this shows that capital punishment in the United States does not meet the principle of fairness found in the Hebrew Scriptures. We cannot say we are following the law given by Yahweh as long as—

- Poor defendants have fewer resources for their defense than the wealthy.
- African-American defendants are often treated more severely than whites committing similar crimes.
- White victims are more likely to be avenged by the death penalty than those of other races.

Whatever else might be claimed for capital punishment in the United States, it cannot be said that it meets the standards of fairness set by the Hebrew Scriptures.

5. Capital punishment may not be used unless there is absolute certainty of guilt.

There is probably no stronger emotional argument against capital punishment than that innocent people may be executed. Even the strongest proponent of capital punishment would admit that the execution of an innocent person would be a terrible miscarriage of justice. The Hebrew Scriptures also show a deep concern about the possibility of executing the innocent. The ancient Hebrews did not have access to modern police methods, and so they felt that eyewitness testimony was the strongest evidence of guilt. However, they went further than demanding an eyewitness to the crime; they demanded a minimum of two or three eyewitnesses.

This was a high requirement for evidence because—

- Only adult males could be witnesses.
- Witnesses could not have any connection to the crime or the people involved.

- Witnesses were not allowed to make inferences from what they had seen.
- Confessions were not allowed.

We thus are justified in saying that the Hebrew Scriptures' requirement for evidence in a capital case was absolute certainty.

The application of capital punishment in the United States certainly does not meet this requirement of certainty. The coming of DNA testing has shown that the American justice system frequently makes mistakes. More than 25 percent of the people the police considered to be prime suspects in violent crimes and who also were tested using DNA technology, have been found to be innocent.[31]

Since the 1976 reinstatement of capital punishment, eighty-seven death-row inmates have been released because they were innocent.[32] This averages out to more than three per year, more than one percent of the six thousand men and women who have been placed on death row during that time. The stories of these falsely convicted people include forced false confessions, mistaken or perjured witnesses, and misconduct by police and prosecutors.[33] This proves that numerous mistakes have been made and continue to be made. Sadly, the number undoubtedly represents only a fraction of many other innocent death-row inmates whose cases have not been overturned. It is certain that some of those who have been executed were innocent.[34]

One would expect that the high number of mistakes known to have occurred would make state legislatures, Congress, and the court system anxious to prevent this kind of injustice. However, the opposite is true. Many states place strict time restrictions on the introduction of new evidence after a person has been sentenced to die. This time restriction may be as short as twenty-one days.[35] In other words, even if incontrovertible evidence of a person's innocence is found twenty-two days after he has received a death sentence, the courts are not required to reopen the case.

In spite of increasing evidence of the number of mistakes made in capital cases, state legislatures, Congress, and the courts seem more interested in speeding up the appeals process rather than in correcting procedures that lead to the conviction of the innocent.

Since the reinstatement of the death penalty in 1976, sixteen Florida death-row inmates (more than any other state) have been released from prison because they were innocent.[36] Despite this fact, in 2000 the legislature shortened the state appeals process in capital cases.[37] Similarly, in 1996 the U.S. Congress passed and the president signed the Anti-Terrorism and Death Penalty Reform Act, limiting the right of habeas corpus. This law sets a six-month time limit on appeals to the federal courts after state appeals. It also requires federal courts to limit the basis of appeals that they will hear. In many cases, federal courts are to assume that state-court rulings are correct, even when there is evidence that state courts often make mistakes on such rulings.[38]

Even before the Anti-Terrorism and Death Penalty Reform, the U.S. Supreme Court had already limited appeals based on actual innocence. In *Herrera v. Collins* (1993), the majority held that a claim of innocence should not be considered at the federal level unless it could be shown that the claim was a result based on a procedural error at the state level.[39] This case occurred because evidence of Lionel Herrera's innocence was presented in Texas after the state's thirty-day limit for presenting such evidence. The Court held that the federal courts should not interfere with this or similar statutes, even when there was clear evidence of innocence. According to the majority, stopping the execution process should be left to the executive branch at the state level.

However, because of political considerations, many state governors and pardons boards are reluctant to use their power to commute death sentences. Thus Governor Ann Richardson of Texas did not stop Herrera's execution. He died by lethal injection on May 12, 1993. Recognizing such reluctance to commute death sentences, Justice Harry A. Blackmun dissented from the Herrera decision: "The execution of a person who can show that he is innocent comes perilously close to simple murder."

Hence, we have to deal with the mounting evidence that innocent people are given death sentences with some regularity. The justice system has done little to prevent this from happening. All this shows clearly that the application of capital punishment in the United States does not meet the standard for protection of the innocent set by the Hebrew Scriptures.

6. Capital punishment may not be used unless the court examines mitigating circumstances and spares any perpetrator not fully culpable for the crime.

Although the Hebrew Scriptures have tremendous spiritual insights into the human condition, they were written at a time when there was little understanding of the psychological causes of human behavior. The scientific advances of the past two hundred years give us a much better understanding of why human beings behave as they do. The standard of forgiveness at the heart of the message of the Hebrew Scriptures makes it imperative that these new discoveries be taken into account when determining whether or not a person should receive a death sentence.

We will briefly examine four different factors that should mitigate against the use of the death penalty. These are mental retardation, brain injuries, mental illness, and youthfulness of the offender.

Mental retardation is defined as being "significantly subaverage in general intellectual functioning existing concurrently with deficits in adaptive behavior and manifested during the developmental period."[40] The disability of mental retardation includes traits that make it difficult for a mentally retarded person to function adequately in the criminal justice system: communication and memory problems, impulsiveness, limited moral development, lack of knowledge arising from their inability to take in societal information, denial of their disability, and motivational differences that may make them wish to please people they see as important or in authority.

Because of these symptoms of their disability, mentally retarded defendants may give up their rights to an attorney, may exaggerate their role in a crime, or even may confess to crimes they did not commit. Coercive police tactics may more easily intimidate them. More-intelligent codefendants may even use them as fall guys, scapegoats. They are generally poor witnesses whose confusion on the witness stand may appear to a jury as simple dishonesty.[41]

In *Penry v. Lynaugh,* 109 St. Ct. 2934 (1989), the U.S. Supreme Court held that the execution of mentally retarded persons was not unconstitutional, but that mental retardation must be considered in sentencing in capital cases. Despite this ruling, mentally retarded defendants continue to be sentenced to death in disproportionate numbers. Only 3 percent of the population of the United States is mentally retarded, and mentally retarded people are less likely to commit violent crimes than the general population. Yet estimates claim that 10 percent of death-row inmates are mentally retarded.[42]

One study conducted in Mississippi by the law firm of Jenner & Block found that 32 percent of the death-row inmates in that state were at least borderline retarded.[43] Given these statistics, mental retardation appears to be an unacknowledged aggravating factor in capital cases, rather than a mitigating factor.

Brain injuries are a relatively unexplored factor in death-penalty cases. Brain injuries occur from severe head trauma. They may result in the inability to self-monitor one's behavior, difficulty in emotional control, and impulsiveness or lower inhibition.[44] All these characteristics may contribute to criminal activity.

A study of fourteen juvenile death-row inmates published in 1988 found that all fourteen had been in situations in which a head injury could have occurred.[45] Eight of the subjects had injuries serious enough to require hospitalization and/or to cause indentation in the cranium. Neurological and EEG testing showed that nine of the fourteen had serious abnormalities. Twelve of the fourteen reported experiencing severe physical abuse as children. Seven reported receiving blows to the face and head as part of this abuse. Two of the subjects' mothers were alcoholics, and one mother was beaten when pregnant. This may point to fetal alcohol syndrome or injury in utero, which also could have harmed the subjects' brain development.[46]

Mental illness identifies a group of diseases that cause their victims to perceive and react to the world in a way not validated by objective data. Paranoia causes a person to perceive threats where none exists. Schizophrenia may cause its victims to hear voices or have visual hallucinations. Bipolar disorder causes periods of depression alternating with periods of euphoria, when the person is hyperactive and impulsive. Compulsive-obsessive disorders may cause victims to become stuck in unhealthy patterns of thoughts and behaviors, including deviant sexual behavior. Depression may cause a person to consider the world as evil and hopeless, and sometimes lead to suicidal or homicidal thoughts. Both physical and environmental factors can affect the severity of mental illnesses.

The study of juvenile death-row inmates mentioned above found that nine were either psychotic at the time of the evaluation or had been diagnosed as such in childhood. Ten showed signs of paranoia, seven had experienced auditory or visual hallucinations, three had signs of bipolar disorder, and two had attempted suicide. Five had received treatment for mental illness in childhood.[47] It is also significant that five of the inmates had been sexually abused, which can lead to sexually deviant expressions of mental illness.

This study is of a relatively few inmates and all of approximately the same age. Yet none of these findings would surprise those who are familiar with death-row inmates. It is not unusual for defense attorneys to present this kind of information about their clients in the mitigation phase of sentenc-

ing hearings. A common complaint of death-penalty proponents is that the opponents of capital punishment present
such information to blame society and not the perpetrators
for their crimes. Politically, the proponents' argument has
carried much weight. Courts condemn to death many
inmates with mental retardation, brain damage, or mental illness that makes it impossible for them to resist the psychological pressure to commit a crime or to understand the seriousness of their crime.

In some cases these issues have not even been considered.
Defendants or their families may have covered up their mental illness. Defense attorneys may have either failed to recognize the condition as a mitigating factor or have not brought
up these factors for fear of embarrassing the defendant or his
family. Of the fourteen juvenile inmates in the study mentioned above, only five had received pretrial assessments of
their mental and emotional condition. These evaluations
"tended to be perfunctory and provided inadequate and inac-
curate information regarding the adolescents' neuropsychiatric and cognitive functioning."

To discover the truth about abuse, and particularly
about sexual abuse, the authors asserted that only
"painstaking, lengthy interviews inquiring in detail about
injuries, the origin of visible scars, and the existence of
'scars I can't see' would reveal the extent to which they had
been victimized."[48]

In 1984 the U.N. Economic and Social Council adopted
*Safeguards Guaranteeing the Protection of the Rights of Those
Facing the Death Penalty.* This document was designed to clar-
ify the differences between capital punishment that could
still be considered legitimate and "summary and arbitrary
executions." In addition to clearly defining the procedural
rights of defendants, the *Safeguards* named specific groups
that should be exempted from capital punishment. These
included pregnant women, minors, mothers of very young
children, and the insane.

The addition of the insane marked the international community's strongest condemnation of the use of capital punishment for those who are mentally incompetent. A clarifying resolution in 1988 expanded the *Safeguards* to include "persons suffering from mental retardation or extremely limited mental competence."[49]

Although the *Safeguards* do not embody a treaty relationship, they do represent an international standard in opposition to applying capital punishment to the mentally retarded, brain damaged, and mentally ill. After a visit to the United States in 1997, Bacre Waly Ndiaye, the U.N.'s Special Rapporteur on Extrajudicial, Summary, or Arbitrary Executions, stated that executions of the mentally retarded in the United States were "in contravention of relevant international standards." In 1999, the U.N. Commission on Human Rights passed a resolution asking nations "not to impose the death penalty on a person suffering from any form of mental disorder."[50]

This international condemnation of the use of the death penalty on defendants found to be mentally or emotionally disabled has created a contemporary set of mitigating factors that should be considered in capital sentencing. These factors have been steadfastly ignored in the United States. Hence, it is clear that the application of the death penalty in the United States does not sufficiently determine the true culpability of the defendant to meet the principle of mitigation set down in the Hebrew Scriptures.

The youthfulness of offenders is another mitigating factor that should be considered in applying the death penalty. The United States' continued application of capital punishment for crimes committed when the perpetrator was less than eighteen years of age has led to widespread international criticism. Before the twentieth century, children as young as ten could be executed.[51] One focus of modern opposition to the death penalty has been to eliminate the execution of minors.

The opposition to executing children has been based on the modern understanding of child development. Unlike previous generations, we no longer think of children as miniature grown-ups. Instead, we recognize that children must grow through organic mental, emotional, and moral phases in order to take on the traits of a healthy adult. Poor decisions made as a child or adolescent should not be punished as severely because minors have not had the opportunity to develop physically or experientially to be fully responsible for their actions.

The United Nations' *International Covenant on Civil and Political Rights* (art. 6, sect. 5) prohibits the death penalty for anyone under the age of eighteen.[52] Similarly, the Organization of American States in its *American Convention on Human Rights* (art. 4, sect. 5) bans the use of capital punishment for persons under eighteen.[53] The United States signed these treaties but reserved the right not to follow these provisions. Another treaty, the U.N. *Convention on the Rights of the Child*, came into force in 1990. It also prohibits ratifying nations from applying the death penalty to anyone under eighteen years of age. All nations of the world except the United States and Somalia have ratified this treaty.[54]

In two cases the U.S. Supreme Court set a lower age standard for the United States. In *Thompson v. Oklahoma*, 487 U.S. 815 (1988), decided on a five-to-four decision, the Court prohibited executing people for crimes committed when they were less than sixteen years old. The following year, however, the Court held in *Sanford v. Kentucky*, 492 U.S. 361 (1989), that the Eighth Amendment of the U.S. Constitution does not prohibit the death penalty for crimes committed when the perpetrator was sixteen or seventeen years old.

Since 1990, only six countries—Iran, Nigeria, Pakistan, Saudi Arabia, the United States, and Yemen—are known to have executed persons for crimes committed when they were less than eighteen years old.[55] On this issue the United States is clearly out of step with an overwhelming majority of the world's nations, which believe that youth should be an absolute mitigating factor in death-penalty cases. The world standard is eighteen years old.

The Hebrew Scriptures made one of the earliest calls to

consider mitigating circumstances in considering the punishment for a crime. It is true that the sole mitigating factor to be considered was whether the perpetrator of the crime intended to kill the victim. Intent was judged only by the circumstances of the situation and the relationship between the people involved. Modern science has allowed us to look more deeply into human motivation. We now recognize that the issue of intent is much more difficult to determine.

For example, can a paranoid schizophrenic who believes that he has been told by God's voice to kill a stranger, be judged as fully intentional in his action? In the modern setting, the primacy of forgiveness in value system of the Hebrew Scriptures argues that the defendant must be given the benefit of the doubt.

But is this what happens in the United States? The presence of large numbers of mentally retarded, brain damaged, and mentally ill inmates on the nation's death rows proves that mitigating circumstances are *not* being properly considered when the criminal justice system judges defendants with these kinds of disabilities. Indeed, after the attempted assassination of President Reagan by a mentally ill man, who was acquitted of the crime based on his mental condition, a number of states removed from their statutes the possibility of a verdict of "innocent by reason of insanity."

In *Ford v. Wainwright*, 477 U.S. 399 (1986), the U.S. Supreme Court held that if a person is too insane to understand what is happening to him, he cannot be executed. But this ruling does not protect him if he was too insane to fully comprehend what he was doing at the time of his crime.

Thus, our courts are willing to condemn men and women who could not fully understand or resist the impulses that contributed to their crime. This shows that our practice of capital punishment is not in accord with the principle of mitigation found in the Hebrew Scriptures. Furthermore, many states continue to insist on executing people for crimes committed when they were adolescents, in spite of the condemnation of this practice by almost all other nations of the world. This practice displays an arrogant desire *not* to consider mitigating factors in capital sentencing.

7. Capital punishment should not be a form of human sacrifice, executing individuals for reasons other than their own crime.

The Hebrew Scriptures insist on the careful application of the death penalty because the Israelites did not want this practice to be confused with human sacrifices in the religious cults of their ancestors or neighbors. Unlike human sacrifice, capital punishment was not designed to manipulate the gods. Though there was a sense that a serious crime unbalanced the moral scales of the universe, there was no expectation that Yahweh would punish the community if death sentences were not given out. Yahweh indeed tells the Israelites that if they ever ignore the practice of human sacrifice, he will punish the offenders himself:

> If the people of the land should ever close their eyes to them, when they give their offspring to Molech, and do not put them to death, I myself will set my face against them and against their family, and will cut them off from among my people, them and all who follow them in prostituting themselves to Molech. (Lev. 20:4-5)

The effect of such a passage is that the Hebrews could afford to be extra careful in their application of the death penalty. If the community could not determine who was guilty of a crime, or even if they did not punish the guilty person when they knew who it was, Yahweh himself would restore the moral balance of the universe. Yahweh even says, "Vengeance is mine, and recompense. . . . The LORD will vindicate his people" (Deut. 32:35-36). Failure of the Israelites to punish an individual crime would not lead Yahweh to retaliate against the community as a whole.[56]

Indeed, when the people were punished, it was only because the whole community had sinned, often under the leadership of a foolish and wicked king![57]

Yahweh's promise to punish criminals himself emphasizes again that only the individual criminal should be punished for his own crime. Punishing another person for someone else's crime does not rebalance the moral scales. It further unbalances them. The demand for witnesses and the requirement for equal treatment of the rich and poor before the law—both show that under the Hebrew law, the death sentence looked backward in time to the crime rather than forward to manipulating the gods for future considerations. Its purpose was solely one of punishment.

Human sacrifice, on the other hand, was an attempt either to placate gods who were already angry, or to manipulate the gods into providing for the needs of the community. The sacrifice was not necessarily tied to a particular crime, although it was often assumed that a crime of some kind was behind a community's catastrophe. Sometimes the crime was known, but frequently it was not. In either case, a human scapegoat was chosen to pay for the crime or for the future service to be rendered.

The scapegoat, as noted in the first chapter, was usually a person counted as of little worth to the community. Through the sacrificial ritual, however, the scapegoat was given unusual importance. Exceptional powers were attributed to him or her. If the crime was known, the scapegoat was blamed for it, whether or not there was any real connection between the scapegoat and the crime.

As practiced in the United States, capital punishment fails to meet the other standards of the Hebrew Scriptures for administering the death penalty. With regard to this seventh principle, we must ask, Is the American death penalty simply a Christianized form of pagan human sacrifice?

The Gallup Poll conducted in 2000 on support for capital punishment found that 66 percent of Americans supported capital punishment. Ninety-one percent of the people polled felt that over the last twenty years, at least one person had been wrongfully sentenced to death. Those who favored the death penalty estimated that about 10 percent of death-row inmates were actually innocent of the alleged crime. Yet 60 percent said that the death penalty was not imposed often enough.[58]

When the 1999 version of the death-penalty poll was taken, 65 percent of respondents said they believed a poor defendant was more likely to receive a death sentence than a middle-class or wealthy person who had committed the same crime. Fifty percent said they believed an African-American defendant was more likely to get the death penalty than a white defendant for the same crime.[59]

These percentages show that substantial numbers of those who favor capital punishment believe that it is applied against the innocent, and that it is applied unfairly against the poor and minorities. Such willingness to accept violence against people seen as less valuable to society is a trait of human sacrifice. It surely does not meet the standards for the use of capital punishment as specified in the Hebrew Scriptures.

A second trait of human sacrifice appears to be present in the use of the death penalty in the United States: the glorification of the sacrificial victim. Anyone who watches a few evenings of television can see that murder is an important part of American popular culture. Television programs focusing on killing, murder mysteries, and true crime nonfiction are among our most popular forms of entertainment. However, almost all of the stories do not portray murderers as they usually are.

In the popular media, murderers are frequently wealthy and almost invariably highly intelligent. The portrayal of serial killers, in particular, fits this pattern. Hannibal Lector in *The Silence of the Lambs* is typical. He is a brilliant psychiatrist who can easily outsmart the run-of-the-mill police officer. Most of the murderers on the popular *Law and Order* television program also are middle class or wealthy.

Another group of criminals frequently appearing on these

shows are the crime bosses of the Mafia or the Russian mobs, pictured as virtually all-powerful. The police and prosecutors frequently pull in a more-typical, blue-collar criminal as their first suspect. Yet they must use all of their considerable wits to find and successfully prosecute the true killer.[60]

In reality, most murderers come from the lower classes, and most murders are crimes of passion, not of stealth. The typical serial killer has a blue-collar job or is homeless. The reason he is not caught is because his victims are frequently people that society has little interest in protecting. For example, many serial killers have preyed on prostitutes or homosexuals. In addition, the typical serial killer has a lifestyle of frequently traveling or moving to a number of different locations. His murders occur in different places. Because no one cares much about the victims, it takes the police much time to recognize the pattern (the modus operandi).

Even when a criminal has few financial or personal resources, the media find ways to make him seem more unusual and dramatic. The media in Idaho, for instance, have consistently referred to one death-row inmate as "Mad Max." Abandoned quite young by his parents, he had never learned to read and had spent a good deal of his life in state institutions. His friends, other inmates, and prison staff have never referred to him as Mad Max, and he has specifically asked the media not to call him by this name. But by tying him into a popular cult character, the media made him seem dashing and more dangerous than he actually is.[61] In doing so, they have made him a much better villain for their stories.

Because scapegoating requires that all of the ills of society be placed on the victim, society endows that victim with special powers not available to other human beings. American society is unwilling to view the typical death-row inmate realistically, as a badly damaged human being with few psychological, social, or financial resources. Their portrayal of them as nearly superhuman villains is another sign that capital punishment in the United States is more like the pagan practice of human sacrifice, and less like the restricted use of the death penalty seen in the Hebrew Scriptures.

In addition, human sacrifice always has the purpose of either ending a current community catastrophe or of preventing future evil. The typical rational arguments (arguments based on reasoning rather than faith or emotions) for capital punishment are, in fact, attempts to show that capital punishment has a social purpose beyond revenge against the criminal. These two arguments are that an execution deters murder, and that an execution keeps a murderer from repeating his crime.

The argument of deterrence asserts that executions dissuade other potential murderers from committing murder. This argument perhaps had some validity when capital punishment was used as a substitute for the blood feud at the dawn of civilization. When a number of revenge killings might result from a single murder, the state's controlled provision of a single revenge killing may have served to break the cycle of violence, and thus to save lives.

Modern people, however, have moved far away from the self-help concept of justice embodied in the blood feud. Today, society neither encourages nor permits its citizens to seek this kind of revenge. Thus, the deterrence argument theorizes that an execution will serve as a moral lesson for people who know little of the crime and have no relationship with the criminal.

Sociological, psychological, and statistical evidence contradicts this theory. Deterrence depends on several assumptions that simply are not true in the case of potential murderers. First, it assumes that potential murderers are aware of the death penalty and believe it likely that they will be executed if they commit a murder. Second, it assumes that potential murderers are afraid of the death penalty. Third, it assumes that murderers are able to make rational decisions and that murders are rational acts.

Studies of the typical criminal mentality dispute all of

these assumptions. Most criminals do not behave rationally; instead, they act impulsively. They picture themselves as beyond the rules, and assume that they will not be caught or punished for their crimes. Often they see danger as a challenge rather than as something to be feared. Moreover, most murders are committed under the influence of drugs, alcohol, or both, which obviously impairs the murderer's judgment.[62]

Cross-sectional studies compare murder rates in jurisdictions practicing capital punishment against those that do not. Time-series studies examine the murder rates before and after major death-penalty events. Statistically, both have validated the argument that there is no deterrent effect of capital punishment.[63] These arguments against the deterrence effect have been conclusive enough to convince some death-penalty proponents that deterrence is not a strong argument for capital punishment.[64]

The second rational argument for capital punishment is that of prevention. Proponents of this argument say that capital punishment will keep particularly dangerous murderers from killing again. This point does have some validity. A murderer who has been executed will not kill again. However, this rationale assumes that society can make good judgments about the future behavior of individuals. Studies of former Texas death-row inmates who have had their sentences commuted to life, however, found that these inmates were actually less likely to be violent than other inmates.[65] In fact, murderers often become model prisoners who have a positive influence on other inmates.

According to Warden Lewis Lawes, who oversaw 151 executions in New York's Sing Sing prison between 1920 and 1931 and became an opponent of the death penalty, "Murderers make the best prisoners. They are the least troublesome to any warden, and often they accomplish a great deal behind bars."[66] Leo Lalond of the Michigan Department of Corrections said, "After a few years, lifers become your better prisoners. They tend to adjust and just do their time. They tend to be a calming influence on younger kids, and we have more problems with people serving shorter terms."[67] Thus, instead of interrupting the cycle of prison violence, one could argue that executing murderers actually makes the prison environment more dangerous for both staff and other inmates.

Although these two rational arguments for capital punishment have significant weaknesses, they do point to a meaning for it beyond simply penalizing the offender. Capital punishment is a part of what Walter Wink calls the Domination System.[68] This is the array of entities that control our fallen world. Its primary value is power. In this system, status is gained by dominating others.

Hence, the rich, who control resources, are considered as more valuable than the poor. Men are given more status than women. It is better to be physically strong than to be weak. It is better to be in the majority than the minority. It is better to be white than to be black. And the primary instrument of the Domination System is violence.

In this system, most Americans have done quite well. By world standards, we are wealthy. Our health problems are mostly those of overconsumption, not of subsistence. Our military strength seemingly makes us immune from warfare—though terrorists may still crash through our façade. Materially, we are the envy of the world.

Nevertheless, despite our wealth and material success, there is a great fear in our hearts. We know that our strength has not been built on community, but on individualism. Many of us know that we are only a major illness away from poverty. With an economic downturn, our jobs and our security can be lost. We know that our last days or years may be lived out in loneliness. We might be locked away from a society that does not value the wisdom of experience, but only the latest and most up-to-date information, no matter how vacant it might be.

The poor are symbolic of our unease. The homeless, those who have been left behind, make us uncomfortable. They symbolize our own insecurity. When they beg, we want to turn away and not see them, even as we toss a coin to soothe our consciences. We want to clear them out of our cities. We want them to be unseen and unheard. And because we want to be in control, we want to blame them for their condition. After all, if poverty is the result of some moral defect that we do not share, then we do not have to worry about falling into poverty ourselves.

Because of its seemingly random nature, crime also symbolizes our insecurity. So we equate poverty with criminality, and we demand law and order—but not at the cost of providing opportunities for the poor. Although poverty and crime are invariably correlated in the literature of the social sciences and humanities, we do not wish to give up our position of dominance. So we demand that the government make us safe without instituting economic justice.

Many politicians, to bolster their own power, are more than happy to oblige. They provide a method of human sacrifice with which to take away our fear. They lock more and more people away in the human warehouses we call prisons, and occasionally they offer up the ultimate sacrifice—a human killed to satisfy the blood lust of the mob. It does not matter whether the sacrifice actually makes us safer. It does not matter if the victim is guilty or innocent. It does not matter if the process is fair. We are offering up a scapegoat to the god of security, and we believe that somehow this will placate the spirit of violence that controls our society.

But in supporting capital punishment, we participate in the very kind of crime that we fear. We placate the spirit of violence by becoming more violent ourselves. We fear the kind of killing that tortures the victim on the way to being murdered. Yet capital punishment psychologically tortures the victim for years before he is actually executed. We fear the killing of the innocent, yet we support a system that we assume kills the innocent. We claim to be teaching that killing is wrong, but we do it by the very action that we say we abhor. We are imitating the person we despise. To use Girard's term, we are participating in mimetic violence.

There can be no denying, then, that this simply is a form of human sacrifice. It means killing a social outcast to relieve the tension within the community. It makes the claim, based on blind faith and not on empirical evidence, that such a killing will bring about a future benefit. And it demands that people look the other way when their hearts tell them it is wrong to kill another human being.

How different this is from the ancient Hebrews. At their best, the Israelites were willing even to let the criminal go free because they knew that Yahweh would somehow work out justice. On this ultimate principle, then, the administration of capital punishment in the United States fails to meet the standards of the Hebrew Scriptures. Our use of the death penalty cannot be justified by the use of the Hebrew Scriptures. It is a pagan practice and has nothing to do with Yahweh's way of justice and mercy.

5
The Life and Teachings of Jesus

The limitations placed on the use of the death penalty in the Hebrew Scriptures created a new and much more cautious approach to capital punishment than could be found in other Near Eastern cultures of that time. Though the Hebrew Scriptures set strict limitations on the implementation of the death penalty, the New Testament sets a personal moral standard so high for participation in an execution that in truth it forbids followers of Jesus from participating in capital punishment or supporting it.

This opposition to capital punishment is found in the teachings of Jesus, in the stories of Jesus' execution and of other martyrs in the New Testament, and in the epistles with their theology of the atonement and of the state. In this chapter, we investigate the general teachings of Jesus on sin and forgiveness, and then we examine the one story in which Jesus speaks directly about the use of capital punishment.

The Birth Narrative

Capital punishment was an issue for Jesus even before his birth. His mother, Mary, became pregnant before she was married. The Bible says this was the result of a miracle, but the figure of a woman pregnant while still a virgin did not fit the cultural pattern of the Jews. In several Hebrew narratives, birth miracles occurred for women who had long been barren.[1] Mary's story must have seemed implausible. Her pregnancy put her in mortal danger, since she could be found guilty of fornication as an engaged woman, a capital crime (Deut. 22:23-24).

Joseph, engaged to Mary, is a kind and "righteous man." He could seek the death penalty because she is pregnant and he is not the father. Instead, he simply plans to dismiss/divorce her quietly. Even at that, her future would be in doubt. Her guilt is exposed by her obvious pregnancy. If Joseph would divorce Mary, the elders of Nazareth might assume that she is pregnant not by Joseph and might want to put her to death by stoning—although lack of adequate witnesses could be an issue (cf. Deut. 22:23-29). God, however, intervenes and tells Joseph to go ahead with the marriage (Matt. 1:18-25). In doing so, Joseph may be saving Mary from a death sentence (cf. Mishnah Ketuboth 4.3-4). Jesus' birth, then, is the direct result of the forgiveness of a capital crime.

Jesus and the Law

Jesus was a Jew steeped in the teachings of the law and the prophets. Luke 2:41-52 tells the story of the twelve-year-old Jesus staying behind in Jerusalem to learn more about the Jewish faith from the teachers of the temple. The rabbis teaching there were amazed at his understanding and questions, although, contrary to popular tradition, he was not teaching the teachers.[2]

During his temptations at the start of his ministry, Jesus was able to answer the devil with memorized quotes from Deuteronomy (Matt. 4:1-11; Luke 4:1-12). Luke 4:16 says that Jesus went to the synagogue in Nazareth "as was his custom." He was a man well versed in Scripture and the traditions of his people.

This expertise gave Jesus credibility as a teacher and the freedom to approach the law in a new way. The scribes and the Pharisees were inheritors of the great oral tradition of the law. This tradition, eventually crystallized in the written Mishnah and later in the Talmud, recorded their attempts to apply the Torah to real-life situations. Through these interpretations, the scribes and Pharisees found ways to lighten the harsher provisions of the law. In general, their legal opinions softened the heavier regulations by giving detailed instructions for their application that lessened their severity. The witness provisions for capital cases are one example of how the oral tradition mitigated some of the violence the written statutes seemed to demand.

However, because the traditions were quite complex and (in Jesus' day) not readily available in writing, they became the province of a relatively small group of men. These legal experts gained power through their knowledge, and since power tends to corrupt, the oral law was often misused. Jesus was blunt in his criticism of this corruption. In Luke 11:37-54, an exchange takes place in which Jesus warns some Pharisees that they are "full of greed and wickedness," and that while they "tithe mint and rue and herbs of all kinds," they "neglect justice and the love of God." He tells the lawyers or scribes that they "load the people with burdens hard to bear," but "do not lift a finger to ease them." He concludes, "Woe to you lawyers! For you have taken away the key to knowledge; you did not enter yourselves, and you hindered those who were entering."[3]

Jesus' approach to the law was quite different. Rather than humanizing the law through more and more exceptions and interpretations, he looked behind the law for the meaning God was expressing. What he found was God's unconditional love for the world he had created and for each and every human being in it. The purpose of the law was to create a relationship between God and his creations, and to protect the human race, which held a special place in God's love. When asked by a lawyer to name the greatest commandment of the law, Jesus quoted two passages from the Hebrew Scriptures: Deuteronomy 6:5 and Leviticus 19:18.

> He said to him, " 'You shall love the Lord your God with all your heart, and with all your soul, and with all your mind.' This is the greatest and first commandment. And a second is like it: 'You shall love your neighbor as yourself.'

On these two commandments hang all the law and the prophets." (Matt. 22:37-40; Mark 12:28-31)

Jesus referred to this underlying basis for the law when he said that "until heaven and earth pass away, not one letter, not one stroke of a letter, will pass from the law until all is accomplished" (Matt. 5:18; Luke 16:17). In both cases where this saying appears, it is immediately followed by alterations in the law that seek the underlying meaning and extend it beyond its written form.

In Matthew 5:20 Jesus tells his disciples that their righteousness must exceed the righteousness of the scribes and Pharisees in order for them to enter the kingdom of heaven. He then says that anger, harsh words, and pursuing a lawsuit are the equivalents of murder (Matt. 5:21-26). Lust and divorce are equated with adultery (Matt. 5:27-32). Jesus does not allow oaths, which imply a dual standard of truthfulness (Matt. 5:33-37). He expands the limitations on vengeance of the *lex talionis* (law of retaliation), by decreeing that his followers should use nonviolent methods of resisting injustice (Matt. 5:38-42).[4] Finally, Jesus disavows hatred altogether (Matt. 5:43-48).

Luke parallels many of these teachings, including Jesus' statement on divorce (Luke 16:18; cf. cross-references in a Bible or a book of Gospel parallels). In each case, Jesus goes beyond the letter of the law in a way that makes it more loving, nonviolent, truthful, and just. The underlying meaning of the law remains the same, but the application is extended beyond that of the Torah and its interpreters.

Jesus' Relationship to Sinners

Jesus was known for his acceptance of all people. He befriended people whom the letter of the law denigrated or condemned.[5] Many of Jesus' followers were women (Luke 8:1-3). Under the law, women were clearly second-class citizens.[6] Many of the women Jesus befriended were considered to be "sinners." Though in most cases their sin is unspecified, the popular opinion has always been that these women had dubious sexual reputations. Jesus went even farther when he welcomed prostitutes into his company, stating that their faith would allow them to enter the kingdom of God before the self-righteous religious authorities (Matt. 21:31). Significantly for this study, prostitution could have been treated as a capital crime under the law because it was a form of fornication.

In addition, Jesus accepted people with disabilities, even though under the law they were not allowed full membership in the community because a disability was seen as a sign of God's disfavor (Lev. 21:16-24; John 9:1-7). Again and again, Jesus went out of his way to help those with disabilities. In the parable of the great dinner, he notes the religious leader's refusal of the invitation and compares that with the commendable willingness of people with disabilities to accept the gifts of God (Luke 14:15-24).

Jesus even accepted tax collectors, the hated collaborators with the Romans, who helped enforce tax laws that impoverished their own people. He called the tax collector Matthew (Levi) to be one of his disciples (Matt. 9:9; Mark 2:14; Luke 5:27). Jesus' acceptance of Zacchaeus led the tax collector to donate half his wealth to the poor, and repay fraudulent tax collections four times over (Luke 19:1-10). Although Zacchaeus had become wealthy through collecting taxes, Jesus recognized the price he had paid in the loss of respect and friendship of his own people.

Upon the conversion of Zacchaeus, Jesus said, "Today salvation has come to this house, because he too is a son of Abraham. For the Son of Man came to seek out and to save the lost" (Luke 19:9-10). Jesus understood Zacchaeus's deep desire to be reconnected with his community, and it was only his conversion that made this possible. The story is an example of Jesus' remarkable ability to see beyond the surface sinfulness of an individual to the desire for love and acceptance that exists in every human heart.

Jesus' acceptance of tax collectors extended to their overlords, the Romans. Although many Jews frowned on those who associated with Gentiles, Jesus responded positively when a Roman centurion asked him to heal his servant. Jesus was impressed by the centurion's faith in Jesus' ability to order the healing, much as the centurion could order his soldiers. He declared, "Not even in Israel have I found such faith" (Luke 7:1-10; Matt. 8:5-13).

Another time when Jesus responded positively to a Gentile, he appears to have learned about faith and tolerance from a woman (Matt. 15:21-28; Mark 7:24-30). After she asked Jesus to heal her daughter, he stated that his message and healings were for the Jews, and that to give them to the Gentiles would be like throwing food meant for one's children to the dogs. But the woman replied, "Sir, even the dogs under the table eat the children's crumbs." Jesus was struck by her faith, and he healed the child.

These examples illustrate how Jesus was within the prophetic tradition that universalized the message of God's love. Yahweh was not just the God of the Jews, but also the God of all people. The Jews were not chosen because they were stronger or better than other people. Instead, they were to be a unique sign of God's love and forgiveness offered to everyone. The prophets had shown this in such passages as Isaiah 2:2-4 (quoted in chap. 3, above).

Though the prophets universalized God's message outward to other nations, Jesus extended the message not only to Gentiles, but also internally to people separated from the community while still living within it. In a sense, those whom the law denigrated or condemned had become the community's internal Gentiles, the enemies within. Jesus abolished this separation. For him, all stood equally needy of God's love and forgiveness.

The Universality of Sin

Much as Jesus saw behind the words of the law to its deeper meaning, he also looked beneath the surface of sin to see its universal implications. The underlying meaning of the law was God's abiding love for the world and the human race; the universal meaning beneath individual sins was humankind's universal desire to be their own god. The temptation the serpent offered Eve in the garden of Eden was that she could "be like God, knowing good and evil" (Gen. 3:5). If we are like God in this sense, that means we can make up our own rules. We can decide what is right and wrong, good and evil. Rather than following God's way for us, we follow our own way. We put ourselves at the center of the universe, rather than recognizing that we serve God.

Our desire to make our own choices about good and evil, however, has been disastrous. Since our determinations of good and evil are not in accord with God's way, our choices alienate us from God and the good world that God created. The result is inequity, injustice, famine, hatred, crime, violence, war, environmental degradation, and many other forms of evil. However, these are only symptoms of the deeper problem—our desire to be in control of our own lives with no regard for how this might affect other human beings or the world around us.

Thus, when Jesus looks beneath the surface of sin, he sees that all sin is interconnected. One cannot isolate sin to one aspect of life. Because a person's sins are minor in the eyes of the world does not mean that he or she is not a sinner. It does not give the "minor" sinner the right to judge the sins of another. Again and again, Jesus demands that his followers be humble when they consider the sins of someone else. In Matthew 7:1-5 (Luke 6:41-42), Jesus warns his disciples not to judge or condemn others.[7]

He follows that warning with a parable. It is the story of a person who claims to see a speck of sawdust in his neighbor's eye, but has an entire log stuck in his own eye. Jesus asks his followers how a person can even see the speck of sawdust when she or he is blinded by the log. Through the parable, Jesus tells his followers that they must first overcome their own sins before they can address the sins of others.

This brings us back to the parallels Jesus draws between what are considered as serious crimes, and everyday occurrences of conflict and lust. On the social level, a murder is certainly more serious than an insult. But the hatred causing the insult is the same as the hatred causing the murder. Hatred sets oneself at the center of the universe. It says that my enemy has no value to anyone else, including God, because that enemy is *my* enemy. How he is to be treated, then, is my decision, based on my desires and concerns. If I wish, I may harm him with gossip and insults or lawsuits. If I am able and I can get away with it, I might also kill him. In so doing, I no longer have to regard him as a separate human entity. He is merely an object, which I can choose to keep or cast aside. He is no longer a human being, whom I must value as a child of God.

Similarly, Jesus equates lustful thoughts with adultery. Looking upon another person as an object for sexual gratification dehumanizes that person, whether or not one acts upon the lustful desire. The person is treated as an instrument for pleasure, not as a complete human being. The first step toward adultery is a lustful thought. Adultery is merely an extension of these thoughts.

Partners in adultery become each other's sexual objects. Each partner is selfish and has no long-term commitment to the other. They do not care how their liaison will affect others—particularly their spouses and families. The important thing for them is that their own sexual desires are met.

Jesus' approach to the law extended it to our inward thoughts. These thoughts, whether of violence or lust, are the first step toward violent or lustful behavior. Because of the depth of our sinfulness, this approach means that God could legitimately condemn us all for our sins.

The Forgiveness of Sins

Although we all are sinners, God does not condemn us. His answer to sin, as seen both in the Hebrew Scriptures and in the life and teachings of Christ, is a militant and life-changing love. God's love challenges our mind-set of violence and vengeance. "Love your enemies," Jesus tells his disciples, "and pray for those who persecute you, so that you may be children of your Father in heaven; for he makes his sun rise on the evil and on the good, and sends rain on the righteous and unrighteous" (Matt. 5:44-45).

Jesus says that if we want to return to God's way, we must imitate God's love and forgive our enemies, just as God has forgiven our sins. He tells us that to know God's forgiveness for ourselves, we must extend forgiveness to others: "If you forgive others their trespasses, your heavenly Father will also forgive you; but if you do not forgive others, neither will your Father forgive your trespasses" (Matt. 6:14-15).

According to the creation stories in Genesis, Yahweh created a world that was totally interconnected. Every creature had its place. When humans brought sin into the world, our connections with God, with each other, and with the natural order were broken. When we seek vengeance for wrongs done to us, we are simply imitating the behavior of our enemies. We escalate the level of violence rather than reducing it. We widen the break between ourselves and others instead of repairing relationships with them.

Jesus recognized this and told his disciples that they should break the vicious cycle of violence by refusing to imitate the violent behavior of those who hurt them. He asked us to reconnect with those who have hurt us. We can do this only by forgiving them. The world can be put back together as God originally created it only by repairing the damage, not by imitating its violence. Vengeance is merely an imitation of the violence that has been done to us. Forgiveness in the face of this violence allies us with God as he works to repair our broken relationships in a fallen world.

Peter asked Jesus whether disciples were required to forgive an enemy as many as seven times, apparently doubting that such forgiving is possible. Jesus replied that they must forgive seventy-seven times[8]—so many times then that they would lose count.

Just as the real story of the Hebrew Scriptures is Yahweh's

steadfast love for his people, the real story of the New Testament is God's love for all people, despite their sins. As human beings, we like to justify ourselves by making favorable comparisons between ourselves and others. We exonerate ourselves by pointing to the sins of others: "I may be a sinner, but at least I have not committed *that* sin." Jesus' teaching, however, no longer allows such comparisons. For Jesus, an insult is the same as a murder, and a lustful thought is the same as adultery. Sin is sin. For one sinner to condemn another is the height of arrogance; it simply compounds one's own sinfulness.

The Woman Caught in Adultery

John 8:2-11 most clearly teaches this lesson against condemning others. In the story of the woman caught in adultery, Jesus directly addresses the issue of capital punishment. This is one of the most famous and beautiful stories of Jesus' compassion:

> Early in the morning [Jesus] came again to the temple. All the people came to him and he sat down and began to teach them. The scribes and the Pharisees brought a woman who had been caught in adultery; and making her stand before all of them, they said to him, "Teacher, this woman was caught in the very act of committing adultery. Now in the law Moses commanded us to stone such women. Now what do you say?" They said this to test him, so that they might have some charge to bring against him. Jesus bent down and wrote with his finger on the ground. When they kept on questioning him, he straightened up and said to them, "Let anyone among you who is without sin be the first to throw a stone at her." And once again he bent down and wrote on the ground.
>
> When they heard it they went away, one by one, beginning with the elders; and Jesus was left alone with the woman standing before him. Jesus straightened up and said to her, "Woman, where are they? Has no one condemned you?" She said, "No one, sir." And Jesus said,

"Neither do I condemn you. Go your way, and from now on do not sin again."

Most commentators on this passage agree that it was not an original part of John's Gospel. Yet it was an important and authentic story that the early church felt should be included in the canon.[9] The account is not in the earliest Greek manuscripts of John, though two leave a blank space where it would appear. It is also not included in early Syriac, Coptic, or Egyptian versions or in some of the earliest Latin versions. However, Jerome included it in the Vulgate, published in the fourth century, and both Ambrose and Augustine knew the story.

This text is also quoted in a third-century work called the Apostolic Constitutions. The church historian Eusebius says that an early second-century Christian named Papias told "a story of a woman accused of many sins before the Lord." Augustine states that the story was removed from the Gospel because certain readers thought it condoned adultery. Some scolars think this explains its absence from early manuscripts.[10]

The story itself has a number of elements that lend it authenticity. Presumably, the woman's trial has been held the day before the story unfolds. In accord with the provisions of the Mishnah, the judges have spent the night discussing the case. The case is according to formula: the woman has been caught in the act, though we are told nothing about the witnesses. Therefore, the judges quickly find her guilty and sentence her to death.

On the way to the place of execution by stoning, however, witnesses on her behalf are sought out. Thus, it is not unusual for the group to stop and ask for thoughts from a teacher, known for his compassion. The story, however, states that there is a darker reason behind their request for Jesus' opinion. The scribes and Pharisees want to trap Jesus into saying something blasphemous.[11]

According to provisions of the Torah and the Mishnah, Jesus has a number of options at this point. He could take a legal approach to the matter. The woman's male codefendant in the case is not present. Jesus could ask what has happened to him and why he is not being stoned. If the man is not going to be executed, this would be a violation of the fairness required by the law.[12] On that account, Jesus may be able to demand mercy for the woman. He also could ask to hear the witnesses. A withering cross-examination of the witnesses might discredit the case against the woman.

Jesus, however, does not propose traditional legal remedies, even though this would have been the safest way to handle the "test" he was being given. In accord with his teachings on sin and forgiveness, he again asks his hearers to go beyond the letter of the law. Jesus takes his time. We can imagine that the mob on its way to an execution is in a blood frenzy. Jesus knows that this mood must be broken if they are to respond with mercy. So he bends down and calmly writes something in the dirt. In doing so, he begins to de-escalate the violent emotions of the crowd. We can imagine that the members of the crowd, like some Bible commentators, become curious about what he is writing.[13]

The action moves the crowd away from their blood lust to fresh curiosity, from their emotions to their reason. It is also a sign that Jesus recognizes the game his enemies are playing and is refusing to play along.[14] From a personal perspective, it also gives him time to think about how he will respond.

When Jesus finally replies, his words are perfectly in accord with the totality of his teaching: "Let anyone who is without sin be the first to throw a stone at her." He upholds the law. The woman has committed a serious sin and deserves the death sentence, as the law stipulates (Lev. 20:10; Deut. 22:22). She has placed her own lustful desires at the center of her universe, without thinking of how her behavior would affect others.

The pain that she has caused her husband, the danger in which she has placed her children's future, the potential conflict which she has brought between her family of origin and her husband's family—all these she has made secondary to her own self-centered sexual appetite. She was willing to sacrifice all these things because she decided that she could replace God's law of love with her own shortsighted view of right and wrong.

Jesus does not condone her behavior, nor does he make excuses for it. His answer shows he assumes that the woman is responsible for her own conduct. He does not seek psychological or sociological causes that might mitigate her action. He admits no extenuating circumstances. For Jesus, sin is sin.

In no way does Jesus deny that the woman deserves punishment. But then he extends God's answer to sin. Who has the right to enforce the death sentence imposed by the law? Only persons who have not broken the law themselves. Any person who has broken the law stands in need of God's forgiveness. In his teaching, Jesus guarantees us that God loves us and will forgive us. But for that guarantee to be made to us, it must be made to all. If God does not love or forgive our enemy, whom we perceive as a sinner, then his love is conditional. He will love us only as long as we don't commit a certain level of sin. But what is that level? We cannot know, since we cannot know fully the mind of God.

As Walter Wink put it,

> If . . . we believe that the God who loves us hates those whom we hate, we insert an insidious doubt into our own selves. Unconsciously, we know that a deity hostile toward others is potentially hostile to us as well. And we know, better than anyone, that there is plenty of cause for such hostility. If God did not send sun and rain on everyone equally, God would not only not love everyone, but love no one.[15]

Christ brings the good news that there is no level of sin which God cannot or will not forgive.[16] His love is unconditional. Just as God forgives us, he will forgive our enemies. Just as God forgives our enemies, he will forgive us. There cannot be one without the other.

Jesus appeals to this principle. If you do not need God's mercy, he essentially tells the crowd, then you do not need to show mercy. But if you are a sinner, and thus in need of God's mercy, then show mercy to this adulterous woman, for she is a sinner who needs mercy as well. Here his message was not new. It had been made in the Hebrew Scriptures. Yahweh is repeatedly described as compassionate and merciful and always willing to forgive the sinful people of Israel. Isaiah states this in typically beautiful language:

> Seek the LORD while he may be found.
>   Call upon him while he is near;
> let the wicked forsake their way,
>   and the unrighteous their thoughts;
> let them return to the LORD, that he may have mercy on them,
>   and to our God, for he will abundantly pardon.
> For my thoughts are not your thoughts,
>   nor are your ways my ways, says the LORD.
> Far as the heavens are higher than the earth,
>   so my ways are higher than your ways,
>   and my thoughts than your thoughts. (Isa. 55:6-9; cf. Ezek. 18)

Just as Yahweh is merciful, he calls upon his people to be merciful as well. Micah (6:8) asks, "What does the LORD require of you but to do justice, and to love kindness, and to walk humbly with your God?" Zechariah (7:9) resonates with it: "Render true judgments, show kindness and mercy to one another; do not oppress the widow, the orphan, the alien, or the poor; and do not devise evil in your hearts against one another." The prophets repeatedly demand that the Israelites show mercy on society's most devalued members, the poor and the outcast.

Because Jesus' words echo so much of the Hebrew tradition, the elders recognize it first. They are acquainted with the story of Yahweh's forgiveness and have pondered on it. Jesus' brief response is enough to convince them that what they are doing is wrong. It may be that some, like Rabbis

Tarfon and Aqiba two hundred years later, have already found the death penalty to be incompatible with the mercy of the God of Israel.[17] All they need is a final argument from Jesus. The younger men follow, partly in imitation of their teachers, who they believe to be more learned and less sinful than themselves. It would indeed be an act of pride to claim that they are not sinful when their older and wiser teachers admit their sins.

Finally, Jesus is left alone with the woman. "Has no one condemned you?" he asks. "No one," she replies. Then Jesus adds his own forgiveness to the crowd's: "Neither do I condemn you." But as she leaves, he admonishes her to take advantage of the second chance that has been offered to her: "Go on your way, and from now on, do not sin again." Can this woman change her life? Haven't the risks she has taken—even endangering her life—shown her to be a hard-core sinner? Will Jesus' simple admonition be enough? We cannot know. But what Jesus has done for her is to show that he believes a new life is possible for her. He has opened the door to that new life for her. She now has an opportunity to walk through it and live in a way pleasing to God.

John 8:2-11 applies Jesus' teaching about forgiveness to a capital case. Until recently, few commentators beyond such pacifistic groups as the Anabaptists have interpreted this passage as a message against the death penalty.[18] Christian proponents of capital punishment seem to have taken five basic approaches to rejecting such an interpretation, all of which, in my opinion, are fallacious.

Argument 1

The first argument attacks the placement of this story in the canon.[19] Yes, the story is a relatively late addition to the Scriptures, but it has become an accepted part of the New Testament at least from the fourth century. It was included in the canon by no less an authority than Jerome. There is evidence that the story was well-known before that time and may have been included in earlier copies of the New Testament.

In addition, the story itself is much beloved by Christians and has been used for centuries as an example of Jesus' compassion. "Casting the first stone" is deeply imbedded in our language as a phrase associated with self-righteous behavior. Despite some discomfort about whether the story might be construed as accepting adultery, early Christians obviously felt that the narrative had great merit. They believed the story made an important contribution to explaining who Jesus was. Because of this, they found a place for it within the canon in its final form. In my opinion, most Christians would reject the notion that this story is not a part of the biblical canon.

Argument 2

In a second point against using the story of the adulterous woman as a teaching against the death penalty, some claim that general ethical principles cannot be accurately deduced from biblical narratives.[20] We agree that it is dangerous to establish ethical standards from biblical stories taken out of context. Yet the use of this story to support Jesus' disavowal of capital punishment is not such a case. As shown above, this story is not of an isolated incident from Jesus' life. Instead, it is a practical application of his general teachings on forgiveness.

Within this context, the story can be seen as a narrative illustration of Jesus' teachings. It is therefore logical to conclude that when Jesus taught his disciples not to judge or condemn others, he also was teaching them not to participate in legal processes that allowed or forced them to judge and condemn.

Argument 3

A third tactic for disavowing this story as a teaching on the death penalty is holding that the execution of the woman was not a legal execution. Instead, some claim it was a legal lynching, carried out primarily to trap Jesus. Therefore, runs this argument, Jesus was stopping an illegal killing rather than a judicial execution. As already stated, however, the woman had committed a capital crime, and the procedure for the execution was being carried out in accord with the normal operations of the Jewish judicial system. The mob aspects of the case were a normal occurrence, just as in the past mobs attended public hangings or today demonstrate outside modern prisons in which executions are taking place.

In other words, this appears to have been a fully legal execution being carried out under a legal system in many ways more diligent in seeking the truth than the modern American system. Hence, Jesus' intervention stopped a legal execution fully sanctioned by the Jewish authorities.

Furthermore, if Jesus had felt that the execution did not meet the legal standards set by the Hebrew Scriptures, it would have been safer for him to challenge it on these grounds, rather than on the more radical approach he took. If the execution was legally questionable, he could have cross-examined witnesses and thoroughly challenged procedures. The fact that Jesus never challenged the legality of the execution indicates that it fit within the framework of the law.

Argument 4

A fourth approach has been to try to negate this story's relevance for the modern debate on capital punishment. Some claim that the crime of adultery is not as serious as the crimes for which we apply death sentences—most commonly murder.[21] They imply that Jesus stopped the execution of an adulteress, but that he would not have stopped the execution of a murderer. As already pointed out in chapter 2, however, adultery was a very serious crime in Jesus' time. Barclay quotes rabbis who said, "Every Jew must die before he commits idolatry, murder, or adultery."[22] For the Jews of that time, adultery was a deadly serious crime, ranking with idolatry and murder.

When the prophets condemn the sinfulness of the Israelites, the metaphor most often used is of adultery, not of murder. This certainly implies the serious nature of the crime in the eyes of Jesus' contemporaries. In fact, it was perhaps the most grievous crime a woman could commit because it threatened both her husband and her children; it had the potential of drawing her family and her husband's family into a deadly feud. The seriousness of the crime can be inferred from the continued use of the death penalty for adultery in some Muslim countries today, along with the "honor killings" of women who have brought shame onto their families through the suspicion of adultery.

Murder, on the other hand, was not necessarily considered to be the most serious crime. Both the Greeks[23] and the Romans[24] seem to have used banishment as a typical punishment for murderers, even while punishing some crimes against property with death. Cain's banishment for the murder of Abel may also indicate that among the ancient Hebrews, banishment was the typical punishment for intragroup murders. Numbers 35:31, which required the death penalty for murderers, was a departure from this practice. This law was likely created because of the strong likelihood that murder would be avenged with murder, creating a cycle of violence. The requirement of the death penalty for murder was a way of de-escalating a possible feud in which many might die (see chap. 2).

In the story of John 8:2-11, Jesus is not arguing that adultery does not deserve a death sentence under the law. Indeed, his words imply that it does. For Jesus, however, deserving death and receiving death are two different things. By essentially asking the mob to imitate God's forgiveness, he stops the punishment called for by the written and oral law. There is no indication anywhere in the Bible that Jesus made distinctions between crimes. It is therefore reasonable to assume that his forgiveness of the grievous crime of adultery shows that he would also have forgiven other serious crimes, including murder, a crime listed as only one of the trio of most serious crimes (adultery, idolatry, murder) for the Judean people.

Argument 5

A fifth argument for disregarding this story in the discussion of contemporary capital punishment is that executing a criminal under the modern system does not require us to throw the first stone. Thus, we can personally forgive the criminal but still support the state's right to take his life as the punishment for his crime. This is the classic argument for Christian participation in capital punishment, and it can be traced back to the theology of Augustine in the fifth century.

Writing shortly after the sack of Rome in 411, Augustine justified Christians' use of violence by creating a distinction between private conduct and behavior required from a citizen of the state. This is a position that has often been called the two-kingdom theory. As citizens of the kingdom of God, we cannot kill our fellow human beings. But when our duty as citizens of the state requires our participation in such killing, this duty excuses our otherwise sinful participation because we have become necessary instruments to keep the law and order that God has ordained. Augustine said,

> There are some exceptions made by divine authority to its own law, that men may not be put to death. . . . He to whom authority is delegated, and who is but a sword in the hand of him who uses it, is not himself responsible for the death he deals. . . . They who wage war in obedience to the divine command, or in conformity with His laws, have represented in their persons the public justice or the wisdom of the government, and in this capacity have put to death wicked men; such persons have by no means violated the commandment, "Thou shalt not kill."[25]

This approach obviously runs counter to the narrative. Following Augustine's reasoning, Jesus should have allowed the execution to go forward because it was an official act of the state. The mob would simply be doing what the state asked of them. Under his own moral standard, Jesus could have legitimately acted as the executioner since he was "without sin" (John 8:7; Heb. 4:15; 1 Pet. 2:21-24). He did not do so, even though the state had sanctioned the killing. Instead, the woman was not killed and was actually allowed to leave with no further punishment.

The notion that killing can be the final step in a process of love and forgiveness is strange indeed. In Matthew 7:15-20, Jesus takes a pragmatic approach to such belief systems in his comments about false prophets. "Are grapes gathered from thorns or figs from thistles? In the same way, every good tree bears good fruit, but the bad tree bears bad fruit." It seems absurd to say that an act of forgiveness can still call for the suffering, torture, and death that is "the fruit" of capital punishment. Certainly, in my experience with death-row inmates, they do not feel in any way forgiven by the society that is taking their lives. It is simply dishonest for us to say that we have forgiven a criminal, but that we still demand secondhand deadly revenge on him from the state.

However, this two-kingdom theory has had a tremendous impact on Christian social ethics. It will be worth a bit more time to examine it further. Although the proponents of this approach to Christian ethics most frequently appeal to the Hebrew Scriptures and the epistles, they also cite at least one of Jesus' sayings for support. This is Jesus' comment about paying taxes in Matthew 22:15-22. The saying comes from a confrontation between Jesus and a group of Pharisees and Herodians. They wish to trap Jesus into saying something seditious, which would force the Romans to imprison or execute him. So they ask him whether it is lawful to pay taxes to the emperor.

Jesus asks for one of the coins used in paying these taxes. It is a silver denarius bearing a portrait of the emperor. He asks his questioners, "Whose head is this and whose title?" When they answer that it is the emperor's, Jesus replies, "Give therefore to the emperor the things that are the emperor's, and to God the things that are God's."

The traditional interpretation of this story is that Jesus

was supportive of the government. He drew a distinction between duties to God and duties to the state, and in so doing refused to challenge the state. There are a number of problems with this interpretation, however. The tone of the Gospels is one of great tension between Jesus and the government. Matthew's account of the birth of Jesus states that King Herod tried to kill Jesus, even as a child. Jesus' kinsman and forerunner John the Baptist was executed by Herod Antipas, tetrarch of Galilee and Perea at the time.

On several occasions, Jesus himself is critical of the government. When told that Herod wishes to kill him, Jesus publicly attacks the king by calling him a fox, which was a risky insult against a powerful ruler (Luke 13:32).[26] Jesus also is critical of Pilate, claiming that some Galileans Pilate massacred were not deserving of their death because they were no more sinful than anyone else (Luke 13:1-3). Jesus also tells his disciples that they must not behave as powerful government authorities do:

> You know that the rulers of the Gentiles lord it over them, and their great ones are tyrants over them. It will not be so among you; but whoever wishes to be great among you must be your servant, and whoever wishes to be first among you must be your slave; just as the Son of Man came not to be served but to serve, and to give his life as a ransom for many. (Matt. 20:25-29; Mark 10:42-45)

The most important proof that Jesus' teachings were considered dangerous to the status quo, however, is the cross. Jesus was executed for sedition. His message was considered to be dangerous to the smooth functioning of the state. Pilate and the Jewish leaders determined that Jesus' message was in fact a revolutionary attack on their government. They decided that the Jesus movement must be crushed through Jesus' execution.

If we assume that Jesus' message was considered dangerous, it seems reasonable that other interpretations can be placed on his comments about taxation. In another view,

Jesus was suggesting that God's people should not accept Roman money at all. Such coins were clearly idolatrous. Many of them bore the graven image of a man whom many worshiped as a god. This incident may also relate to the time (29-31) when Pilate, ignoring Jewish sensitivities, issued Judean coins illustrated with pagan symbols. While the Judean coins did not depict the head of the emperor (as in Matt. 22:20-21), Jews likely felt uncomfortable using them.[27] Yet any refusal to accept denarii or other money depicting pagan images as legitimate payment would have been a serious act of civil disobedience. It could have thrown the entire Judean economy into chaos.

This interpretation is supported by the fact that his enemies wanted to ask questions they hoped he would answer seditiously. They had "malice" and wanted to "entrap him in what he said," so they could denounce him to the Romans (Matt. 22:15, 18). If the Pharisees and Herodians thought Jesus would give an answer supporting the government, they would have had no reason to ask the question about taxation. At his trial, Jesus was even accused of claiming to be a king and of telling his followers not to pay taxes to the emperor. Hence, from the government's point of view, Jesus' message about paying taxes was suspect (Luke 23:2).

Even if Jesus was not advocating an act of civil disobedience, his statement placed an important limitation on the authority of the government over his followers. The coin bore the image of the emperor; it therefore belonged to the emperor. Human beings were created in the image of God;[28] they therefore belonged to God. Under this interpretation, the emperor could legitimately demand payment of taxes using coins bearing *his* image. But the government could not demand the life of a human being, because human beings belonged to God, whose image they bore.

Hence, the government could not legitimately ask its citizens to take a human life. When it did so, it overstepped the limits God had set on it. As we shall see in chapters 7 and 8,

Paul and other early Christian theologians also believed that the legitimate authority of the government was limited, and that it did not include the taking of human life.

Perhaps the ultimate question about capital punishment for Christians who wish to model their lives on the life of Christ is this: "Would Jesus be an executioner?" It takes a strange reading of the words and deeds of Jesus to say that he would accept such a role. Jesus' message was one of love and forgiveness, the antithesis of the hatred and vengeance that underlie the use of capital punishment.[29]

John 8:2-11 tells of a time when he was specifically given the opportunity to endorse the death penalty. He refused to become an executioner himself, and he also touched the consciences of others so that they too turned away from this act of vengeance. Anyone who recognizes this would find it difficult to believe that Jesus would approve of his modern followers' support of capital punishment.

The final act of Jesus' life, his own execution, further upholds this contention. So it is to Jesus' crucifixion and other New Testament executions that we will now turn our attention.

6
New Testament Executions

The Crucifixion of Jesus

The central event of the New Testament is an execution. The stories and sayings of Jesus all lead to the crucifixion. The later acts of the apostles and their epistles all point backward to the crucifixion as well as to a future when Jesus will return. Since we recognize the centrality of Jesus' execution, it is remarkable that the church has, for most of its history, ignored the lessons this event and other executions in the New Testament have to teach us about capital punishment. From the early fourth century, the church has tied its fate to that of the governmental authorities; these rulers have always desired to use the death penalty as their ultimate weapon for social control.

Thus, to support its allies, the church has refused to talk about the crucifixion as a killing initiated and carried out by the government. Instead, the church has focused on Jesus' crucifixion as an act of atonement, interpreting it as bringing God's grace to individual believers but having little relation to rulers' use of the death penalty.[1] Hence, we need to examine details of the crucifixion and other executions reported in the New Testament. Such an examination shows that the apostolic church, through whom we have received the New Testament, understood these executions to have important spiritual and political lessons to teach

Christians about governments and their use of this extreme sanction.

The portrayals of Jesus' crucifixion in the popular media, including films and television, often give a distorted view of what happened. According to this view, the crucifixion occurred under the provisions of a primitive legal system that allowed Jewish and Roman authorities free reign in their dealings with criminals. In addition, this portrayal pictures the men responsible for Jesus' execution as extraordinarily weak or evil. The implication of this view is that a modern judicial system, such as ours, would have protected Jesus. The media assume that modern democratically elected leaders provide a higher moral level of leadership than the Jewish and Roman authorities afforded at that time.

However, this view does not reflect the historical reality. Both the Jewish and Roman legal systems were highly developed and provided numerous legal protections for defendants. In chapter 2, we have already discussed the Jewish law and its oral interpretations in some depth. The level of evidence required in a capital case, the provisions for cross-examination, and the harsh penalty for false witnesses—all this process gave defendants a good chance of being acquitted in Jewish trials. The Jewish law was not a hypothetical system that covered up how things were really done. The lifestyle of the Jews, as based on the law, had given them a reputation for living according to high moral standards—moral standards attractive to many Gentiles who found nothing like them in their own religions.

The Roman law also provided protections for defendants, particularly for Roman citizens, but for others as well. Paul, a Roman citizen, used these provisions on at least two occasions to protect himself from arbitrary punishment (Acts 22:22-29; 25:1-12). The Roman law was so well developed that a moratorium on the death penalty for citizens occurred in the first century B.C. because the courts allowed to impose death sentences were rarely called into session.[2] Around the same time, exile replaced death as the punishment for homicide.[3] Pilate, the Roman prefect over Judea and charged to follow Roman law and enforce it, is portrayed as reluctant to impose the death sentence on Jesus; he felt that the evidence against Jesus was insufficient.[4]

Thus Jesus was crucified under the two most advanced legal systems of his time. Moreover, his execution occurred in a country known for its high moral standards and under the rules of a powerful empire distinguished for its administrative competence. It was an empire that had brought a much higher degree of law and order than the Mediterranean world had ever seen before. Jesus' execution, in other words, occurred under judicial systems quite capable, in theory, of protecting an innocent man. But these systems failed.

The execution of Jesus was based on political decisions made by men influenced by their own self-interest and also thinking that Jesus' death was necessary for the public good. The Jewish religious leaders accused Jesus of the capital crime of blasphemy, but he was executed by the Romans for sedition.[5] This indicates the complexity of the political climate in which Jesus lived and died. Judea was a colony of Rome. As in all colonies, the colonizers depended on native collaborators to help them understand the local political situation and to keep it under control.

In Judea, the leading collaborators were the Sadducees, the religiously conservative group that controlled the priesthood and the temple. Providing religious goods and services, such as selling animals for sacrifice in the temple, was a lucrative business for the Sadducees. Jesus' attack on these practices represented a threat not only to the Sadducees' religious prestige, but also to their economic welfare. It was no wonder that they wanted to get rid of him.

But Jesus was a popular religious leader, and it was Passover, a time when nationalist feelings were running particularly high. Jesus entered Jerusalem to the acclaim of the crowds (Matt. 21:1-11; Mark 11:1-11; Luke 19:28-39; John 12:12-19). According to the synoptic Gospels, shortly after this event Jesus made his most aggressive attack on the corruption of the temple by driving out the moneychangers and sellers of sacrificial animals (Matt. 21:12-17; Mark 11:15-19; Luke 19:45-48).

Though the Gospels describe the cleansing of the temple as an individual act, religion professor Bruce Chilton speculates that up to two hundred followers of Jesus may have been involved.[6] At least the texts imply that large numbers of people supported this action: after all, the temple authorities did not believe they could arrest Jesus without causing civil unrest. At the same time, Jesus was disrupting the temple business at its busiest and most profitable time of the year. Something had to be done and done quickly.

The determination to bring Jesus to execution was a decision carefully made by men who felt that they had the best interests of their people at heart (John 11:45-53).[7] It was carried out by a Roman official who believed that the execution was necessary to protect law and order. The conflict had been brewing for some months. Jesus was aware that the most powerful temple leaders considered him to be a dangerous radical. Several times he predicted that he would be put to death.[8] Jesus showed his political acuity by predicting that the Jewish council, the Sanhedrin, would not execute him themselves, using traditional Jewish methods, but that the Romans would crucify him.[9]

The movement of Jesus from his arrest to the hearing before the Sanhedrin and to the hearing before Pilate, appears to be carefully planned. Jesus was captured at night, when his arrest would cause the least public uproar. Luke 22:6 says that Judas was hired to betray Jesus specifically so that the arrest could take place when no crowd was present. According to Mark 15:25, Jesus was crucified at nine o'clock the next morning. Between these two events, he had a hearing before the Sanhedrin, two hearings before Pilate, and a hearing before Herod.

Over the years, there has been much debate about whether Jesus' hearing before the Sanhedrin was actually a legal proceeding.[10] If the hearing before the Sanhedrin was a trial, it clearly had many aspects that ran counter to the law. According to the Hebrew Scriptures, conviction demanded at least two eyewitnesses giving essentially the same story. Luke reports no witnesses against Jesus (Luke 22:66-71). Mark's account states that the witnesses against Jesus did not agree with each other, which means that their testimony should have been discounted (Mark 14:55-59).

Matthew 26:59-61 also reports false witnesses, but says that eventually two witnesses (the necessary number for conviction; Deut. 17:6) came forward who agreed that Jesus had made a statement about being able to destroy and rebuild the temple. Matthew does not report such words coming from Jesus, though Jesus does assert his authority over the temple (21:12-16; 12:6) and predicts its destruction (24:2; 23:38; cf. John 2:19-22, where Jesus says he will rebuild the "temple," referring to his resurrection).

There is no report that this false testimony about destroying the temple was contradicted. However, if rigorous cross-examination had been applied, there should have been some question about why only two witnesses had heard such statements when so many others had been present. The court should not have admitted the statements of any witnesses if they contradicted testimony from other witnesses. Neither Mark nor Matthew reports that the false witnesses were punished as required (Deut. 19:18-19).

There is some question about whether the rabbinical laws found in the Mishnah would have governed a trial held 170 years before they were written down. Yet it seems clear that these laws were based on custom and practice considerably older than the writing of the Mishnah itself. It is therefore not unreasonable to assume that at least some of the laws would have applied to Jewish trials at the time Jesus was executed. If so, there are many disparities between the laws and the way the hearing before the Sanhedrin was held.

The accounts of Matthew and Mark report that the hearing before the Sanhedrin was held at night, which is against the rules described in the Mishnah (Sanhedrin 4.1).[11] Some have held that the meeting described in Matthew and Mark was a preliminary hearing of some kind and that Luke describes the real trial. Even if the Sanhedrin tried Jesus offi-cially on Friday morning, however, he could not have been legally executed until at least Sunday, at the earliest. The Mishnah requires the Sanhedrin to wait overnight for a final vote of condemnation, and therefore prohibited beginning a trial on the day before a Sabbath or a festival.[12] If Luke's ver-sion is correct, Jesus' hearing was Friday, the day before the Sabbath and at the beginning of Passover. There was no overnight wait.

Moreover, Jesus' hearing violated many of the rules for the treatment of witnesses found in the Mishnah. The Mishnah encouraged rigorous cross-examination of witness-es, but there is no report of any cross-examination of wit-nesses at this hearing. In the Gospels, no one asked the obvi-ous question about why only two of many witnesses heard Jesus' statements about the temple. Those speaking in favor of the defendant were supposed to speak before those who wished to speak against him. There is no report of anyone speaking in favor of Jesus. Judges were not allowed to act as witnesses against the defendant. Yet after Jesus makes a state-ment, the high priest exclaims, "He has blasphemed! Why do we still need witnesses? You have now heard his blasphemy. What is your verdict?" (Matt. 26:65-66; Mark 14:63-64; Luke 22:71).

These violations of the law are so obvious that they should have caused considerable religious turmoil during the Passover festival, but no objection to them is reported. The only logical explanation is that the Sanhedrin did not claim to hold a trial, but only a hearing. The leaders' purpose was to turn public opinion against Jesus and convince the Sanhedrin's more reluctant members that Jesus should be turned over to the Romans.

Perhaps the account of John captures the meaning of the hearing most accurately.[13] He does not report a hearing before the Sanhedrin at all, but only a nighttime interview with the high priest Annas (John 18:19-24). If the so-called trial was only a meeting between Jesus and Annas and a few other leaders, the purpose may have only been to confirm a decision already made. Instead of trying Jesus for blasphemy, they intended to accuse him of sedition and let the Romans execute him.

The reason for this decision was threefold. Without doubt, the Sanhedrin did not want to take responsibility for executing a popular religious leader of a seemingly large number of followers.[14] Some of Jesus' disciples were associated with the Zealots, a group of radical Jews. The Zealots were willing to use violence to punish those they felt were traitors to their own nation.[15] The execution of a popular religious leader, particularly one who at times appealed to nationalist feelings, was likely to result in violent repercussions. This was especially true if the arrest and execution took place around the time of Passover, an intensely nationalistic holiday.

The second reason was timing. As stated above, for the Sanhedrin to try Jesus on a capital charge, he would have to be tried during the daylight hours on Friday (perhaps illegal, on Passover eve) and could not have been executed until at least Sunday, well into the Passover Week (M. Sanhedrin 4.1 also implies that executions could not be carried out during the festival, but we do not know if these provision applied then).[16] According to Matthew 26:5 (Mark 14:2), the chief priests and elders were acutely aware of the timing of the execution in relationship to the Passover: "Not during the festival, or there may be a riot among the people."

During the Passover, the law would need to be scrupulously observed. The greatest Jewish legal scholars would be present, so any deviation from the law and its traditional interpretations would be observed and commented upon. Because of the intense religious feelings aroused by the festival, such deviations would almost certainly lead to civil unrest.

Any delay in the execution would also have given Jesus' supporters time to organize his defense and would make the already-tense situation worse. As collaborators with Rome, the priests were interested in keeping the peace, especially during the Passover festival. Their concerns are expressed clearly in John 11:48: "If we let him [Jesus] go on like this, everyone will believe him, and the Romans will come and destroy both our holy place and our nation." They had convinced themselves that they had a national crisis on their hands. They needed Jesus out of the way and fast, but their own religious traditions kept them from carrying out an execution as quickly as they wanted.

The third reason the Jewish leaders wanted the Romans to carry out the death sentence was that a crucifixion had religious significance as a form of execution. Crucifixion equaled hanging on a tree, a punishment cursed by the law.[17] If Jesus had been executed in this manner, it would have discredited him and the movement gathering around him.[18] If timing and the manner of execution had not been issues, the Sanhedrin probably could have tried Jesus officially and ordered his execution by stoning.

The synoptic Gospels do not mention the Romans prohibiting the Jews from imposing death sentences. John 18:31 reports that the Jewish leaders said, "We are not permitted to put anyone to death." The Romans probably did not allow the Jewish courts to impose death sentences without their approval.[19] However, this permission does not appear to be have been difficult to obtain. The near execution of the woman caught in adultery (John 8:2-11) and the execution of Stephen for blasphemy (Acts 6:8-8:1) show that the Jewish courts were allowed to impose capital sentences, at least in some cases involving violation of Jewish law.

In John 19:6, Pilate tells the Jewish leaders that they could crucify Jesus themselves if they wished to. Some have assumed that Pilate was simply mocking the Jewish leaders, who could not legally execute Jesus themselves.[20] Another interpretation is that Pilate was ignorant of the Jewish law requiring execution by stoning for blasphemy, and he was making a bona fide offer to allow the Sadducees to execute Jesus themselves.

However, there is a third possibility: Pilate might have been making a bona fide offer based on his knowledge that Jewish leaders had used crucifixion as a method of execution in the past, and that some contemporary Jews were calling for crucifixion as the punishment for some crimes. Hasmonean rulers in Palestine had used crucifixion during the previous century, and Josephus reported that Alexander Jannaeus crucified eight hundred persons.[21] One of the Dead Sea Scrolls, the Qumran Temple Scroll, names three crimes worthy of crucifixion: blasphemy, betraying one's people to a foreign nation, and bringing evil on one's own people.[22] The author of the scroll also believes that Israel had used the punishment of crucifixion throughout its history.[23]

While Pilate may have been serious in suggesting that the Jewish leaders crucify Jesus, problems would have remained for the Jewish leadership if they had followed this course. There is no sign that the mainstream of Jewish leaders had accepted crucifixion as a form of execution for blasphemy. If the punishment was considered an innovation, it could have caused an uproar during Passover Week, particularly if the populace saw it as imitating a hated Roman practice. By having the Romans carry out the crucifixion, the leaders diverted blame from themselves in case there was a violent reaction, while still giving them the benefit of the religious condemnation of those who were "hung." Thus, a Roman execution provided the best solution to a number of perceived problems.

Therefore, the temple leaders took Jesus to the Roman governor Pilate, who because of the early hour had probably been kept informed of the situation throughout the night. They attempted to show Pilate that Jesus' alleged blasphemy was also sedition. These leaders argued that Jesus was making a political claim to be "King of the Jews," which could be interpreted as a direct challenge to the emperor, who had the sole right to confer such leadership positions. Luke 23:2 relates an accusation that Jesus had forbidden his followers from paying taxes to the emperor, which would have been a major economic attack on the Roman governance of the colony.[24]

Apparently Pilate at first was not convinced of the charge of sedition.[25] He offered alternatives, such as having Jesus flogged. Luke 23:6-12 reports that he tried to foist the problem off on Herod. However, nothing worked. Then public opinion, as fickle then as it is now, turned. The crowds, probably at the urging of the agents of the temple leadership, began to call for Jesus' death. Perhaps the final straw was when the temple officials told Pilate, "If you release this man, you are no friend of the emperor. Everyone who claims to be a king sets himself against the emperor."

When the argument was stated this bluntly, Pilate must have considered the personal consequences for himself. On one hand, the Roman rules for evidence had not been met. Pilate repeatedly had stated as much. Allowing Jesus to be executed on an unproved charge would be a violation of the Roman law he was supposed to uphold. On the other hand, there were the political considerations. By protecting this poor, itinerant street preacher, Pilate was risking a major riot that could easily turn into a full-scale insurrection. He was also alienating the powerful priests who helped him keep the native population in line.

In addition, his failure to execute Jesus might be used as an accusation against him. The temple leaders had implied that they would portray it as a failure of his loyalty to the emperor. No doubt they had powerful friends willing to take the tale to Rome.[26] Weighing these consequences, Pilate decided to ignore the legal requirements in order to meet the political needs of the moment. He ordered the death of a man he believed to be innocent. The Jewish and Roman laws failed to protect this most innocent man. Battered by the onslaught of perceived political necessity, the greatest systems of human justice crumble.

As Pilate vacillated about what to do, a curious event occurred. In a last-ditch effort to save Jesus, Pilate turned to a custom by which one prisoner of the people's choice was released at Passover. Pilate appealed to the crowd that Jesus be that choice. But the people demanded the release of Barabbas, a notorious prisoner (Matt. 27:16), bandit (John 18:40), insurrectionist, and murderer (Mark 15:7; Luke 23:18).

Outside the Gospel accounts, there is no evidence of the custom of freeing a criminal at the time of Passover, so the custom must have been short-lived if it existed at all.[27] Pilate may have simply invented the custom on the spot. Matthew 27:15-17 and John 18:39 state that Pilate initiated the discussion of releasing Jesus, but when he did, the crowd called for Barabbas.

Another explanation might be that there was a custom of an amnesty for minor criminals as a Roman sign of goodwill at Passover. Mark 15:6-8 reports that the crowd called for the release of a prisoner. But when Pilate used such a call in an attempt to release Jesus, this crowd took the opportunity to call for the release of Barabbas instead. In the earliest manuscripts, Luke 23:13-25 does not mention the custom of releasing prisoners at all. It states that the crowd's demand to release Barabbas came as a response to Pilate's offer to flog Jesus and then let him go. It does not make sense for a Roman governor to release a dangerous criminal, particularly one with revolutionary leanings, even once a year.[28]

Perhaps in offering to release one prisoner accused of sedition, Pilate opened the door for the crowd to demand the release of another criminal accused of the same crime. Such an event is not something that would have been a common practice. The release of Barabbas instead of Jesus was extraordinary.

Barabbas is not mentioned by name again in the New Testament, so it is doubtful that he became active in the early church. But the symbolic meaning of his release is clear. The liberation of Barabbas is a foreshadowing of the discussion of atonement. Here is an obvious example of a sinner spared by the death of Jesus. Like many criminals, Barabbas may have justified his crimes as acts of social justice, and his popularity with the crowd may indicate that there was some truth to this rationale. But in the end, Barabbas was a dangerous criminal, a bandit, a murderer. He was a violent man who was willing to take human life.

His life, however, was spared through the crucifixion of Jesus. Jesus literally took his place on the cross. Thus Jesus' death saved a man who deserved the death sentence, according to both Jewish and Roman law. The death of Jesus gave the murderer Barabbas another chance. So a murderer was the first beneficiary of Jesus' atoning act on the cross.

This benefit was not merely some spiritual succor in the next life. Barabbas was given his life in the here and now. He was given an opportunity to change his ways in this world, not an eternal life in the next. Indeed, since we never hear of Barabbas again in the Scriptures, we cannot be sure what use he made of his second chance. But we do know that Jesus' death came between him and his execution. Jesus' death saved a murderer sentenced to die. This story, which appears in all four Gospels, shows that the early church understood Jesus' death to be a redeeming act for all human beings, and that this redemption should have practical consequences in the way that we treat even the worst of sinners.

After the story of Barabbas comes the crucifixion itself. The description of Jesus' execution shows that little has changed in human nature over the last two thousand years. Just as crowds gather outside modern prisons to celebrate death and mock the person being executed, Jesus was mocked and derided. Indeed, the execution was so cruel that Jesus began to pray Psalm 22, which begins, "My God, my God, why have you forsaken me?" (Matt. 27:46; Mark 15:34).

Despite the pain and humiliation of the cross, however, Jesus continued to proclaim and practice God's forgiveness.

Luke 23:34 reports that Jesus prayed for forgiveness for those who were torturing and killing him: "Father, forgive them; for they do not know what they are doing." Later, he promised salvation to one of the criminals being executed with him, after the thief requested that Jesus remember him when he came into his kingdom (Luke 23:43).

What lessons, then, do the descriptions of the crucifixion of Jesus have to teach us about capital punishment? The first lesson is that human justice systems, even at their best, are not perfect. They can be corrupted by economic, political, and personal considerations. When this occurs, they become unjust. If they are allowed to use the death penalty, they may impose it on even the most-innocent people.

The second lesson of the crucifixion is that the death of Jesus was meant to atone for the sins of all human beings, including murderers. The first person saved by the blood of Jesus was Barabbas, a murderer. Jesus' salvation is not just something that happens in the coming world. Salvation came to Barabbas in the here and now. It gave him a chance to turn away from his sinful life, even though there was no indication that Barabbas was a particularly good candidate for this offer of salvation.

The third lesson is that even though Jesus was put to death in a most cruel way for crimes he had not committed, he did not call for revenge. If anyone had a right to condemn his killers, it was Jesus. But Jesus did not seek revenge. He did not call from the cross for his followers or for God to avenge his death. Instead, he prayed for his killers to be forgiven. Moreover, even on the cross, he offered forgiveness to his fellow sufferers. Virtually the last act of Jesus' life was to offer solace. The repentant thief was not condemned; he was comforted. No one can read the accounts of the crucifixion and come away with the conclusion that Jesus would want his followers to inflict on others the kind of suffering inflicted on him.

The Execution of John the Baptist

The story of John the Baptist's execution appears in Matthew 14:1-12 and Mark 6:14-29. John, of course, was the immediate forerunner of Jesus. Luke 1:36 states that John and Jesus were kinsmen, and the three synoptic Gospels say that John baptized Jesus (Matt. 3:13-17; Mark 1:9-11; Luke 3:15-22). John lived and ministered in the desert, and apparently did not visit the towns or cities, so his ministry was considerably more ascetic than Jesus' was.

Jesus clearly admired John but drew a distinction between their styles of ministry in Matthew 11:7-19 (Luke 7:18-35). In part, he said, "For John came neither eating or drinking, and they say 'He has a demon'; the Son of Man came eating and drinking, and they say, 'Look, a glutton and a drunkard, a friend of tax collectors and sinners!'" All the Gospels go to some pains to report how John himself declared that he was not the Messiah (Matt. 3:11-15; Mark 1:7-9; Luke 3:16-17; John 1:19-28; 3:25-30). Perhaps the Gospels are countering claims of John's followers in those early-church years that he was the Messiah (cf. Acts 19:1-7).

Despite John's asceticism, he was willing to speak prophetically about the current situation in Galilee. In particular, he condemned the Tetrarch Herod Antipas for marrying his brother Philip's wife, Herodias.[29] Such a condemnation had political overtones in a country that jealously protected its religious heritage. It is not surprising that Herod had John arrested, at the insistence of his wife. Though Herod was willing to arrest John, he was not ready to execute him. Mark 6:20 states that Herod feared John and respected his righteousness. Matthew 14:5 gives a more cynical view, saying that Herod wanted to kill John but feared the public reaction because John was regarded as a prophet.

Then a strange turn of events occurred while Herod was celebrating his birthday. On a whim, he offered his step-daughter "up to half his kingdom" for a dance that pleased him and his guests. Guided by her mother, she asked for the head of John the Baptist. Mark reports that Herod did not want to carry out the execution, but he also did not want to go back on his public oath. He therefore ordered the execution. John was beheaded, and Herodias had her revenge.

The story leaves the reader with many questions. There is no doubt that in this case the execution had political overtones. John had offended and perhaps even endangered the political position of a powerful person. His continued existence made him dangerous, but his popularity provided him with some protection. However, the powerful have ways of getting what they want. The story tells of a simple, perhaps drunken, response to a request from a political favorite. But the final denouement of the story was undoubtedly the result of weeks or months of palace intrigue. Herod may have recognized that his wife's political friends had gained power, and that those who wished to protect John had lost strength. The imprisonment of John had taken his ministry out of the public spotlight, and perhaps Herod now felt safer in doing away with a prophet whom many had forgotten.

In the story, there is no mention of a trial. Had John been tried and found guilty of sedition? We cannot know. Perhaps this was an extra-judicial execution, one that occurred outside normal legal channels. Such events occur in tyrannical regimes, but normally tyrants like to cloak their political executions with some degree of procedure—a show trial to prove that the condemned is getting what he or she deserves. The existence of judicial capital punishment makes such show trials possible.

If there is no "legitimate" use of the death penalty, extra-judicial or pseudo-judicial executions are less justifiable. It is not surprising, for example, that when Benito Mussolini came to power in Italy, he reinstated the death penalty. Although he had the dictatorial power to murder whomever he pleased, the existence of judicial capital punishment allowed him to justify his crimes as legal executions. John the Baptist was in the prison of a tyrant, probably charged with a capital crime. It was a short step from there to an execution that merely carried out what everyone was expecting anyway.

What, then, does the execution of John the Baptist have to teach Christians about the death penalty? Like the execution of Jesus, John's execution was a political event. It was used to eliminate a political enemy and to assuage a political friend. John's execution also teaches us that capital punishment opens the door to less-judicial forms of execution. The existence of the death penalty allows its misuse. Its violence is used to justify other forms of violence that are less concerned with the rights of the accused.

Capital punishment may begin as a serious attempt to punish the guilty without destroying the innocent. But by the very nature of its unlimited violence toward individuals, it opens the door to extrajudicial violence. John the Baptist may have been executed on a whim, but such an execution would have been less possible if judicial capital punishment had not been in place to sanction it.

The Two Thieves

On the first Good Friday, Jesus was not the only person executed. All the Gospels report that two bandits were also executed with him that day (Matt. 27:38-44; Mark 15:27-32; Luke 23:32-43; John 19:18). Matthew and Mark report that the thieves joined the others who mocked Jesus. John reports that the bandits were crucified with Jesus but gives no further information about them. Only Luke reports a conversation between Jesus and the thieves. It is worth giving the passage in its entirety.

> One of the criminals who were hanged there kept deriding him and saying, "Are you not the Messiah? Save yourself and us!" But the other rebuked him, saying, "Do you not fear God, since you are under the same sentence of condemnation? And we indeed have been condemned justly, for we are getting what we deserve for our deeds, but this man has done nothing wrong." Then he said, "Jesus, remember me when you come into your kingdom." He replied, "Truly I tell you, today you will be with me in Paradise." (Luke 23:39-43)

Crucifixion was a particularly painful form of execution. The hands or wrists were nailed to the crossbar of the cross, and the feet were nailed to the upright post. The arms were also tied, so that the weight of the body would not tear the nailed hands off the crossbar. The weight of the body pulled it down, which stressed the arms and chest and made it difficult to breathe. In response, the condemned man would push his weight back up until fatigue would force the body down again. Thus, the condemned man would move his body up and down over the rough wood of the cross for many hours. The wood would scrape his back raw.

Before the crucifixion, the victim was usually flogged, which would increase the pain of rubbing the back on the cross. The blood and sweat of the condemned man would attract insects, and there was no way for him to brush them away. Death might take several days. It might come from suffocation, exhaustion, or infection from the wounds.

Under these conditions, the dialogue between Jesus and the two thieves took place. The first criminal joined the crowd in deriding Jesus, but what he requested was perfectly understandable. He was seeking physical salvation, though he doubted that it would come, and this fostered his cruelty. Yet anyone who reads the story carefully and considers the agony that he must have been in cannot condemn this thief. Nor did Jesus condemn him. He is included in Jesus' plea for forgiveness for those who were torturing him.

In the second thief we see a miracle. Here was self-admittedly an evil man nearing death and in agony. Matthew and Mark tell us that the good thief had also taunted Jesus, but according to Luke, he repented. As death came close, he suddenly understood what Jesus had been saying. Perhaps it was Jesus' statement of forgiveness that opened this thief's eyes. Against all odds, he recognized Jesus as the Savior and requested the salvation that Jesus offered. In response to that request, Jesus assured him of God's grace. It is one of the most powerful and dramatic conversion stories ever told.

If nothing else, this narrative should humble us. It teaches us that we cannot know the future salvation story for any other individual. One primary assumption of the death penalty is that we can determine the future of a human being. As a corollary, many assume that some people are so evil they are not worth saving. To put it bluntly, the use of capital punishment implies that there are some human beings who are beyond God's reach, and that society can determine *with certainty* who those people are. Such assumptions show the *hubris* of human culture.

This simple story of a single paragraph undermines these prideful assumptions. When all Jesus' friends and followers abandon him and stand back from him, a condemned criminal, under the most dire and painful of conditions, volunteers to give Jesus comfort and to defend him. How can this not lead us to question our ability to know the motivation and character of our fellow human beings? Why does one thief doubt and the other believe? Who can answer this question?

If the first thief had been given a bit more time, might he too have come to accept Jesus as his Savior? If he had not been placed in a situation of complete pain and despair, could he have been more open to the message Christ brought him? Again, we must stand in silent unknowing before such questions.

And what about the second thief? If he had been executed a day earlier, would his punishment not only have been death on earth, but eternal death as well? Wouldn't the good thief also have been cut off from Jesus by a death sentence carried out a single day earlier? Can anyone answer such a question?

We know that many men and women on death row have conversion experiences. The more cynical among us may question the sincerity of some of these conversions. Nevertheless, who has the right to say that any particular one is not genuine? A fundamental belief of Christianity is that people, even the worst of people, can be reached by the salvation offered by Jesus. Based on that salvation, we also believe that people can change. They can become better people—people more oriented toward life and love and away from death and violence.

When we take a human life through the death penalty, particularly if the condemned person has not yet received salvation, we step between that person and Jesus. We take away their chance to know their Savior and to know salvation and the better life it can bring. Jesus warned against putting stumbling blocks in the way of those who were seeking him. "It would be better for you if a millstone were hung around your neck and you were thrown into the sea than for you to cause one of these little ones to stumble" (Luke 17:2; Matt. 18:6; Mark 9:42). The story of the two thieves shows that even condemned criminals are counted among "these little ones," and that capital punishment can, in fact, be just such a stumbling block that Jesus condemned.

The Stoning of Stephen

The story of Stephen is told in Acts 6:8-8:1. Stephen was one of seven Hellenistic Jewish Christians chosen to oversee the distribution of food for the church at Jerusalem. In addition, Stephen was a powerful speaker and debater for the church. It was Stephen's leadership and speaking abilities that eventually drew the attention of the authorities. He was accused of blasphemy and tried before the Sanhedrin.

Acts 7 records a remarkable speech Stephen made in his own defense, summarizing the history of the Hebrews and showing that Jesus was the culmination of that history. Perhaps because he knew that the results of the trial were a foregone conclusion, Stephen pulled no punches in his speech. He demonstrated again and again that the Hebrews had rejected the salvation offered to them.

Stephen's speech did not have the effect of calming the crowd. Indeed, it made them all the angrier. Acts 7:57-60 states that they rushed together against him and then dragged him out of the city and stoned him. Stephen, however, remained steadfast, and his last words echo those of Jesus on the cross, "Lord, do not hold this sin against them."

The speed with which the execution was carried out violated many of the laws governing capital punishment. There was apparently no overnight wait for the vote to convict, nor is there any hint of using normal procedures for appeal on the way to the place of execution. Stephen's last words to the court before his condemnation, therefore, have the ring of prophecy. "You are the ones that received the law as ordained by angels, and yet you have not kept it" (Acts 7:53).

Stephen's execution may best be described as a legal lynching. There was a trial, but the verdict and sentence were predetermined. The Christians had become an increasingly serious threat to the Jewish leadership. The trial of Stephen is the third trial described in Acts.[30] The first is the trial of Peter and John in Acts 4:1-22. The result is a warning. The next is the trial of the apostles in Acts 5:17-42. This ends with their flogging. Now Stephen's trial ends with his execution. The kind of anger expressed in the rush to execution shows the unpopularity of the new sect. As a result, the authorities ignore the law—the very thing they are trying to uphold.

Again, political considerations override the protections of the law. From the Jewish leadership's point of view, Stephen was a leader in a new and dangerous cult. They considered the cult itself to be blasphemous. It attacked the symbolic heart of their religion—the sacrificial ritual of the temple. In doing so, it appeared to threaten the special relationship between the Jews and their God. But the Jesus movement was also growing rapidly. Under these extraordinary circumstances, extraordinary measures needed to be taken. The provisions of the law that protected these criminals had to be set aside. They thought they had to break the law in order to save it.

In the case of Stephen, we see another danger of the death penalty. Stephen's trial and execution had many of the trappings of the law, but it was stripped of the law's essential protections. The witnesses threw the first stones, but the witnesses had been set up. Stephen had been allowed to speak, but there had been a rush to judgment, and the appeals process had been short-circuited.

This is one message of the execution of Stephen. With the best of intentions, the authorities may be tempted to use the death penalty as a method for keeping undesirables under control. They tend to ignore inconvenient parts of the law that make it difficult to achieve convictions or carry out executions. That temptation can be overwhelming when the majority feels under threat.[31]

The ease with which African-Americans were executed in the nineteenth and twentieth century American South shows that, in many cases, the protections of the law were ignored. The less protection the law provided to this group, the less reason for the more-violent members of white society to even bother with the law. Real lynching, rather than legal lynching, was the result.[32] When prejudice is combined with the blood lust symbolized by the death penalty, reason becomes meaningless, mercy becomes meaningless, the law becomes meaningless. That is a lesson from the stoning of Stephen.

The Killing of James

Acts 12:1-5 describes a violent persecution of the Christians by Herod Agrippa I. The persecution included the execution of James, the brother of John.[33] "He had James the brother of John killed with the sword" (Acts 12:2). The use of the sword may indicate that James was beheaded as an apostate.[34]

Herod Agrippa had been brought up in Rome, but on his return to Palestine, he appeared to become an observant Jew. This conversion may have had political overtones, but it was genuine enough to cause him to take some political risks in protecting the people he governed. He had been instrumental in forestalling a plan by the insane Emperor Caligula to place his own statute in the temple, an act that would have almost certainly caused a Jewish revolt against Rome.[35] Therefore, Herod had a good reputation among the Jews. His persecution of the unpopular Christians undoubtedly added to his reputation.

In the story of the execution of James, the New Testament again portrays the use of capital punishment as a political tool. This was not like Pilate's reluctant use of the death penalty against Jesus, and the Sanhedrin's rush to judgment against Stephen. Instead, Herod's use of the death penalty appears to be a calculated, proactive deed by a shrewd politician. He knew the Christians were a hated minority. Thus, to identify himself with an act that enforced the persecution of the Christians would make him more popular. So he had James executed specifically to increase his popularity with his subjects. He would have done the same to Peter, if Peter had not made a miraculous escape.[36]

Even if we assume that the new Christian sect genuinely outraged Herod, his action illustrates another New Testament message about capital punishment. The death penalty can be used as a tool for ambitious politicians. There is nothing in the story suggesting that the early church had attacked or threatened the government of Herod. They were simply a convenient target Herod could use to enhance his own political position. Executing Christians improved his position with his countrymen at virtually no political cost. Herod could condemn Christians, much as modern politicians can demonize drug dealers or serial killers. He was simply going along with the crowd.

In the modern United States, the use of capital punishment for personal political purposes can easily be demonstrated. In nearly every national campaign, candidates invariably assure the voting public that they support the death penalty. As a part of the campaign, a candidate will occasionally even demonstrate this support by an official act of arbitrarily rejecting an appeal from death row.[37]

The execution of the apostle James and modern executions for political gain both illustrate the final lesson of these New Testament executions. Political leaders, even those who may have many good accomplishments, cannot be trusted with the death penalty. It is too easy for leaders to use executions for their own political gain by targeting the unpopular and unprotected. The practice of scapegoating is alive and well, and as long as it is, capital punishment will always be used as a tool by the ambitious.

The Meaning of New Testament Executions

The writers of the New Testament told stories of executions from the point of view of potential victims, rather than from the viewpoint of mainstream society. Every story casts a negative light on the execution it describes. In cases where we are given any details about the trials leading up to the executions, the law is ignored or subverted in favor of political needs. Moreover, capital punishment is repeatedly shown to be a political tool of the powerful that is used primarily on people who challenge the status quo or who can be scapegoated for political gain.

Capital punishment is shown to be something that gets in the way of the work of the church. It is either used against members of the church, or as in the case of the two thieves, it prevents the message of salvation from reaching some who most need it. In the execution of Jesus, the violence of the death penalty is contrasted with the forgiveness of the Savior, even as he dies on the cross. Stephen, taking his cue from Jesus, forgives his executioners even as he falls under their barrage of stones.

The difference is clear. On one side is the world, with its violence and deceit, represented most clearly in the use of the capital punishment. On the other side we see Jesus and his followers, frequently the victims of the death penalty, and yet offering love instead of hate, forgiveness instead of revenge.

While the Gospels and Acts show executions in a negative light, the epistles provide a theological justification for opposing capital punishment. Now we turn to those epistles.

7
Atonement and the Powers

Jesus was the founder of Christianity, but the apostle Paul was its greatest proselytizer, gathering in many converts. Paul was proof in and of himself that "God's foolishness is wiser than human wisdom."[1] Early in his life, Saul/Paul would have seemed the least-likely person to become the greatest advocate for Jesus Christ. He began his relationship with Christianity as its enemy. Saul participated in the execution of Stephen and became a leading persecutor of the church in Jerusalem (Acts 7:58-8:3).

The Atonement

Years later, Paul told Herod Agrippa II, "I not only locked up many of the saints in prison, but I also cast my vote against them when they were being condemned to death" (Acts 26:10). After participating around Jerusalem in harassing believers in Christ, he sought and obtained permission to extend to Damascus this persecution of those belonging to "the Way." On the road to Damascus, however, he had a miraculous conversion experience. To the amazement of all, he was changed from being a leading persecutor of the church to become its most powerful advocate (Acts 9).

Paul refers to his activities as a persecutor of the church in Galatians 1:13-14 and Philippians 3:4-6. In both cases, he explains that his actions came from a mistaken zeal for the traditions of his people. Paul's early persecution of the church undoubtedly weighed heavily on him. In 1 Timothy 1:12-16, the writer, speaking in Paul's name,[2] expresses what Paul must have felt about his activities as a persecutor:

> I am grateful to Christ Jesus our Lord, who has strengthened me, because he judged me faithful and appointed me to his service, even though I was formerly a blasphemer, a persecutor, and a man of violence. But I received mercy because I had acted ignorantly in unbelief, and the grace of our Lord overflowed for me with the faith and love that are in Christ Jesus. The saying is sure and worthy of full acceptance, that Christ Jesus came into the world to save sinners—of whom I am the foremost. But for that very reason I received mercy, so that in me, as the foremost, Jesus Christ might display the utmost patience, making me an example to those who would come to believe in him for eternal life.

Paul had a sense of guilt for the blood he helped shed as a judge in capital cases against the earliest Christians. That guilt provided him with emotional underpinning for his theology of God's grace through the atoning death of Christ. Paul's sinful taking of human life could never be made right. There was no human way he could take it back. Therefore, if he were to be made right with God and his fellow human beings, it would have to be through the forgiveness of God, through God's grace, not through his own action.

From studying the Hebrew Scriptures, Paul believed that Yahweh was a God of justice as well as mercy. Sin ripped apart the moral fabric of the universe; it had to be made right. The traditional way to make it right was through sacrifice. The most primitive cultures allowed the sacrifice of the "outsider" to make amends for the sins of the people. If something offended the gods, a person who had little value to society could be offered up as a payment. By choosing the weakest members of society for sacrifice—prisoners of war, foreigners, people with disabilities, children, unmarried women, criminals—society guaranteed that there would be no blood revenge for the killing (see chap. 1, above). The gods were appeased, and no further cycle of violence was initiated.

As a scholar of the law, Paul was aware that Yahweh, the Hebrew God, had outlawed this most primitive kind of sacrifice. Yahweh told the Hebrews that he himself would be the avenger for the weak; therefore, the weak could no longer be used as surrogate sacrificial victims. The law replaced the substitutionary form of human sacrifice with an elaborate system of animal sacrifice for minor sins, and capital punishment for more serious offenses.

In capital punishment, the person committing a major sin was held directly responsible to rebalance the moral scales of the universe through his or her death. Thus an execution was a form of human sacrifice, but one in which a person was directly linked to the offense against God and society. It no longer carried the instrumental purpose of placating the gods who might otherwise punish the community for the crime.

Paul and other early Christians came to understand that Jesus took his followers a further step away from sacrificial justice. In the death of Christ, they saw a final sacrifice, the sacrifice of the fully righteous man, whose death paid for all human sins. Paul thought of Jesus as the new Adam. Adam began as sinless, but he sinned and thereby made all humans the captives of sin and death. In committing the first sin, Adam and Eve initiated a vicious cycle of sinfulness. Those who had been sinned against sought revenge, thereby escalating the level of violence and cruelty. In their parents' arms, children learned selfishness, ethnocentrism, and hatred.

Wealth for the few at the expense of suffering for the many became the accepted norm. Material goods gained value over the needs of people. Coldhearted individualism took the place of community. Each new level of sinfulness led others to imitate it, either for revenge or self-protection, which in turn led to even more innovations in evil.

From the beginning God recognized human sin as a vicious cycle that could not be addressed in kind. The cycle had to be broken by someone who refused to play the game of imitating the sinfulness of others. So Jesus came into the world. Like Adam, Jesus was also sinless. But rather than sinning, Jesus took on the punishment for human sin, thus breaking the cycle by which sin and death hold all human beings captive. Although sinned against, Jesus refused to seek revenge, even lawful revenge. By refusing to play the sin game, Jesus showed us the way to freedom.

Paul elaborates this most fully in Romans 5:15-19:

> The free gift is not like the trespass. For if many died through one man's trespass, much more surely have the grace of God and the free gift in the grace of the one man, Jesus Christ, abounded for many. And the free gift is not like the effect of one man's sin. For the judgment following one trespass brought condemnation, but the free gift following many trespasses brings justification. If, because of the one man's trespass, death exercised dominion through that one, much more surely will those who receive the abundance of grace and the free gift of righteousness exercise dominion in life through one man, Jesus Christ.
>
> Therefore, just as one man's trespass led to condemnation for all, so one man's act of righteousness leads to justification and life for all. For just as by the one man's disobedience the many were made sinners, so by the one man's obedience the many will be made righteous.

Many contemporary Christians may feel uncomfortable with this passage because it addresses the issue of original sin. We may well ask how a loving God can hold us responsible for sins we did not commit. However, this interpretation of the Fall of human beings is an explanation for something that is quite apparent in our lives. The doctrine of original sin simply recognizes the fact that all human beings are sinners. Because the world is sinful, sin is something into which we are all born.

From earliest childhood, we learn the ways of sinfulness by osmosis from our parents and our culture. Even in young children, naturally egocentric, we see growing signs of self-ishness and violence, though childhood innocence and pow-erlessness often obscures their expression. Growing into adults, humans become both more virulent and subtle in their sinning. Sin takes on a life of its own. We believe that circumstances compel us to commit sins—that we are often forced to choose the lesser of two evils. We often feel trapped into sinning against our will. Thus Paul explained,

> I do not understand my own actions. For I do not do what I want, but I do the very thing I hate. Now if I do what I do not want, I agree that the law is good. But in fact it is no longer I that do it, but sin that dwells within me. For I know that nothing good dwells within me, that is, in my flesh. I can will what is right, but I cannot do it. For I do not do the good I want, but the evil I do not want is what I do. (Rom. 7:15-19)

Paul understood sin to be a disease so pervasive in human nature and society that only the most-powerful antidote could reduce its power and eventually eliminate it. That antidote, according to Paul, was the atoning death of Jesus on the cross. It was the sinless man taking onto himself the sin of the human race—past, present, and future. This death represents God's forgiveness of our sins.[3] In Christ's death, there is a radical restatement of the message of the Hebrew Scriptures. God loves his people despite their failures, their mistreatment of each other, their injustices, and their violence.

God understands that we are trapped; we are in a cycle of sinfulness from which we cannot escape by ourselves. Therefore, he takes the first step for us. Through the crucifixion of his Son, God makes it possible for us to be free. This strange and beautiful notion is set forth by Paul most clearly in Romans 5:6-11:

> While we were still weak, at the right time Christ died for the ungodly. Indeed, rarely will anyone die for a righteous person—though perhaps for a good person someone

might actually dare to die. But God proves his love for us in that while we still were sinners Christ died for us. Much more surely then, now that we have been justified by his blood, will we be saved through him from the wrath of God. For if while we were enemies, we were reconciled to God through the death of his Son, much more surely, having been reconciled, will we be saved by his life. But more than that, we even boast in God through our Lord Jesus Christ, through whom we have now received reconciliation.[4]

To fully understand the power of this passage, we must read it from the perspective of a parent. Many of us would like to think that we would be willing to sacrifice our own lives for the life of a friend, or if we stretch it, even the life of a stranger. We picture ourselves, for example, rushing into a burning building to save a child. However, if the person we are asked to save is an enemy, one who has deliberately and cruelly harmed our family members, we must admit it would be much less likely that we would exchange our lives for theirs.

Now, however, we must take the analogy a step further. While we might be able to offer our own lives for the sake of another, most parents would not be willing to sacrifice their child's life to save someone else. Certainly such a risk does occasionally happen, as when Gentile parents in the Holocaust endangered their own children to save Jews. But these sacrifices are so remarkable because they rarely occur.[5]

Now, however, we must up the ante one more time to understand God's sacrifice. How many parents would be willing to sacrifice their child to save someone who had deliberately injured or killed other members of their family? This level of sacrifice is virtually unheard of in the human realm. A person who would do such a thing would be considered mentally ill or even criminal. Indeed, it is such a strange notion that Paul uses it to contrast the way God sees the world with the way humans see it.

The message about the cross is foolishness to those who are perishing, but to us who are being saved it is the power of God. For it is written,
"I will destroy the wisdom of the wise,
and the discernment of the discerning I will thwart."
Where is the one who is wise? Where is the scribe? Where is the debater of this age? Has not God made foolish the wisdom of the wise? For since in the wisdom of God, the world did not know God through wisdom, God decided, through the foolishness of our proclamation, to save those who believe. For Jews demand signs and Greeks desire wisdom, but we proclaim Christ crucified, a stumbling block to Jews and foolishness to Gentiles, but to those who are called, both Jews and Greeks, Christ the power of God and the wisdom of God. For God's foolishness is wiser than human wisdom, and God's weakness is stronger than human strength. (1 Cor. 1:18-25)

In short, in the crucifixion of Jesus, God shows the human race that he will not seek revenge on us for our sins; he will not imitate our violence. Instead, he asks us to imitate his forgiveness, which according to the wisdom of the world leaves us vulnerable and without control of our lives. But a strange thing happens, Paul informs us, when we open ourselves to the Spirit by imitating God's love and forgiveness. We can see beyond events to their deeper spiritual meaning. In Paul's words,

Those who are unspiritual do not receive the gifts of God's Spirit, for they are foolishness to them, and they are unable to understand them because they are spiritually discerned. Those who are spiritual discern all things, and they are themselves subject to no one else's scrutiny.
"For who has known the mind of the Lord
so as to instruct him?"
But we have the mind of Christ. (1 Cor. 2:14-16)

In other words, when we accept Christ's message of love and forgiveness, and when we step out in faith to live that message, then we begin to see the world differently. We start to break the cycle of violence and revenge. We are able to see our enemies as human beings much like us. We see beyond their sinfulness to that part of them that remains in the image of God. As a result, we begin to understand that their evil actions are, to some extent, mirrors of our own evil.[6] We no longer want retribution; we begin to look for reconciliation. Paul summarized this transformation:

> From now on, therefore, we regard no one from a human point of view; even though we once knew Christ from a human point of view, we know him no longer in that way. So if anyone is in Christ, there is a new creation: everything old has passed away; see, everything has become new! All this is from God, who reconciled us to himself through Christ, and has given us the ministry of reconciliation, that is, in Christ, God was reconciling the world to himself, not counting their trespasses against them, and entrusting the message of reconciliation to us. So we are ambassadors for Christ, since God is making his appeal through us; we entreat you on behalf of Christ, be reconciled to God. For our sake he made him to be sin who knew no sin, so that in him we might become the righteousness of God. (2 Cor. 5:16-21)

This does not mean that forgiveness is easy or automatic. Howard Zehr says, "Forgiveness is not an emotion; it is not an event; it is a journey."[7] Someone who has lost a family member to a terrible crime will not "get over it in time." But they may, through the grace of God, find a measure of spiritual understanding and comfort. Anger and fear are the first reaction to such a crime. The desire for revenge is a natural response to the horror of the murder of a loved one. But to discern the spiritual meaning of the crime through the mind of Christ, the victim's loved ones must set out on a journey of forgiveness. Only this can bring the deepest level of consolation and understanding.[8]

Paul himself was a frequent victim of violence. He

describes some of the violence used against him in 2 Corinthians 11:23-25:

> Are they ministers of Christ? I am talking like a madman—
> I am a better one: with far greater labors, far more imprisonments, with countless floggings, and often near death.
> Five times I have received from the Jews the forty lashes
> minus one. Three times I was beaten with rods. Once I
> received a stoning.

It is sure that Paul did not get over these events easily. His letters show a man prone to anger, likely having to resist the temptation to violence all of his life. He said of his resentment at injustice, "Who is made to stumble, and I am not indignant?" (2 Cor. 11:29). Often as we read Paul's letters, we come to understand that he is giving a message to himself as well as to the church to which he is writing. This is the case in Romans 12:14-21, where he echoes some of the words of Jesus:

> Bless those who persecute you; bless and do not curse
> them. Rejoice with those who rejoice, weep with those who
> weep. Live in harmony with one another; do not be
> haughty, but associate with the lowly; do not claim to be
> wiser than you are. Do not repay anyone evil for evil, but
> take thought for what is noble in the sight of all. If it is possible, so far as it depends on you, live peaceably with all.
> Beloved, never avenge yourselves, but leave room for the
> wrath of God; for it is written, "Vengeance is mine, I will
> repay, says the Lord" [Deut. 32:35]. No, "if your enemies
> are hungry, feed them; if they are thirsty, give them something to drink; for by doing this you will heap burning
> coals on their heads." Do not be overcome by evil, but
> overcome evil with good.

Here is nothing of the merely meek and mild Christian. Paul was a militant, just as Jesus had been. For Paul, love became a weapon. Forgiveness became a form of vengeance. It exposed the enemy to himself; it confronted the enemy with the result of his sin; it brought the healing power of shame to him. Paul often used the language of warfare in describing the Christian life, but the goal of Paul's warfare was not destruction of the enemy; it was the enemy's reclamation and restoration.

> Indeed, we live as human beings, but we do not wage war according to human standards; for the weapons of our warfare are not merely human, but they have divine power to destroy strongholds. We destroy arguments and every proud obstacle raised up against the knowledge of God, and we take every thought captive to obey Christ. (2 Cor. 10:3-5)

Paul was a man in a unique position. He had practically been an executioner. Then he became subject to a trial leading toward capital punishment; eventually, according to Christian tradition, he was executed. The same zeal that he brought to persecuting the church, he brought to defending it, but with this very important difference: he no longer allowed himself to harm his opponents. Like many persecutors, Paul had rationalized his violence: his executions of Christians were for the benefit of the people as a whole. Upon his conversion, he came to realize that each and every individual was important to God. Christ had paid the price for every crime. Jesus' atoning sacrifice had already made the world right.

To demand a further sacrifice was in effect a denial of the efficacy of the work of God's grace through Christ. It implied that there were some human beings whose sins were not covered by God's sacrifice of his own Son. Demanding further sacrifice would create such a division in the efficacy of the atonement as to leave open to question the efficacy of Christ's sacrifice for each individual sin. The demand for further sacrifice would essentially reinstate, or leave in force, salvation by works of the law. If some sins are not forgiven through the death of Christ, and we cannot be certain what those sins might be, then any violation of the law we make may lead to our destruction. Thus, if some sins are not covered by

Christ's atonement, we must follow the law without deviation, and we are again trapped in legalism.[9]

On the other hand, if Christ's sacrifice pays for all sins,
then our response to a murderer should not be a demand for
a human sacrifice to make the world right through his punishment. Christ's sacrifice on the cross has *already* balanced
the moral scales. So our reaction should be one of militant
(strongly active) love to disarm the violence of the criminal
and eventually restore him as much as possible to society.[10]
This was, of course, exactly what happened to Paul himself.
He was a murderer of Christians, persecuting the church. But
through the grace of God, he saw his error. He may have seen
this grace most clearly in the Christians he had condemned,
who expressed their forgiveness for him as they were led
away to execution!

The church, though at first doubtful about his conversion,
allowed him to become part of their community. The result
was a spectacular missionary career that firmly planted the
Christian message in the world of the Gentiles. If the church
had accepted the wisdom of the world, rather than the way
of Christ, there would have been no forgiveness for Paul. At
least, he never would have been allowed to become a part of
the church. At worst, the church would have imitated Paul's
own violence and would have had him assassinated. So
Paul's life itself was the result of the grace he taught.

Paul was not the only New Testament writer who
focused on the atonement. The writer of the letter to the
Hebrews addresses the issue of the finality of Jesus' sacrifice, making it clear that no further sacrifice is needed. The
audience for this letter was Christians of Jewish background, and the letter assumes a thorough knowledge of
the Hebrew Scriptures.[11] All through Hebrews 9–10, the
writer compares the sacrifice of Christ with the sacrifices
conducted under the Mosaic Law. In each example, he
shows that the sacrifice of Jesus provides a final solution to
the problem of sin, while the sacrifices of the priests only
gave temporary solutions.

He concludes his argument in Hebrews 10:11-18:

> Every priest stands day after day at his service, offering
> again and again the same sacrifices that can never take
> away sins. But when Christ had offered for all time a sin-
> gle sacrifice for sins, "he sat down at the right hand of
> God," and since then has been waiting "until his enemies
> would be made a footstool for his feet." For by a single
> offering he has perfected for all time those who are sancti-
> fied. And the Holy Spirit also testifies to us, for after say-
> ing,
> "This is my covenant that I will make with them
> after those days, says the Lord:
> I will put my laws in their hearts,
> and I will write them on their minds,"
>
> he also adds,
> "I will remember their sins and their lawless deeds no
> more."
> Where there is forgiveness of these, there is no longer any
> offering for sin.

Like Paul, the writer of Hebrews believed that Christ's
sacrifice solved the problem of sin for all time. No further
sacrifice was needed. The offering of a human sacrifice for
major crimes, like animal sacrifices for minor offenses, now
had no spiritual purpose. The author of Hebrews believed
that God would still punish those who turned their back on
Christ's sacrifice (he was particularly concerned with apostasy), but the sacrifice required by the law was no longer appli-
cable. God, not humans, would now be responsible for setting right the moral structure of the world when sin occurred
(Heb. 10:26-31).

John also addressed the atonement clearly. In 1 John 2:1-2
he stated that Christ's sacrifice atoned for all sins:

> My little children, I am writing these things to you so that
> you may not sin. But if anyone does sin, we have an advo-
> cate with the Father, Jesus Christ the righteous; and he is
> the atoning sacrifice for our sins, and not for ours only but
> also for the sins of the whole world.

Later in the same letter, John ties the atonement directly to the idea of loving one's fellow human beings:

> Whoever does not love does not know God, for God is love. God's love was revealed among us in this way: God sent his only Son into the world so that we might live through him. In this is love, not that we loved God but that he loved us and sent his Son to be the atoning sacrifice for our sins. Beloved, since God loved us so much, we also ought to love one another. No one has ever seen God; if we love one another, God lives in us and his love is perfected in us. . . .
>
> There is no fear in love, but perfect love casts out fear; for fear has to do with punishment, and whoever fears has not reached perfection in love. We love because he first loved us. Those who say, "I love God," and hate their brothers and sisters, are liars; for those who do not love a brother or sister whom they have seen, cannot love God whom they have not seen. The commandment we have from him is this: those who love God must love their brothers and sisters also. (1 John 4:8-12, 18-21)

John's conception of Christ's atonement for our sins, like the conceptions of both Paul and the author of Hebrews, is that the atonement was once and for all. It applied to all sins and was for all time. John was particularly astute in attaching God's love to human love. For John, the effects of the grace of God on those who accepted Jesus' sacrifice for themselves would be the ability to pass that grace on to others, through their love for others. John uses particularly strong language in addressing Christians who claim God's forgiveness for themselves, but who refuse to forgive others. Such people, John said, are liars. Their claims to love God are refuted by their hatred of their fellow human beings.

One purpose of John's letter was to counter a form of heresy called Docetism. It counted Christ as a visible spirit and claimed that Christ only seemed to be human, to suffer, and to die on the cross.[12] The result of such spiritualism was to devalue the world of the material, which in turn made it possible to discount works of charity and love. If the material world was not important, then there was no need to worry about the material needs of one's brothers and sisters. John was thus especially interested in making the message of Jesus concrete in the world, where people lived and struggled. God's love was made material in the body of Jesus; therefore, his love would have effects in the material world. Through loving each other, God's love would become visible.

Moreover, John had the psychological insight that fear and hatred were interconnected. If we fear a person, then we also hate him. When our love of God becomes the center of our lives, we no longer fear, because our hope is centered on God. But if we hate someone, we must also in some way fear that person. Such fear shows our lack of faith and hope in the future that God offers us.

The teaching of the atonement offered to everyone negates the sacrificial purpose of the death penalty that was accepted by the Hebrew Scriptures. In addition, the New Testament writers' emphasis on love of one's neighbor as well as love of God disallows Christian participation in a social practice as brutal as capital punishment. This will be confirmed when we examine the writings of the Ante-Nicene Fathers on the issue of the death penalty.

The Cosmic Powers

At the same time, the early Christians' insistence on showing God's love did not prevent them from recognizing the need for social controls. Paul, in particular, wrote of the need for social organization, often called "the principalities and powers" (Eph. 6:12, KJV), "cosmic powers" (NRSV), or "authorities" and "rulers" (for brevity, I group them as "the powers"). According to Paul, the powers are the spiritual entities lying behind the visible structures of society. They provide structure to human interactions and prevent social chaos. This New Testament understanding of social organization has become increasingly important in recent years, and several major theological works have been written on the subject.[13]

A basic understanding of the powers is that when God created human beings, the powers were also created. These are spiritual forces standing behind all human organizations, language, and ideas. Like all things created by God, they were part of God's good creation.[14] These powers are manifested in such material entities as families, schools, corporations, and nations, as well as in intellectual entities such as ideas, intellectual movements, and ideologies. They are necessary for human survival. Though we may occasionally become aware of the presence of the powers through a form of revelation, we know them primarily in their physical manifestations.[15] Through these physical manifestations, they provide us with goods and services we need for living. They give us a means of communication with each other. They provide order and protect us.

However, in the Fall of human beings, the powers also fell. Like individual human beings, the powers desire to accumulate more authority and control for themselves. They want to put themselves in the place of God, and they attempt to separate God from his people.[16] For example, the national powers (those manifested in individual nations) demand to be worshiped like gods. They require people to take oaths of allegiance and demand absolute loyalty. "My country, right or wrong," becomes the motto of all nations. In the area of criminal justice, a governmental power may overstep its legitimate responsibility to protect its citizens, and misuse its authority to punish its critics and keep dissidents in line.

Jesus' death on the cross was the beginning of the redemption of the powers as well as the redemption of individual human beings. Colossians 2:13-15 shows how the redemption of human beings is related to the redemption of the powers:

> When you were dead in trespasses and the uncircumcision of your flesh, God made you alive together with him, when he forgave us all our trespasses, erasing the record that

stood against us with its legal demands. He set this aside, nailing it to the cross. He disarmed the rulers and authorities [powers and principalities] and made a public example of them, triumphing over them in it.

The crucifixion and resurrection are the beginning of the defeat of the powers. These two events show first that the powers are in rebellion against God, and second that the rebellion will ultimately fail. As seen in chapter 6 (above), Christ's crucifixion demonstrates the failure of the best legal systems of the time to protect a truly innocent man. The crucifixion unmasked and continues to unmask the powers behind such systems, which claim to have human good as their objective, but which instead are willing to sacrifice the innocent to maintain their ungodly control. The crucifixion shows that the powers are more interested in their own survival and self-aggrandizement than in justice. Their illusions have been stripped from them by their crucifixion of Jesus. They are now exposed for what they really are.[17]

However, the ultimate redemption of the powers is yet to come. Where Christ is preached, the gospel constantly challenges the powers, even when the church fails in its duty to resist their unholy claims. There is always an element of resistance to the idolatry of the powers. When the final redemption comes, the powers will not be destroyed; they will, like human beings, be renewed within their rightful place under God. Human life will always require the organization of these spiritual forces, but when redemption is complete, the powers will act as the servants of God rather than the challengers of God.

Thus Paul prophesies in 1 Corinthians 15:24-27,

> Then comes the end, when [Christ] hands over the kingdom to God the Father, after he has [dethroned] every ruler and every authority and power. For he must reign until he has put all his enemies under his feet. The last enemy to be [neutralized] is death.[18]

For Paul, the powers had been created to be the servants of God and human beings. The Fall, however, had brought these spiritual forces into rebellion against God, as they attempted to usurp the role of God in human society. The powers are necessary for human survival, but in the present world they have become a necessary evil because they are likely to demand more than what is legitimate. The sacrifice of Christ on the cross will eventually bring them back under control.

With this background, we turn to the passage of the New Testament to which death penalty proponents most often appeal, Romans 13:1-7:

> Let every person be subject to the governing authorities; for there is no authority except from God, and those authorities that exist have been instituted by God. Therefore whoever resists authority resists what God has appointed, and those who resist will incur judgment. For rulers are not a terror to good conduct, but to bad. Do you wish to have no fear of the authority? Then do what is good, and you will receive its approval; for it is God's servant for your good. But if you do wrong, you should be afraid, for the authority does not bear the sword in vain! It is the servant of God to execute wrath on the wrongdoer. Therefore one must be subject, not only because of wrath but also because of conscience. For the same reason you also pay taxes, for the authorities are God's servants, busy with this very thing. Pay to all what is due them—taxes to whom taxes are due, revenue to whom revenue is due, respect to whom respect is due, honor to whom honor is due.

Christian proponents of capital punishment point to Romans 13:4, which says, "But if you do wrong, you should be afraid, for the authority does not bear the sword in vain! It is the servant of God to execute wrath on the wrongdoer." While this passage indicates Paul's acceptance of the state's right to punish criminals, it cannot be inferred that this also extends to the right of the state to practice capital punishment. The word translated *sword* in this passage is *machaira,* which was actually more of a long dagger than a sword. Soldiers performing police duties carried it as a sign of authority.[19] It was not an instrument of execution for the Romans, who mostly used crucifixion to execute noncitizens.

The Roman church to which Paul was writing included Jewish Christians. No doubt many of the Gentile members were slaves or from the lower classes and had not attained Roman citizenship.[20] If Paul had wished to make a statement supporting capital punishment, he would probably have referred to crucifixion rather than the short sword.

Romans 13:1-7 is immediately preceded by Paul urging the Roman church not to seek revenge (quoted above; Rom. 12:19-21). It is immediately followed by a passage that plays off the concept of paying what is owed, found in Romans 13:7:

> Owe no one anything, except to love one another; for the one who loves another has fulfilled the law. The commandments, "You shall not commit adultery; You shall not murder; You shall not steal; You shall not covet"; and any other commandment, are summed up in this word, "Love your neighbor as yourself." Love does no wrong to a neighbor; therefore, love is the fulfilling of the law. (Rom. 13:8-10)

It is unlikely that immediately preceding this kind of message, Paul would come out with a statement in support of the death penalty. This is particularly true when the situation of the early church is more carefully considered. The Romans had executed Jesus. In the case of Jesus, Paul certainly would not have felt that the "rulers are not a terror to good conduct, but to bad." The church was subjected to sporadic but deadly persecutions.

The New Testament itself shows that two leaders, Stephen and James, were executed in the first years of the Christian movement. Peter was incarcerated and threatened with execution. In 49, Emperor Claudius expelled the Jews from Rome, likely because of controversy over the Christian faith.[21]

No doubt, Jewish Christians were well aware of, and angered by, the oppression occurring in Palestine at the time Paul wrote his letter to the Christians in Rome. Moreover, Christian tradition states that all of the apostles, with the possible exception of John, were martyred. Paul himself would later be executed.

It is therefore no surprise that most of the teachings about the government in the New Testament are not positive. Romans 13:1-7; Titus 3:1;[22] and 1 Peter 2:13-17[23] seem to speak favorably of the state. But in the Gospel accounts of Jesus' temptation, the nations of the world are shown to be under the power of the devil, who offers them to Jesus if he will fall down and worship the devil (Matt. 4:8-11; Luke 4:5-8).

In Revelation 13, John allegorizes Rome and its emperors as the beast of Satan.[24] The passage goes into detail about how the Roman imperial cult demanded the loyalty Jews traditionally had given to God alone. The emperors, particularly Nero, desired to be called divine names, such as "Lord," "Savior," and "Son of God."[25] The imperial cult used the death penalty and economic coercion to force people to participate in its idolatry.

> [A second beast, representing the priesthood of the imperial cult][26] performs great signs, even making fire come down from heaven to earth in the sight of all; and by the signs that it is allowed to perform on behalf of the beast, it deceives the inhabitants of earth, telling them to make an image for the beast that had been wounded by the sword and yet lived;[27] and it was allowed to give breath to the image of the beast so that the image of the beast could even speak and cause those who would not worship the image of the beast to be killed. Also it causes all, both small and great, both rich and poor, both free and slave, to be marked on the right hand or the forehead, so that no one can buy or sell who does not have the mark, that is, the name of the beast or the number of its name.[28] (Rev. 13:13-17)

This view of government in Revelation 13 can hardly be considered positive, and it seems difficult to reconcile John's view with Paul's. However, they are reconciled in the early church's concept of the powers. The powers are both necessary and prone to evil. In Romans 13, Paul accepts the necessity of the government. The government does keep some evil people in check. It does protect a certain normalcy of human life and provides a reasonably consistent social and political environment in which we can live. For this reason, believers should support the government, which is under God and hence accountable to God (Rom. 13:1).

Nevertheless, the government also has a strong tendency to overstep its limits. It uses its power to abuse its citizens—to force itself into a position of unrighteous authority that coerces political, social, and religious conformity to its values, all in the name of law and order.

For the early Christians, this second view of the government was more prevalent, based on their own experiences. Paul's comments on the government must be read in this light. Beginning in Romans 12, Paul cautions the Roman church not to be co-opted into following the prevailing immoral cultural norms of the city. He then cautions against division in the church, which under the threat of persecution could be fatal. He follows with a discussion on how the Roman Christians should handle themselves when under persecution. They are to support each other, and they are not to fall into hatred of the persecutors. They are to overcome evil with good.

Then comes the passage about the government, at the beginning of Romans 13. In it, Paul continues to address a church under real or threatened persecution by the Roman government at a specific point in its history. Though Claudius expelled Jews from Rome in 49, some Jewish Christians have returned by the time Paul is writing Romans (in 54-58; e.g., Prisca and Aquila, Rom. 16:3). Their continued Christian witness might lead to further unrest and then harassment for the church. The believers at Rome were tempted to react violently or at least to do things that the government could construe as subversive activity, in sympathy with persecuted Christians anywhere and with rebels in Judea. The inclusion of 13:1-7 in Romans shows that this temptation was real.[29]

However, if the Roman Christians resort to violence against the government, that would lead to the destruction of the Roman church. It would also be the complete antithesis of the message of love that Jesus preached. Paul therefore appeals to the aspect of the powers that focuses on their necessity. The power of government was created for human good. Hence, resisting the government would bring forth all the dangers of political chaos.

Furthermore, Paul tells the Roman church, "If you do what is wrong," if you take part in a revolt against the government, then you should expect the wrath of the government. It will send the armed police, who will violently break up the revolt, probably killing many rebels in the process. This interpretation certainly is more in line with the use of the short sword that Paul mentions.

Again, it needs to be remembered that Paul was writing to a specific church at a specific point in its history. Apparently Paul did not feel that the situation called for nonviolent resistance to the government at this point. He told the church to continue to pay taxes and revenues and to show respect and honor to those to whom such was due. Paul tells them to pay what is due (Rom. 13:6-7). The implication is that if the government goes beyond the limits of its duty to organize and protect, then payments can and should be withheld.[30] At that point, all that is owed is love, and making that payment fulfills the entire obligation of the law.

Paul's ministry itself shows that the traditional interpretation of this passage, which insists on unquestioning obedience to the government, is not what Paul meant. Paul constantly had run-ins with the authorities. He was jailed numerous times, flogged, and nearly stoned to death. Such a history hardly shows an unquestioning obedience to the government. Many government officials thought of Paul as a troublemaker. In the end, he paid the price of martyrdom, being executed by the state.[31] Paul himself clearly did not obey governments without question.

If we read Romans 13:1-7 in its context, then, it cannot be read as an endorsement of government violence. Instead, it is a caution to Christians tempted to use violence in a revolutionary action against the state. This passage, in other words, has little to say directly about capital punishment, except possibly to say that rulers would likely use it on those who revolted against the government. Here Paul does not endorse the government's potential act of executing "wrath on the wrongdoer," though he does call that authority "the [unknowing] servant of God" (Rom. 13:4; cf. Jer. 25:9).

Paul and other apostolic writers do not address the issue of capital punishment directly for three reasons. First and most important, the teachings of Christ about love and forgiveness are diametrically opposed to the practice of the death penalty. Therefore, the early church assumed that its members would not participate in this or other forms of bloodshed.[32]

Second, the Christians had little control over the government. The Roman Empire was not a democracy, and most early Christians did not come from the ranks of the powerful. There was no need to talk about changing the laws on the death penalty since they could not do it—though they might speak out prophetically to proclaim God's wisdom to "the rulers and authorities" (Eph. 3:10).

Third, the Christians were not required to participate in capital punishment, which was carried out by the military. There was no draft, and Christians were not compelled to be part of the execution process. It was not an issue forced on them.[33] For the apostolic church, the government was at best a necessary evil and at worst a vicious persecutor. Its functions were not something in which Christians participated.

Like the Gospels, then, the apostolic teachings in the epistles and Revelation present an ethic definitely contrary to the practice of capital punishment. Who can read the beautiful love chapter of 1 Corinthians (13) and believe that Paul was a man who could endorse the willful and brutal killing of a fellow human being? He eloquently states,

> Love is patient; love is kind; love is not envious or boastful or arrogant or rude. It does not insist on its own way; it is not irritable or resentful; it does not rejoice at wrongdoing, but rejoices in the truth. It bears all things, believes all things, hopes all things, endures all things. Love never ends. (1 Cor. 13:4-8)

How can such language be equated with the psychological torture and vengeance that are a part of an execution? Only by the most extreme twisting of language can this jump be made. As we shall see in the next chapter, there is certainly no indication that the earliest Christians, those closest to Paul in time and culture, ever jumped to this conclusion of supporting capital punishment.

8
Early Church Fathers Interpreting the Bible

Since the fourth century, the main body of the Christian church has accommodated the needs of various nation states, in exchange for a privileged position as their civil religion. Among those accommodations has been an acceptance and then an endorsement of capital punishment, one of the government's most powerful tools for social and political control. For seventeen centuries, church leaders and intellectuals have found ways to ignore much of biblical teaching in order to justify the death penalty. It is no wonder, then, that until recently the typical layperson assumed that the Bible provides unequivocal support for capital punishment.

However, the church was not always a proponent of capital punishment. The leaders who took the reins of the church directly from the apostles never wrote anything favoring this practice. It was also assumed that Christians would not participate in it or other forms of bloodshed. To participate in capital punishment in the Roman Empire, one had to act as either a judge or a member of the military, since the military provided the executioners. During the first century and a half of the church's history, there is no evidence that Christians entered either government service or the military. At this stage of the church's history, helping to carry out capital punishment was thus not an issue for Christians.

Apostolic Fathers

Christian writers of the first century universally forbade all kinds of bloodshed, some of which were perfectly acceptable to pagan society. The Didache (Teaching of the Twelve Apostles), perhaps already composed late in the first century,[1] divided human conduct into two ways: the way of life, the Christian way; and the way of death, the way of the world. This text condemns several kinds of private bloodshed, including murder, abortion, and infanticide, as aspects of the way of death. Although it does not mention public forms of homicide, later writings make it reasonable to assume that these forms of killing would also have been prohibited.[2]

Since Christians of the first century faced intermittent persecution, it may well have been that the temptation to violence was to revolution rather than the judicial death penalty. Christian writers, however, were continuously writing against violence, even when it seemed justified. In a letter to the church at Ephesus, Ignatius (d. ca. 107) says,

> Pray continually for the rest of mankind as well, that they may find God, for there is in them hope for repentance. Therefore allow them to be instructed by you, at least by your deeds. In response to their anger, be gentle; in response to their boasts, be humble; in response to their slander, offer prayers; in response to their errors, be "steadfast in the faith" [Col. 1:23]; in response to their cruelty, be gentle; do not be eager to retaliate against them. Let us show ourselves their brothers by our forbearance, and let us be eager to be imitators of the Lord, to see who can be the more wronged, who the more cheated [1 Cor. 6:7], who the more rejected, in order that no weed of the devil might be found among you, but that with complete purity and self-control you may abide in Christ Jesus physically and spiritually.[3]

Thus Ignatius called for believers to have kind and gentle responses to cruelty they were suffering. They were not to retaliate. Given Ignatius' attitude against the use of violence in the heat of the moment and for self-defense, it is difficult to believe that he could have approved of the cold-blooded killing required of a judge or executioner. [4]

Justin Martyr

Justin Martyr (110-165) was the first post-apostolic writer who spoke directly of capital punishment. His protest against the death penalty was primarily directed against the execution of Christians, but its biting nature implies a more universal condemnation. He begins his argument by stating that because Christians fear God and recognize that God sees all they do, they are the least likely people to commit crimes. In his view, if all people believed that God was watching their behavior, the world would be a better place.

Justin then gives an interesting insight into criminal thinking and the state's reaction to it. Addressing the Roman authorities, he says that most criminals assume they can escape the detection of their crimes by the state, since they know the state is only made up of men. But if they believed in God, they would know that their crimes would always be seen and punished by him. Hence, they would live more positively. Justin questions whether the authorities really want a better society, since they seem to enjoy the punishments they dole out:

> But you seem to fear lest all men become righteous, and you no longer have any to punish. Such would be the concern of public executioners, but not of good princes.[5]

The argument Justin makes is one that is repeated throughout the writings of the early theologians. Christianity has a gentling influence on society—an influence that will make criminal punishments less necessary. In addition to this more-common message, there are two rather unique features of this passage. First, Justin reminds the Roman authorities that they are simply human and cannot control all that happens in society. He also claims that they seem to prefer punishment above rehabilitation, and thus think more like executioners than wise rulers. This is probably the bluntest and most honest condemnation of the Roman authorities' mind-set made by the early church. It is little wonder that Justin ended his life as a martyr.

Protests Against Christians in the Military

According to noted church historian Roland Bainton, there is no evidence of Christian participation in the military until 170-180. This nonparticipation appears to have been a deliberate choice of the Christians in this era.[6] As the church gained greater numbers of adherents, its members began to be integrated into mainstream Roman life. The rigor of the church's stance against bloodshed diminished. The evidence shows that around 170 more Christians began to enter the army. In 174 the Thundering Legion contained Christian soldiers, recruited from what is now Armenia. The Syrian ruler Agbar IX made Christianity his official state religion in 202, which implied that Christians could be part of all government functions, including military life.[7]

When Christians began joining the Roman army by the late second century, they also were joining the ranks of potential executioners. This change brought more theological attacks against Christian participation in state-sponsored bloodshed, including capital punishment. It is remarkable that not a single extant Christian writing from this era supports Christian participation in state-sponsored bloodshed, and particularly in executions. This in itself is evidence of the early church's strong and continuing opposition to Christian participation in capital punishment. Since the church later came to affirm Christian involvement in executions, it undoubtedly would have preserved early statements in support of the death penalty if they had existed.

Tatian, Theophilus, Athenagoras, Minucius Felix

Early Christian writers universally condemned the gladi-

atorial contests, used as a means of capital punishment for
some criminals. Tatian (110-172) wrote a withering attack on
the games in his "Address to the Greeks." Here is part of his
challenge:

> Do such exhibitions as these redound to your credit? He
> who is chief among you collects a legion of blood-stained
> murderers, engaging to maintain them; and these ruffians
> are sent forth by him, and you assemble at the spectacle to
> be judges, partly of the wickedness of the adjudicator, and
> partly of that of the men who engage in the combat. And
> he who misses the murderous exhibition is grieved,
> because he was not doomed to be a spectator of wicked
> and impious and abominable deeds. You slaughter animals
> for the purpose of eating their flesh, and you purchase men
> to supply a cannibal banquet for the soul, nourishing it by
> the most impious bloodshedding. The robber commits
> murder for the sake of plunder, but the rich man purchas
> es gladiators for the sake of their being killed.[8]

Theophilus (115-181) used the church's disavowal of gladiatorial spectacles to deny reports of Christian violence.
Because of a misunderstanding of the meaning of the com-
munion meal, rumors spread that Christians practiced cannibalism. Theophilus quotes Christ's admonition to "love your
enemies" (Matt. 5:44) and the instructions to pray for those in
authority found in 1 Timothy 2:2. Then he asks rhetorically
whether those who follow such instructions can support violence in their religious ritual:

> Consider, therefore, whether those who teach such things
> can possibly live indifferently, and be commingled in
> unlawful intercourse, or, most impious of all, to eat human
> flesh, especially when we are forbidden to witness shows
> of gladiators, lest we become partakers and abettors of
> murder.[9]

Around 177 the Greek Christian Athenagoras wrote *A Plea
for the Christians*, addressed to the emperors Marcus Aurelius
Anoninus and Lucius Aureilus Commodus. In this apology

for Christianity, he also responded to accusations of Christian cannibalism.

Athenagoras began by appealing to the peaceful traditions of the Christians, quoting both Matthew 5:43-48 and Luke 6:27-38.[10] Then he argued that such a peaceful people could not eat human flesh because they would first have to kill the human. Citing the fact that slaves of Christian masters had never reported such activities, he went on to state the Christian abhorrence of bloodshed more generally:

> For when [the slaves of Christian masters] know that we cannot endure even to see a man put to death, though justly, who of them can accuse us of murder and cannibalism? Who does not reckon among the things of greatest interest the contests of gladiators and wild beasts, especially those of which are given by you? But we, deeming that to see a man put to death is much the same as killing him, have abjured such spectacles. How, then, when we do not even look on, lest we should contract guilt and pollution, can we put people to death?[11]

Athenagoras's condemnation of killing, though specifically aimed at gladiatorial games, was more general and not just directed at these spectacles. He refers to seeing men killed justly, which implies the execution of criminals. He felt that any kind of participation in the killing of a human being was forbidden to Christians. Athenagoras took a separatist position. He did not call for the end of the state's homicidal practices, as Tatian seems to do, but he said that Christians could not participate in them.

Some may wonder whether such a statement represents true opposition to the death penalty. However, in maintaining that Christians could not participate in public homicides acceptable to most Romans, Athenagoras was clear in his belief that they were immoral. Although society was still using these practices, he believed such practices were opposed to Christian ethical teaching. A refusal to participate in a social practice on moral grounds is a strong statement of one's moral evaluation of the practice, whether or not one specifically calls for an end to it. The original readers of his *Plea* would have recognized that he opposed the practice of public homicide, whether that was in the gladiatorial ring or in some other form of capital punishment.

Minucius Felix, writing in Rome around 205, made a more-concerted attack on the Roman morality. Writing in a dialogue form, he aggressively denounced Roman ethical practices. He was blunt in his criticism of Roman religion and its claim that it was the basis of the empire's power. After listing a number of immoral practices, Minucius stated, "Therefore the Romans were not so great because of their religion, but because they were sacrilegious with impunity."[12]

Like Athenagoras, Minucius also responded to the accusation of Christian cannibalism. He pointed to the Jewish ritualistic draining of the blood of animals that apparently was still practiced by his congregation as evidence that Christians could not engage in human bloodshed. "To us it is not lawful either to see or to hear of homicide; and so much do we shrink from human blood, that we do not use the blood even of eatable animals in our food."[13]

Tertullian

Tertullian of Carthage (145?-220?) wrote more on the church's attitude toward violence than any of the other Ante-Nicene fathers. Like the writers already mentioned, Tertullian responded to accusations of Christian violence, but he did so much more extensively and systematically. In one instance, he pointed out that the Christians could represent a threat to the empire if they chose that way, but they did not choose to do so.

> If we are enjoined, then, to love our enemies, . . . whom have we to hate? If injured, we are forbidden to retaliate, lest we become as bad ourselves: who can suffer injury at our hands? In regard to this, recall your own experiences. How often you inflict gross cruelties on Christians, partly

because it is your own inclination, and partly in obedience to the laws! How often, too, the hostile mob, paying no regard to you, takes the law into its own hand, and assails us with stones and flames! .... Yet, banded together as we are, ever so ready to sacrifice our lives, what single case of revenge for injury are you able to point to, though, if it were held right among us to repay evil by evil, a single night or two with a torch or two could achieve an ample vengeance? . . .

If we desired, indeed, to act the part of open enemies, not merely of secret avengers, would there be any lacking in strength, whether of numbers or resources? . . . For what wars should we not be fit, not eager, even with unequal forces, we who so willingly yield ourselves to the sword, if in our religion it were not counted better to be slain than to slay? Without arms even, and raising no insurrectionary banner, but simply in enmity to you, we could carry on the contest with you by an ill-willed severance alone. For if such multitudes of men were to break away from you, and betake themselves to some remote corner of the world, why, the very loss of so many citizens, whatever sort they were, would cover the empire with shame; nay, in the very forsaking, vengeance would be inflicted.[14]

In this passage, Tertullian bases his stance on Jesus' teaching to love our enemies (Matt. 5:44; Luke 6:27). He asserts that, according to human wisdom, the Christians had every right to retaliate against their enemies, and they could do so effectively. But because they followed Jesus' teaching, they remained peaceful.

Tertullian's general principles of nonviolence carried over into a rejection of the death penalty. In his treatise *On Idolatry*, Tertullian expresses his skepticism about whether Christians can hold public office. He sets some requirements for those who wish to do so. The list itself is ironic, since Roman officials were expected to engage in most, if not all, of the activities listed:

Let us grant that it is possible for anyone to succeed in moving, in whatsoever office, under the mere *name* of the

office, neither sacrificing nor lending his name/authority
to sacrifices; not farming out victims; not assigning to others the care of temples; not looking after their tributes; not
giving spectacles at his own or the public charge, or pre-
siding over the giving of them; making proclamation or
edict for no solemnity; not even taking oaths: moreover
(what comes under the head of *power*), neither sitting in
judgment on anyone's life or character, for you might bear
with his judging about *money*; neither condemning or fore-
condemning; binding no one, imprisoning or torturing no
one—if it is credible that all this is possible.[15]

Notice that Tertullian includes a specific prohibition on
participating in a capital trial, sitting in judgment on anyone's life. He is especially sensitive about vicarious participation in sin. Tertullian states that as moral infractions
become more serious, Christians need to be more careful in
keeping their distance from them. For serious infractions,
such as when a human life is taken, Christians need to be
careful that they do not provide any kind of support for the
action. In his words, "For although the fault be done by
others, it makes no difference if it is done *by my means.*"[16]
Thus, even though a judge does not actually carry out the
execution of a condemned person, he bears moral responsibility because his participation lends legitimacy to the
execution.

Tertullian was adamantly opposed to any Christian participation in the military. His opposition was based on a
number of related reasons, but focused primarily on the practice of idolatry and the sanctioning of violence. While other
Christian writers tried to make a distinction between nonviolent service within the military and violent service,
Tertullian condemned all participation:

Inquiry is made about this point, whether a believer may
turn himself unto military service, and whether the military may be admitted into the faith, even the rank and file,
or each inferior grade, to whom there is no necessity for
taking part in sacrifices or capital punishments. There is no

agreement between the divine and the human sacrament, the standard of Christ and the standard of the devil, the camp of light and the camp of darkness. One soul cannot be due to two *masters*—God and Caesar.

And yet Moses carried a rod, and Aaron wore a buckle, and John (Baptist) is girt with leather, and Joshua the son of Nun leads a line of march; and the People warred: if it pleases you to sport with the subject. But how will *a Christian man* war, nay, how will he serve even in peace, without a sword, which the Lord has taken away? For albeit soldiers had come unto John, and had received the formula of their rule; albeit, likewise, a centurion had believed; *still* the Lord afterward, in disarming Peter, ungirded every soldier. No dress is lawful among us, if assigned to any unlawful action.[17]

The passage begins with the assumption that if soldiers participate in the violent duties of the military, including capital punishment, they cannot be church members. The discussion here is whether someone in the military who does not participate in bloodshed could be a member of the church. For Tertullian, the Didache's division between the two ways (life and death) becomes the camp of light and the camp of darkness; he rejects any participation in the camp of darkness. According to his view, the military's function is bloodshed, and so Christians must not participate in it at all. While acknowledging the militarism within the Hebrew Scriptures, he points to Jesus' refusal to allow Peter's use of the sword at the time of his arrest as the final word against Christian participation in violence (Matt. 26:52).

Tertullian argues against participation in the military again in *The Chaplet*, or *De Corona*, and again he mentions the military's relationship with capital punishment as a specific reason for Christians to reject such participation. He starts with a question: "Now, to come down to the very heart of the question about the soldier's crown, should we not first examine the right of a Christian to be in the military service at all?" After some further comments about the problem of idolatry in the military, he asks rhetorically:

> Is it likely we are permitted to carry a sword when our
> Lord said that he who takes the sword will perish by the
> sword? Will the son of peace who is forbidden to engage in
> a lawsuit espouse the deeds of war? Will a Christian,
> taught to turn the other cheek when struck unjustly, guard
> prisoners in chains, and administer torture and capital
> punishment?[18]

Again Tertullian appeals to Jesus' refusal to allow violence
at the time of his arrest (Matt. 26:52). He also mentions the
Pauline prohibition against suing in the court
(1 Cor. 6:1-8) as well as Jesus' command to turn the other
cheek (Matt. 5:39; Luke 6:29). Tertullian believes that soldiers
could become Christians, but when they do so, they have to
leave the military as soon as possible. He feels that otherwise
they would constantly be under temptation to rationalize
their participation in activities violating the morality of
Christian life.[19]

Some have argued that Tertullian's opposition to participation in the military was the result of his conversion to
Montanism. This was a Christian movement centered in
Phrygia and eventually considered heretical by many in the
mainstream church. It insisted on a much more rigorous
Christian ethic than Catholic orthodoxy. However, there is no
difference in Tertullian's position on participation in the military in his writings from before he adopted Montanism and
those that followed his conversion. *On Idolatry* was written
before his conversion; *The Chaplet* was written afterward.[20]

Hippolytus

Tertullian rejected anyone continuing in active military
duty from participating in church membership. A bit later,
the Apostolic Tradition (ca. 215), written by Hippolytus
(c. 170-235), only rejected soldiers who would not accept the
Christian prohibition on killing and oaths:

A soldier who is in authority must be told not to execute men; if he should be ordered to do it, he shall not do it. He must be told not to take the military oath. If he will not agree, let him be rejected.[21]

This statement allows some flexibility in the church's attitude toward soldiers becoming members of the church. It likely reflects the increasing pressure on the church to allow Christian participation in the military. Since the military performed functions that in modern society would be considered policing activities, this statement appears to have allowed soldiers carrying out such duties to join the church.[22] But it is clear that Christian soldiers were not allowed to help carry out death sentences.

Clement of Alexandria

In the third century, there appears to be a softening in the Christian opposition to participation in government bloodshed. Clement of Alexandria was the only early Christian leader who seemed to condone the state's use of capital punishment, although he did not allow Christian participation in carrying out executions. In *The Stromata* he says,

> When [the law] sees anyone in such a condition as to appear incurable, posting to the last stage of wickedness, then in its solicitude for the rest, that they may not be destroyed by it (just as if amputating a part of the whole body), it condemns such a one to death, as the course most conducive to health.[23]

Shortly afterward in the same work, Clement writes,

> But [the law] is the highest and most perfect good, when one is able to lead back any one from the practice of evil, to virtue and well-doing, which is the very function of the law. So that one falls into incurable evil—when taken possession of, for example, by wrong or covetousness—it will be for his own good if he is put to death.[24]

One must be careful not to make too much of this statement. The context of the passage is a defense of the Hebrew Scriptures, which had come under attack from Marcion and other critics of orthodox Christianity. These voices regarded the Hebrew Scriptures as too cruel and arbitrary to be included in the Christian canon. *The Stromata* is not a treatise on the role of worldly government. The law referred to in the passage is the Mosaic Law, rather than law in general.[25] With this understanding, the punishment of death referred to in the passage may have been death brought on by God for sin, rather than the death penalty inflicted by the state.

Thus, these chapters are not a defense of capital punishment by worldly governments, but an attempt to deal with a traditional problem of scriptural interpretation. This seems especially reasonable when one of the incurable evils mentioned by Clement is covetousness. The prohibition of covetousness is the last of the Ten Commandments, but it is not a capital crime. Instead, it is an inner sin, which the state does not count as a crime. Clement could not have been suggesting that the state should execute people for this sin, which is in the mind.

Even if Clement was supporting the government's use of capital punishment, however, he was doing so at a time when pagans controlled the state. Thus if he endorsed capital punishment, that endorsement would have been based on the assumption that the government and populace were pagan. He did not endorse Christian participation in executions. Indeed, in discussing the equality of men and women, he suggested that men should be like women in rejecting violence and military training, quoting Christ's commandment to "turn the other cheek" (Matt. 5:39; Luke 6:29).[26] In this passage, Clement rejects Christian participation in the military, which must also mean rejecting Christian participation in capital punishment since it was carried out by the military.

Moreover, in several passages Clement upholds Christian forgiveness in the face of evil. He states that the Christian "never cherishes resentment or harbors a grudge against anyone, though deserving of hatred for his conduct."[27] Clement further rejects actions based on such thoughts. "He acts unrighteously who retaliates either by word or deed, or by conception of a wish, which, after the training of the Law, the gospel rejects."[28] In a sermon, Clement specifically rejects Christian violence as a reaction to sin, "Above all, Christians are not allowed to correct with violence the delinquencies of sins."[29]

Origen

Christian abstention from governmental duties, including military service, was widespread enough to evoke criticism from the enemies of Christianity. Celsus, a Greek philosopher, wrote a work called *True Discourse* around 178. It was an all-out attack on the early Christians. All we know of Celsus' work are the quotes and answers made to it by Origen (185-254) in his great defense of Christianity entitled *Against Celsus*.

Because Celsus was hostile to Christianity, his accusations that Christians refused to participate in civil government or the military are especially important in determining the typical Christian attitude toward capital punishment. If these accusations are true, then the Christians could not have participated in the imposition of death sentences. Celsus would not have accused the Christians of refusing to participate in the government and military if it could have been easily refuted. And Origen makes no attempt to refute the accusation, thus lending credibility to its accuracy.

It is believed that Origen wrote *Against Celsus* late in his life (ca. 246), at a time when Christian participation in the military and public life was becoming more widespread.[30] Origen, however, continued to take a position against such participation. In response to Celsus' demand that Christians should participate in the government and military, Origen said,

But we recognize in each state the existence of another national organization, founded by the Word of God, and we exhort those who are mighty in word and of blameless life to rule over Churches. . . . And it is not for the purpose of escaping public duties that Christians decline public offices, but that they may reserve themselves for a diviner and more necessary service in the Church of God—for the salvation of men.[31]

Origen's rationale was clearly countercultural. He suggested that the church, as a separate but visible institution, set an example of higher morality and spirituality for the rest of society to follow. Origen suggested that this civilizing influence of the church was more important for the maintenance of order than public service and particularly military service. He pointed out that pagan priests were excused from military service, and he claimed a similar right for all Christians.

As we by our prayers vanquish all demons who stir up war, and lead to the violation of oaths, and disturb the peace, we in this way are much more helpful to the kings than those who go into the field to fight for them. And we do take our part in public affairs, when along with righteous prayers we join self-denying exercises and meditations, which teach us to despise pleasures, and not to be led away by them. And none fight better for the king than we do. We do not indeed fight under him, although he require it; but we fight on his behalf, forming a special army—an army of piety—by offering our prayers to God.[32]

While not condemning government violence outright, Origen did not believe Christians should participate in it. His demand that Christians not participate in the military definitely precluded them from involvement in applying the death penalty.

Origen spoke specifically about the death penalty in his differentiation between Jewish and Christian ethics. He countered Celsus' assertion that the God of the Jews was different from the God of the Christians. Yet he admitted that the different situation of the ancient Jews and the Christians demanded a different ethic. Because the Jews had a land of their own, they were allowed to make war and use capital punishment. The Christians, however, were to live separate from the state, and therefore such violence was not allowed to them. "For Christians could not slay their enemies, or condemn to be burned or stoned, as Moses commands, those who had broken the law, and were therefore condemned as deserving these punishments."[33]

Cyprian of Carthage and Arnobius

While Origen and Clement seemed to hold a position more accommodating to the state, other Christians retained a much more critical attitude. In 246, writing with the enthusiasm of a recent convert, Cyprian of Carthage echoed the criticisms of Tatian, Minucius Felix, and Tertullian in his attacks on state-sponsored bloodshed. In a letter to fellow Christian Donatus, Cyprian shared his vision of the world:

> Observe the roads blocked by robbers, the seas beset by pirates, wars spread everywhere with the bloody horrors of the camps. The world is soaked with mutual blood, and when individuals commit homicide, it is a crime; it is called a virtue when it is done in the name of the state. Impunity is acquired for crimes not by reason of innocence but by the magnitude of the cruelty.[34]

Cyprian continued with a condemnation of the gladiatorial games, which were, as stated earlier, a form of capital punishment masked as entertainment:

> A gladiatorial combat is being prepared that blood may delight the lust of cruel eyes. . . . Man is killed for the pleasure of man, and to be able to kill is a skill, is an employment, is an art. Crime is not only committed but taught. What can be called more inhuman, what more repulsive?[35]

In a letter to Cornelius, Cyprian offers the Christian alternative to killing. He tells of the bravery of Christian martyrs, and he states the Christian prohibition on killing, even when such killing might be justified. Cyprian says the adversary perceived that

> [the Christians] cannot be conquered, but that they can die; and that by this very fact they are invincible, that they do not fear death; that they do not in turn assail their assailants, since it is not lawful for the innocent even to kill the guilty.[36]

As the Roman Empire became increasingly Christianized, Christian writers claimed a civilizing influence for their religion, particularly as it related to violence. Sometime between 304 and 310, Arnobius wrote,

> For since we in such numbers have learned from the precepts and laws of Christ not to repay evil with evil, to endure injury rather than to inflict it, to shed our own blood rather than to stain our hands and conscience with the blood of another, the ungrateful world now long owes to Christ the blessing that savage ferocity has been softened and hostile hands have refrained from the blood of a kindred creature.[37]

Lactantius

Christians continued to oppose participation in capital punishment up to and after the conversion of Constantine in 313, but around this time they became less likely to condemn the imposition of the death penalty by the state. Lactantius, probably writing in the early-fourth century, seems particularly double-minded on the subject. He begins one passage with an attack on the gladiatorial games, but then expands his condemnation to include all forms of state-sponsored homicide:

> Being imbued with this practice [gladiatorial contests], they have lost their humanity. Therefore they do not spare even the innocent, but practice upon all that which they

have learned in the slaughter of the wicked. It is not therefore befitting that those who strive to keep to the path of justice should be companions and sharers in this public homicide. For when God forbids us to kill, He not only prohibits us from open violence, which is not even allowed by the public laws, but He warns us against the commission of those things which are esteemed lawful among men.

Thus it will be neither lawful for a just man to engage in warfare, since his warfare is justice itself, nor to accuse anyone of a capital charge, because it makes no difference whether you put a man to death by word, or rather by the sword, since it is the act of putting to death itself which is prohibited. Therefore, with regard to this precept of God, there should be no exception at all; but that it is always unlawful to put to death a man, whom God willed to be a sacred animal.[38]

Here Lactantius specifically prohibits Christians from bringing a capital charge, which could result in death. He uses an argument similar to Tertullian's in forbidding this action. It makes no difference whether one accuses or condemns someone of a capital offense or actually executes the accused. From God's point of view, both are prohibited because both lead to the killing of a human being. Lactantius also seems to be comparing these forms of killing to sacrifice, referring to humans as sacred animals, which are not to be sacrificed.

Lactantius introduces the interesting argument that capital punishment and other forms of public bloodshed do not deter crime, but actually encourage violence. This thesis, often called the brutalization theory, was revived by modern opponents of capital punishment in the eighteenth century and has been an important argument against the death penalty ever since. Here it appears in embryonic form, perhaps for the first time.

However, in his *Treatise on the Anger of God*, primarily an attack on the Stoic concept of an unmoved and unemotional god, Lactantius not only condones but also seems to demand that rulers use the death penalty to protect society:

> They are deceived by no slight error who defame all censure, whether human or divine, with the name of bitterness and malice, thinking that [God] ought to be called injurious who visits the injurious with punishment. But if it is so, it follows that we have injurious laws, which enact punishment for offenders, and injurious judges who inflict capital punishments on those convicted of crime. But if the law is just which awards to the transgressor his due, and if the judge is called upright and good when he punishes crimes—for he guards the safety of good men [when he] punishes the evil—it follows that God, when He opposes the evil, is not injurious; but he himself is injurious who either injures an innocent man, or spares an injurious person that he may injure many.[39]

Later in the treatise, however, Lactantius returns to a more gentle view of both men and God:

> How many who were in early life base, and condemned by the judgment of all, afterwards have turned out praiseworthy? But it is plain that this could not happen if punishment followed every offense.
>
> The public laws condemn those who are manifestly guilty; but there are great numbers whose offenses are concealed, great numbers who restrain the accuser either by entreaties or by reward, great numbers who elude justice by favor or influence. But if the divine censure should condemn all those who escape the punishment of men, there would be few or even no men on earth.[40]

Lactantius's ambivalence about the state's use of violence may have been a reflection of the time in which he lived. With the conversion of Constantine in 313, only ten years after the severe persecution of the church under Diocletian, Christians experienced a whipsaw of emotions. From what appeared to be their darkest hour, Christianity became not only tolerated but accepted as the foremost religion in the Roman Empire. Undoubtedly, many Christians felt a surge of gratitude to the emperor. But Constantine's conversion also tied the fate of the church to that of the ruler, who wished to use both the military and capital punishment to control his empire.

The Christian church never denied that the government had a legitimate role to play in keeping order in the world. But until the time of Constantine, the government was viewed as a necessary evil, and the church's role was to remind the state of its limitations under God's rule. Now that the state appeared to represent God's protecting arm for the church, the church's role became confused. Supposedly, the Roman Empire was the church's ally, and the church's strength depended on the power of the state. Therefore, leaders thought compromises had to be made.

Lactantius gave the government the right to impose the death penalty in some cases, but he still maintained that Christians could not be involved. Like many Christians of his time, Lactantius must have been feeling his way in the brave new world of state-supported Christianity. Regardless of what we may think of his solution, it is obvious that even under a Christian emperor, Lactantius felt that Christians must not be involved in putting anyone to death or even in accusations or judgments leading to capital punishment.

The First Christian Theologians and the Bible

The first Christian theologians were quite familiar with the biblical writings. Tertullian and Clement of Alexandria wrote treatises defending the inclusion of the Hebrew Scriptures within the Christian canon, and all of the writers allude to biblical principles of nonviolence as standard teachings of the church.

Until the fourth century, no Christian writer accepted Christian participation in bloodshed of any kind. They condemned personal violence; they also were against taking part in violence approved by the state and sometimes required by the state.[41] Living in a time when being counted as Christians necessarily meant persecution and hardships, they held onto their biblical faith in order to maintain this unpopular belief. The condemnation of capital punishment by these writers indicates that the earliest Christians, those closest to Jesus in history, believed that Jesus' message was one of peacefulness; the good news (gospel) of Jesus Christ prohibited taking part in bloodshed, including the death penalty.

Modern Christian proponents of the death penalty, who insist that Jesus' teachings did not prohibit Christian participation in capital punishment, rarely mention the opinions of these important early Christian leaders. They ignore these teachers who risked martyrdom rather than participate in the violence of the state.

Instead, modern death-penalty proponents cite Augustine, the fifth-century theologian who in his teachings tries to justify Christian participation in both war and capital punishment. Augustine helped the church accommodate itself to the state while the church was trying to win a more secure position for itself.

At the same time, death-penalty advocates ignore Augustine's own ambivalence about the death penalty. This track, more true to the gospel, led him to call for restraint, even while proposing theoretical justification for Christian involvement in executions. In one sermon Augustine advises,

> "Man" and "sinner" are two different things. God made man; man made himself a sinner. So, destroy what man made, but save what God made. Thus, do not go so far as to kill the criminal, for in wishing to punish the sin, you are destroying the man. Do not take away his life; leave him the possibility of repentance. Do not kill so that he can correct himself.[42]

In a series of letters to the judges of some heretics who had murdered a Catholic priest and mutilated another, Augustine states,

> If there were no other punishment, . . . extreme necessity might require that such men be put to death, although, as far as we are concerned, if no lesser punishment were pos-

sible, . . . we would prefer to let them go free, rather than avenge the martyrdom of our brothers by shedding their blood. But, now that there is another possible punishment by which the mildness of the Church can be made evident, and the violent excess of savage men be restrained, why do you not commute your sentence to a more prudent and more lenient one?[43]

By studying the convictions of the earliest Christian theologians, we thus find a firm basis for an interpretation of the Bible in our own time that calls for Christians to shun participation in capital punishment. The testimony of these brave church leaders was that Jesus had rejected violence in all its forms. Because of this, as his followers, we are no longer allowed to judge and kill our fellow human beings, no matter what their crime.

The Early Church's Challenging Witness

The writings quoted above show that like Jesus himself, the leaders of the early church did not avoid confrontation with the political powers that ruled their society. They spoke out courageously and bluntly about social evils. In particular, they spoke against the society's use of violence to achieve its ends. Capital punishment was a part of that violence, and it was included in the catalog of social evils that the early church fathers condemned.

It is important to note, however, that this political witness was based on an *experience* of something better. These men lived the word of the gospel, and then they spoke it. Because they lived in Christian communities, they were surrounded by a better alternative. They frequently pointed to this alternative. Roman pagan society had also seen this difference, and as a result, the Christian writers appealed to it with little fear of contradiction.

Christians were known as a gentle, helpful, and moral people. Again and again, their writers call those who accuse them falsely of violence to look at the evidence with their own eyes. "How can people who refuse to attend gladiatorial games because of their violence possibly be cannibals?" "How can people who refuse to use violence even when they and their families are persecuted be expected to kill for the state?"

This is not the time or the place for a full-scale exploration of what this evidence may say about Christians taking part in political action today, but it does suggest some lessons from the early church. First, our political witness must always be based on our experience of the life of Christ. We must never feel that we can witness under our own authority, but only under that authority that Christ gives us. This frequently means that Christian witness against the death penalty must be different from that of its secular opponents.

Christians must be careful of the truth and therefore must use facts and figures carefully. Christians must always recognize the humanity of their opponents, and they should always be looking for common ground and common understanding with them. If they do these things, they will also avoid the third temptation—the temptation to violence, either physical or emotional against their opponents. For Christians, people must always be put before ideas.

A second general principle is that Christian political witness must be based on a daily way of life that is opposed to violence. Like the early church, we must be willing to live our lives nonviolently, constantly seeking out and confronting the injustices that surround us and infect our own hearts. Our witness will be strengthened by our general reputation for gentleness and moral living. Christians should test their thoughts and actions within the cauldron of their community, and they must be willing to listen carefully to the judgment of their brothers and sisters.

Third, a Christian political witness will be strongest when it grows out of personal calling. Many oppose the death penalty and the violence it represents. Yet relatively few are willing to take the risk of personal involvement—such as meeting with victim families or becoming a spiritual adviser for a death-row inmate. How much better we will understand the issues if we do take the risk of such personal involvement—a personal involvement that Jesus himself advocates in Matthew 25:31-46.

Finally, we must recognize that the Christian political witness has always been a part of the Christian tradition. It is not, as some would have us believe, a step away from orthodoxy, made by the social gospel preachers of the early twentieth century. Here we see the earliest Christians speaking out and taking risks to battle the social evils of their day. We could track and follow similar witnesses throughout the history of the church.

For those who oppose the death penalty and other forms of violence, we can take heart that our position is near the headwaters of the mainstream of Christian history. We are not stepping away from tradition in opposing the death penalty but back into our most pure and primitive tradition.

9
Conclusion

For 1,700 years most Christians have believed that the Bible supports capital punishment. By taking a few proof texts that seem to support the death penalty, church leaders were able to make participation in this brutal and cruel social practice acceptable to church members. These same leaders still claimed to serve the Prince of Peace. In this book, we have looked at those proof texts more closely in their historical context. We have also showed how the concept and practice of capital punishment does not fit with other important biblical doctrines, such as teachings on forgiveness and the atonement.

As an attempt to limit the violence of the blood feud, the Hebrew law allowed the Israelites to practice capital punishment. However, the law also set stringent requirements for this practice. First, it required that the court give due consideration of mitigating factors before using the death penalty. Then it demanded that capital punishment could only be applied when there was absolute certainty of the guilt of the accused. Finally, it required that capital punishment be applied fairly and without prejudice. When the application of capital punishment does not meet these standards, it no longer is Yahweh's sanctioned punishment for a crime, but a form of human sacrifice—a practice strictly forbidden in the Hebrew Scriptures.

The standards for the use of capital punishment set by the Hebrew Scriptures simply cannot be attained in human society. Human beings are too fallible to achieve these standards. No matter how hard we try, even in the most scientific of settings, we make mistakes in perception and judgment. No matter how much we may desire it to be otherwise, the rich and the poor will always be treated differently. Thus, while the Hebrew Scriptures give us the right to use the death penalty, they set standards for its use that are impossible for us to achieve.

Since that is the case, Jesus' statement about allowing the person without sin to cast the first stone falls directly in line with the teachings of the Torah. "Yes," Jesus said, "you are allowed to stone this woman to death, but only if you yourself have not sinned." Like the Hebrew Scriptures, Jesus allowed capital punishment, but then set requirements for its use that were impossible to fulfill.

What is the meaning of this paradox? On one hand the teaching is of justice: that sin deserves death. On the other hand, the teaching is one of grace: that mercy supersedes justice. The Bible teaches us that God wants to give us better than we deserve.

That is the story of the Hebrew Scriptures, both on the societal level and the individual level. Over and over, the Hebrews as a people reneged on their covenant with Yahweh. Again and again, they paid the price for their faithlessness. But the punishment was never final. Yahweh always left room for repentance and forgiveness. Similarly, Cain, Moses, and David all committed murder. They took human life, something they could never replace. For their crimes, they received severe punishments; but the punishments were not the end of the story. The door was left open for a new life to be built on the ruins of the old.

In the Hebrew Scriptures, we see a pattern. The oldest texts accept the death penalty with little question. The newer writings raise more issues. In the trial of Naboth, the law fails to protect an innocent man (1 Kings 21:1-16). In the apocryphal story of Susanna (Dan. 13, Greek version), false witnesses nearly cause the death of an innocent woman. The later rabbis piled more and more regulations on the capital statutes in the attempt to make them fairer and more reliable.

In the New Testament, Jesus took another tact. Beginning with the love of God as a model, he told us that we should imitate God's forgiveness rather than each other's desire for vengeance. But Jesus did not just teach this idea; he lived it out. Jesus' crucifixion and the other executions of the New Testament illustrate the failures of the human way of vengeance. Though laws exist to protect the innocent from execution, political and personal considerations overwhelm the laws. Sin is stronger than the law. Jesus' way is different. From the cross he forgave those who were killing him. And the basic tenet of Christianity is that forgiveness is stronger than sin; love is stronger than death.

As a spiritual adviser to death-row inmates, I have learned the importance of both justice and mercy in helping an inmate to grow spiritually. It is important for a criminal's spiritual health for him to recognize and understand the evil he has done. At the same time, he must also understand that God's forgiveness is for him as well as for other people.

In my experience, most criminals have an odd mixture of narcissism and low self-esteem, often created by backgrounds in which love and violence were confused. On one hand, they believe that the rules of society do not apply to them, that they are above the common norms of behavior. On the other hand, they feel like complete outcasts, as strangers to other people, often unable to bond to any other human being; yet they deeply crave any kind of affection. In their childhoods, they have typically experienced abuse that taught them to be both manipulative and yet naïve and impulsive.

It is therefore important for criminals to hear and understand the message of justice. They need to confess the pain, fear, and anguish they have caused their victims and their victims' families. But in order to do this, they must also know that forgiveness is possible—that God still loves them.

In one case, I told an inmate who had committed a particularly brutal crime that God did see his murderous act; but

God also saw him as the abused child cringing in fear while his stepfather brutally beat his pregnant mother until she aborted her baby. At the same time, God saw both these things and everything else in this inmate's life, both good and evil. In other words, God did not just see him as a murderer, but as a human being with all the complexity that human life holds.

Proponents of the death penalty do question the level of forgiveness that Jesus demanded of his followers. They point out that in many cases, one who turns the other cheek will receive a beating or worse. They properly ask what turning the other cheek could mean in the case of domestic violence, rape, and murder.

Protecting society from violent criminals is certainly a legitimate role of government, as Paul demonstrated in his teaching on the principalities and powers (see chap. 7, above). But that protection must come with an opportunity for repentance and redemption if it is to meet the standards set by Jesus. Forgiveness does not mean letting a criminal get away with murder, but it does mean giving that criminal an opportunity to find a new way of life in which his or her former need for violence is given over to God.

The early Christians came to understand that in Jesus' sacrifice of himself, the cycle of vengeance had been broken. The moral universe that had been damaged by sin was repaired once and for all. God had found a way to break through our perpetual sinfulness. Jesus' death on the cross was the final payment for sin—a final sacrifice that made unnecessary other forms of sacrifice, including the human sacrifice that we call capital punishment (see chap. 7, above). Jesus showed us that salvation from sin lay in forgiving the enemy, not in getting even by imitating the enemy's wickedness. When we forgive, we see new possibilities both for our enemy and for ourselves.

Does this mean that we cannot protect ourselves from violent criminals? The powers and principalities have been given the legitimate authority to protect us. Using the

Hebrew Scriptures' concept of banishment as a model, prisons may be an appropriate method of keeping truly dangerous persons from hurting others. However, God's justice is always restorative. That being the case, the true function of prison should be to reclaim lost persons, not just to punish or warehouse them.

Death-penalty proponents may argue that restorative justice is impossible, and that it puts us at risk. But God often asks his people to believe the impossible, even at great risks to themselves. Abraham is told to leave his homeland for a place unknown to him based on a vague promise from Yahweh. Moses is told to return to Egypt to oppose the great power of the Pharaoh for the benefit of slaves.

Mary is told that though unwed she will become pregnant with Jesus, in a society where such a transgression could cause a woman to be stoned to death. Jesus is asked to continue to believe in God's power even as he faces death on the cross. The disciples are asked to preach that a man who has been executed as a criminal was resurrected and is the true Son of God. Tertullian summed up the early Christian faith quite simply, "We believe because it is impossible."

When we accept God's call to live a life of love and forgiveness, however, we see that what might have seemed impossible is possible. Abraham's journey led to the founding of a great and enduring people. Moses was able to free descendants of Abraham from slavery. Mary's child was the Messiah. Jesus was raised by God's power. The early church grew by preaching the impossible. And I have seen murderers who are turning their lives around. With God, the impossible becomes the practical.

In turning away from the death penalty, modern Christians do not turn their back on tradition. For the first three hundred years of its existence, the church did not support the use of capital punishment. The church taught its members that they could not participate in it. In the final analysis, Christian rejection of the death penalty is not a rejection of tradition; it is a return to the original tradition taught by Jesus and his first disciples.

In his poem "Little Giddings," T. S. Eliot wrote these beautiful lines:

> We shall not cease from exploration,
> and the end of all our exploring
> will be to arrive where we started
> and know the place for the first time.

For Christians, the Bible is the ever-new beginning of our knowledge of God. Regarding capital punishment, may God give us the courage to explore our beginnings again and to know that place again where love overcomes death and forgiveness overcomes violence. Amen.

Notes

Preface

1. Frank Newport, "Support for the Death Penalty Drops to Lowest Level in 19 Years, Although Still High at 66%" (Princeton, N.J.: Gallup News Service, in "Poll Analyses," Feb. 24, 2000; on-line).

2. Gardner C. Hanks, *Against the Death Penalty: Christian and Secular Arguments Against Capital Punishment* (Scottdale, Pa.: Herald Press, 1997).

3. John Howard Yoder, *The Politics of Jesus* (Grand Rapids: Eerdmans, 1972), 13.

4. The incongruity of Governor George W. Bush blessing both Karla Faye Tucker and Gary Graham, as the state of Texas executed them, is symbolic of this divide between faith and practice.

5. John T. McNeill, "Asceticism Versus Militarism in the Middle Ages," *Church History* 5 (Mar. 1936): 3-28.

6. Walter Wakefield and Austin P. Evans, *Heresies of the High Middle Ages: Selected Sources Translated and Annotated* (New York: Columbia Univ. Press, 1969), 227, 234, 345. Also Thieleman J. van Braght, *The Bloody Theater or Martyrs Mirror of the Defenseless Christians* (Dutch original, 1660; 3d English ed., Scottdale, Pa.: Herald Press, 1938; reprint, 1987), 281-2.

7. John Driver, *Radical Faith: An Alternative History of the Christian Church* (Kitchener, Ont.: Pandora Press; and Scottdale, Pa.: Herald Press; 1999), 137-8.

8. Cornelius J. Dyck, *Spiritual Life in Anabaptism: Classic Devotional Resources* (Scottdale, Pa.: Herald Press, 1995), 109-10; Driver, *Radical Faith*, 239-40.

9. Auguste Jorns, *The Quakers as Pioneers in Social Work* (Port Washington, N.Y.: Kennikat, 1969), 169-70.

10. These statements appear in J. Gordon Melton, *The*

Churches Speak on Capital Punishment: Official Statements from Religious Bodies and Ecumenical Organizations (Detroit: Gale Research, 1989); and American Friends Service Committee, *The Death Penalty: The Religious Community Calls for Abolition* (Philadelphia: American Friends Service Committee, 1998). Some church statements are also included in an appendix in my book *Against the Death Penalty*.

11. A 1991 Gallup Poll found that 77 percent of Catholics and Protestants supported capital punishment compared to 76 percent of the total population. Eighteen percent of the general population opposed the death penalty; 16 percent of Catholics opposed it; 17 percent of Protestants opposed it. George Gallup Jr., *The Gallup Poll 1991* (Wilmington, Del.: Scholarly Resources, 1992), 129.

12. Robert L. Young, "Religious Orientation, Race and Support for the Death Penalty," *Journal for the Scientific Study of Religion* 31/1 (Mar. 1992): 76-87.

1. The Hebrew Scriptures in Context

1. John Howard Yoder, *The Original Revolution* (Scottdale, Pa.: Herald Press, 1971), 94.

2. The property value of an unmarried woman who was not a virgin—no matter what the cause of her condition—decreased sharply. She became a liability rather than an asset to her father, who would want to give her in marriage to connect to another family. Not only would it be difficult to arrange a good marriage contract for her, but also her condition brought dishonor on the family. A woman who had been raped might even be expelled from her family.

The law in Deuteronomy (22:28-29) actually provides some social protection for the violated woman. She remains an asset to her family, as she will bring in a payment to them. She also will have a place in society as a wife, who will receive some protection from her birth family. The law also prohibits her husband from divorcing her. Otherwise, her family might have cast her out, and she would have no place to go and no protection. In addition, the law sets a limit on the level of revenge that the woman's family can seek. In doing so, it prevents the possibility of a long and deadly blood feud between the family of the woman and the family of the rapist.

3. Chester Starr, *A History of the Ancient World* (New York:

Oxford Univ. Press, 1965), 27.

4. Charles Alexander Robinson, *Ancient History from Prehistoric Times to the Death of Justinian* (New York: Macmillan, 1966), 38.

5. Robinson, 46.

6. Chilperic Edwards, *The Hammurabi Code and the Sinaitic Legislation with a Complete Translation of the Great Babylonian Inscription Discovered at Susa* (1904; reprint, Port Washington, N.Y.: Kennikat, 1971).

7. John Gray, *The Canaanites* (New York: Frederick A. Praeger, 1964), 136.

8. Emmanuel Anati, *Palestine Before the Hebrews: A History, from the Earliest Arrival of Man to the Conquest of Canaan* (New York: Alfred A Knopf, 1963), 427.

9. There appears to be some dispute about the use of human sacrifice in the Canaanite cult. Gray (125) states that there is no indication of human sacrifice in the Canaanite texts. Anati (427) reports that the texts found at Ugarit do indicate that human sacrifice was still practiced by the Canaanites. Lawrence Boadt, *Reading the Old Testament: An Introduction* (New York: Paulist Press, 1984), 223, states that child sacrifice was common during times of crises among the Canaanites.

John Day, *Molech: A God of Human Sacrifice in the Old Testament* (New York: Cambridge Univ. Press, 1989), uses a detailed linguistic analysis of the Hebrew Scriptures and other sources to show that human sacrifice was practiced in honor of the Canaanite god Molech. The Hebrew Scriptures indicate that the Canaanites practiced human sacrifice, and that the Hebrews were not to follow this practice (Deut. 12:29-32). This leads one to conclude that while human sacrifice may have been practiced as an accepted part of the Canaanite religion, this was probably done relatively rarely and only as an emergency measure in the case of grave social crisis. Also see notes 23-27, below.

10. For example, when Adam and Eve are expelled from the Garden of Eden, Yahweh says, "The man has become like one of us" (Gen. 3:22). The use of the plural pronoun implies that there are other divine beings in God's heavenly court. When Jacob flees from Laban, Rachel steals Laban's household gods; this theft becomes a major point of contention between Laban and Jacob. Unlike later prophetic literature, no negative comment is made about these gods (Gen. 31:19-37). Jacob still retains foreign

gods as he travels through Canaan. (Gen. 35:2). Even the first of the Ten Commandments, "You shall have no other god before me [Yahweh]," implies that there are other gods who have some form of existence in reality, not just in the minds of their worshipers (Exod. 20:3; Deut. 5:7).

11. The brief story in Exodus 4:24 is an example. The Lord decides to kill Moses, as he is on his way to Egypt, even though Moses is doing the Lord's bidding. Only Moses' wife Zipporah's quick thinking and prayer save him. While it appears that the Lord is upset by Moses' failure to have his son circumcised, one cannot help but feel the arbitrary nature of God's behavior in this instance. Perhaps at the root of this story is a serious illness or injury that Moses suffered as he prepared for his mission. Ancient life was filled with such uncertainties, much as life is in poverty-stricken countries today. In any case, such uncertainty of life can affect our view of God. If the events of the ancients' lives seemed arbitrary and capricious, it would only be natural to view the gods who presumably controlled these events in the same light.

12. *Harper Study Bible: New Revised Standard Version* (New York: HarperCollins Publishers, 1993), 334. Modern indignation at the *kherem* seems somewhat hypocritical since modern warfare is noted for its failure to make distinctions between military personnel and civilian populations. The strategy of conventional bombing regards the indiscriminate killing of civilians, euphemistically called "collateral damage," as an acceptable and sometimes even desirable by-product. Moreover, for more than fifty years, the most powerful modern nations have, with the approval of the majority of their citizens, pointed nuclear weapons at their enemies. The use of these weapons of mass destruction against the largely civilian populations of Hiroshima and Nagasaki in 1945 far surpassed any atrocities committed by the ancient Hebrews.

13. Walter Wink, *Engaging the Powers* (Minneapolis: Fortress, 1992), 37.

14. Wink, 37.

15. Emrys Peters, "Some structural Aspects of the Feud Among the Camel-herding Beduoin of Cyrenaica," *Africa* 37/3 (July 1967): 261. Quoted in Jacob Black-Michaud, *Cohesive Force: Feud in the Mediterranean and the Middle East* (New York: St. Martin's, 1975), 22.

16. *The Harper Study Bible*, 456.

17. Joseph Ginat, *Blood Disputes Among Bedouin and Rural Arabs in Israel: Revenge, Mediation, Outcasting and Honor.* (Pittsburgh: Univ. of Pittsburgh Press, 1987), 45-59.

18. Jacob Black-Michaud, *Cohesive Force: Feud in the Mediterranean and the Middle East* (New York: St. Martin's, 1975), 125.

19. René Girard, *The Girard Reader*, ed. James G. Williams (New York: Crossroad Publishing Co., 1996), 9.

20. Girard, 11-2.

21. Girard, 83.

22. René Girard, "Generative Scapegoating," in Robert G. Hamerton-Kelly, ed., *Violent Origins: Walter Burkhert, René Girard, and Jonathan Z. Smith on Ritual Killing and Cultural Formation* (Stanford, Calif.: Stanford Univ. Press, 1987), 84.

23. Second Kings 3:27 reports that the king of Moab made a sacrifice of his firstborn son during a battle with the Hebrews.

24. T. H. Gaster, "Sacrifices and Offerings, O. T.," *Interpreter's Dictionary of the Bible,* ed. George A. Buttrick (Nashville: Abingdon, 1962), 4:147-59, especially on "Human Sacrifice," 153-4.

25. Edward Westermark, *The Origin and Development of Moral Ideas* (London: Macmillan, 1906), 466. Quoted in Nigel Davis, *Human Sacrifice in History and Today* (New York: Wil-liam Morrow and Co., 1981), 25.

26. Davis, 52.

27. Human sacrifice was considered to be a way of providing food for the gods. In Ezekiel 23:37, the prophet condemns the sinfulness of Samaria and Jerusalem, "They committed adultery, and blood is on their hands; with their idols they committed adultery; and they have even offered up to them for food the children whom they had borne to me."

28. In 1979, when John Spinkelink was executed in Florida, I heard this part of Genesis 9:6 shouted at anti-death-penalty demonstrators by a pro-death-penalty demonstrator carrying a sign with the same message.

29. The *go'el* had a special responsibility for helping his close kin. Not only was he the avenger of blood in the case of a murder, but he also had special responsibilities if the relative had financial difficulties. Leviticus 25:25-55 explains some of these responsibilities. Another duty was to participate in a levirate

marriage: the next of kin was required to marry a dead man's wife if the couple had no children, so that a child could be procreated to carry on the dead man's family line (Deut. 25:5-10). The story of Onan shows a man who refuses his duty to participate fully in a levirate marriage (Gen. 38:1-11). In the story of Ruth, Boaz cannot marry Ruth until Ruth's late husband's *go'el*, who has both the right and responsibility to marry her, refuses to take her for his wife (Ruth 4:1-12).

30. John Bright, *A History of Israel*, 2ᵈ ed. (Philadelphia: Westminster, 1972), 130-3; cf., e.g., 2 Sam. 11:3, Uriah the Hittite; 24:18, Araunah the Jebusite.

2. The Mosaic Law

1. Bernhard W. Anderson, *Understanding the Old Testament*, 3ᵈ ed. (Englewood Cliffs, N.J.: Prentice-Hall, 1975), 91-93; cf. Exod. 19–24.

2. Anderson, 87-8.

3. Proverbs 31:10-31 expounds on the value of a good wife in Hebrew culture.

4. *Interpreter's Bible*, vol. 1 (Nashville: Abingdon, 1952), 370.

5. The limited sexual understanding of the Hebrews is seen in their test for infidelity when a husband accused his wife of adultery without proof. This test, according to Numbers 5:11-31, was a form of ordeal: The woman was required to take an oath that she had been faithful and then to swallow bitter waters. If she were guilty, she would have "bitter pain, and her womb shall discharge, her uterus drop, and the woman shall be an execration among her people."

6. During his rebellion against his father, David, Absalom raped some of his father's concubines. He did this in a public manner, to show his disrespect for his father (2 Sam. 16:15-23; cf. Deut. 22:30).

7. With the exception of the mother-son incestuous relationship, the law does not specifically provide the death penalty for intra-family incest, such as between father and daughter, or between siblings or other close relatives. Lot's incestuous relationship with his daughters in Genesis 19:30-38 results in the births of the ancestors of Israel's traditional enemies, Moab and Ammon. This indicates that such relationships were condemned. Leviticus 18:6-18 prohibits a long list of incestuous relationships but does not specifically provide the death penal-

ty for any of them. The transgressors are to be "cut off from their people" (Lev. 18:29). Of course, those who committed such transgressions could be condemned to death under the laws of rape, adultery, or fornication.

8. Godfrey Ashby, *Go Out and Meet God: a Commentary on the Book of Exodus* (Grand Rapids: Eerdmans, 1998), 106-7.

9. The change in Abraham's name focuses on the number of progeny that Abraham will have. Sarah is a less archaic form of Sarai, and the new name may be more closely related to Israel. *New Interpreter's Bible*, vol. 1 (Nashville: Abingdon, 1994), 457-9.

10. See 2 Maccabees 6:1-11.

11. Some may object that genocidal regimes, such as the Nazis, actually endorse murder as a societal value. However, such regimes only endorse the killing of people whom they consider to be less than human. The Nazis, for example, considered Jews and other victims of the Holocaust to be subhuman; they therefore regarded killing Jews in much the same way that they would consider killing a dangerous animal. Like any other society, however, these regimes consider intragroup homicides to be the killing of human beings, and they punish the perpetrators as murderers.

12. Chilperic Edwards, *The Hammurabi Code and the Sinaitic Legislation with a Complete Translation of the Great Babylonian Inscription Discovered at Susa* (1904; reprint, Port Washington, N.Y.: Kennikat, 1971).

13. Contrast this with Deuteronomy 23:15-16, which tells the Hebrews not to return fugitive slaves to their owners.

14. Lincoln Keiser, *Friend by Day, Enemy by Night: Organized Violence in a Kohistani Community* (Fort Worth: Holt, Rinehart & Winston, 1991).

15. Leviticus 24:21 gives a provision that also addresses the prohibition of blood money as the punishment for a murder: "One who kills an animal shall make restitution for it; but one who kills a human being shall be put to death."

16. Some death-penalty proponents dispute that the witness requirement in the Hebrew Scriptures is for eyewitnesses, based on Leviticus 5:1 and Exodus 22:13 and the use of stone memorials as "witnesses" of covenants and events, as in Genesis 31:46-49 and Joshua 24:25-27. See Dudley Sharp, "Death Penalty and Sentencing Information in the United States," "Section F: Christianity and the Death Penalty," Justice for All website (Oct.

1, 1997). Leviticus 5:1 does allow witnesses to speak of what they learned of the matter; but this may only mean that in a criminal case, they may be able to provide testimony for the defense, where such evidence would be allowed. The Exodus passage allows physical evidence to be used to show that an animal had *not* been stolen. The use of stone memorials as witnesses obviously has nothing to do with criminal procedure.

On the other hand, where the Bible describes in detail criminal trials, the testimony of two or more eyewitnesses is invariably mentioned (Lev. 24:10-23; Num. 15:32-36; 1 Kings 21:1-16; in the Apocrypha, Susanna 52-59/Greek Dan. 13:52-59; detailed accounts of Jesus' trial, in Matt. 26:57-68; Mark 14:53-65; and the trial of Stephen, in Acts 6:8-16). Moreover, the provisions of the Talmud, discussed in this chapter, show that Jewish experts on the law believed that at least two eyewitnesses were required for prosecuting criminal cases and especially for capital ones.

Mishnah Sanhedrin 9:5 provides a punishment for murderers who committed their crime without adequate witnesses for the court to use the death penalty. The punishment was prison and a diet of "the bread of adversity and the water of affliction" (Isa. 30:20; Jacob Neusner, trans., *The Mishnah: A New Translation* (New Haven, Conn.: Yale Univ. Press, 1988), 604. Further citations from the Mishnah are from this edition.

17. Law 3 in the Code of Hammurabi gives the capital sentence for perjury in a capital trial. See Edwards, *Hammurabi Code.* For the Twelve Tables, see Jan Gorecki, *Capital Punishment: Criminal Law and Social Evolution* (New York: Columbia Univ. Press, 1983), 46-7.

18. "The Talmud is the repository of thousands of years of Jewish wisdom, and the oral law, which is as ancient and as significant as the written law (the Torah), finds expression therein." Adin Steinhalz, *The Essential Talmud,* trans. Chaya Galai (New York: Basic Books, 1976), 4.

19. Neusner, 594.

20. Neusner, xvii-xviii.

21. Mishnah Sanhedrin 3.4.

22. M. Sanhedrin 3.3.

23. M. Sanhedrin 9.3.

24. M. Sanhedrin 9.3.

25. M. Sanhedrin 4.5.

26. M. Sanhedrin 4.1.
27. M. Sanhedrin 4.2.
28. M. Sanhedrin 5.1.
29. M. Makkot 1.9.
30. M. Sanhedrin 5.2.
31. M. Sanhedrin 5.2.
32. M. Sanhedrin 5.3; cf. Susanna 52-59/Greek Dan. 13:52-59: the false witnesses, when Daniel examines them separately, name different trees under which the alleged adultery took place.
33. M. Sanhedrin 4.1.
34. M. Sanhedrin 5:4.
35. M. Sanhedrin 4.1.
36. M. Sanhedrin 5.5.
37. M. Sanhedrin 5.5.
38. M. Sanhedrin 6.1.
39. M. Makkot 1.10.
40. M. Sanhedrin 6.3—7.3.
41. Steinsaltz, *Essential Talmud,* 165.
42. Steinsaltz, 167.
43. Steinsaltz, 167.
44. Steinsaltz, 167.

3. Yahweh's Grace and Forgiveness

1. Barry L. Banstra, *Reading the Old Testament: An Introduction to the Hebrew Bible* (Belmont, Calif.: Wadsworth Publishing Co., 1995), 71: "God created the world a perfect place. The creation, however, was distorted and corrupted by humankind's efforts to achieve autonomy [apart] from God."

2. This text implies a polytheistic worldview and therefore is likely quite ancient. The term translated "sons of God" was later explained as renegade angels who knew no border between heaven and earth. *The HarperCollin's Study Bible* (New York: HarperCollins, 1993), 12.

3. Judges 2:16-23.

4. *Interpreter's Bible,* vol. 1 (Nashville: Abingdon, 1952), 333.

5. *Interpreter's Bible,* 1:518: "It is possible [that the rejection of Cain's offering] was a piece of polemic against the peasant custom of bringing the fruit of the ground as an offering to the Lord (v. 3), instead of the time-honored nomad offering of an animal."

6. *Interpreter's Bible*, 1:519.

7. *Interpreter's Bible*, 1:520. Cain's banishment is described as "a completely cultureless existence."

8. Godfrey Ashby, *Go Out and Meet God: A Commentary on the Book of Exodus* (Grand Rapids: Eerdmans, 1998), 15.

9. Linda Nafziger-Meiser suggested this in a sermon at the Hyde Park Mennonite Fellowship, Boise, Idaho, on July 2, 2000. After Uriah's death, Bathsheba laments for him, likely showing her feelings for her husband. In contrast, there is no mention of Abigail, another of David's wives, mourning the death of her previous husband, Nabal, before marrying David. *Interpreter's Bible*, vol. 2 (Nashville: Abingdon, 1952), 1099, suggests that this incident may have caused Ahithophel's enmity toward David, since Bathsheba was apparently his granddaughter (2 Sam. 11:3; 23:34). It would normally be an honor to have one's granddaughter marry the king. Ahithophel's support of Absalom in his rebellion against David and his advice to Absalom to rape David's concubines hints that Bathsheba had been raped and then forced into the marriage (2 Sam. 16:20-23).

10. Ironically, when Uriah refuses to sleep with his wife, he is following David's own standing order for his troops "on an expedition" (1 Sam. 21:1-6).

11. In general, in the prophetic books, there seems to be a move away from violence. Raymund Schwager, *Must There Be Scapegoats? Violence and Redemption in the Bible* (San Francisco: Harper & Row, 1987), 109-26.

4. Applying Hebrew Scriptures to the Debate

1. Richard C. Dieter, *International Perspectives on the Death Penalty: A Costly Isolation for the U.S.* (Washington, D.C., Death Penalty Information Center, 1999), 20.

2. Andrew Stephen, "In Florida the Killing Is Just Electric!" *New Statesman* 129/4468 (Jan. 10, 2000): 20, quotes Florida Attorney General Bob Butterworth as saying that people who commit murder "better not come to Florida because we might have a problem with the electric chair." "Debate over the Electric Chair," *Current Events* 99/14 (Dec. 17, 1999): 3, quotes Captain Al Sanchez of the Florida State Police: "Lethal injection is too humane for these guys [death row inmates]. I think they ought to suffer a little."

3. The author observed this event.

4. Scott Wesely, "As Otey Executed, 'All Our Souls Are Diminished,'" *Nebraskans Against the Death Penalty Newsletter*, Sept. 1992, 1.

5. "Tucker Death Exposes System Without Mercy," *National Catholic Reporter* 34/16 (Feb. 20, 1998): 28. "Conservatives Rethink Death Penalty," *Christianity Today* 42/4 (Apr. 6, 1998): 19.

6. During the victim-impact statements at the sentencing hearing for one murderer in Coeur d'Alene, Idaho, I observed family members turning to speak directly to the defendant about their anger. At a later Senate hearing on a death-penalty bill, a state trooper stated that the defendant sat "impassively" as family members expressed their feelings about the murder of their loved one. However, the defendant was receiving antipsychotic medication at the time, and courtroom procedures do not allow the defendant to speak to witnesses. He was simply behaving as he was required to do in the courtroom. Earlier he had expressed remorse in a television interview.

7. The third-century Roman jurist Ulpian stated, "Prison ought to be used for detention only, but not for punishment." This appears to have been the standard use for prisons at the time. *Encyclopedia Americana*, vol. 22 (Danbury, Conn.: Grolier Inc., 1998), 621.

8. A series of polls taken in a variety of states in the late 1980s and early 1990s showed that support for the death penalty dropped between 30 and 40 percentage points when life without parole was offered as an alternative. See Gardner C. Hanks, *Against the Death Penalty: Christian and Secular Arguments Against Capital Punishment* (Scottdale, Pa.: Herald Press, 1997), 85-6. National Gallup polls taken in 1999 and 2000 show about a 15 percent drop in support for the death penalty when life without parole is offered as an alternative (Introduction, note 1, above).

9. Pope John Paul II, Mass in St. Louis, Missouri (Jan. 27, 1999). This statement went somewhat further than his encyclical *Evangelium Vitae* (Mar. 25, 1995), in which he stated, "It is clear that, for these purposes to be achieved, *the nature and extent of the punishment* must be carefully evaluated and decided upon, and ought not go to the extreme of executing the offender except in cases of absolute necessity: in other words, when it would not be otherwise possible to defend society. Today, however, as a result

of steady improvements in the organization of the penal system, such cases are very rare, if not practically nonexistent."

10. Amnesty International, *Facts and Figures on the Death Penalty* (London: Amnesty International, 2000), 1.

11. In 1996, Resolution 1097 of the Parliamentary Assembly of the Council of Europe stated, "The willingness . . . to introduce a moratorium [on executions] upon accession [to the Council of Europe] has become a prerequisite for membership of the Council of Europe on the part of the Assembly." Cited in Amnesty International, *International Standards on the Death Penalty* (London: Amnesty International, 1998), 4.

12. Sam Walker, "ABA Vote May Be First Volley in Battle to Check Executions," *Christian Science Monitor* 89/49 (Feb. 5, 1997): 3.

13. Matt Kantz, "Moratorium on Executions Vetoed," *National Catholic Reporter* 35/32 (June 4, 1999): 8.

14. Stuart Taylor Jr., "The Death Penalty: To Err Is Human [moratorium by Gov. George Ryan of Illinois]," *National Reporter* 20/7 (Feb. 12, 2000): 450.

15. For example, Donald Paradis, who was given the death sentence in Idaho, had a public defender who had been out of law school for less than a year and had never tried a major felony, let alone a capital case.

16. In two capital cases in Idaho, attorneys pleaded defendants guilty to first-degree murder without negotiating for non-capital sentences. In both cases, the defendants were given the death penalty.

17. Stephen B. Bright, "Counsel for the Poor: The Death Sentence Not for the Worst Crime but for the Worst Lawyer," *Yale Law Journal* 103 (1994): 1,835-83.

18. As of April 2000, according the Death Penalty Information Center, 43 percent of current death-row inmates were African-American. Further information can be found on the DPIC web-site.

19. Brandon S. Centerwall, "Race, Socioeconomic Status, and Domestic Homicide," *The Journal of the American Medical Association (JAMA)* 273/22 (June 14, 1995): 1,755 (4). A study reported in this article showed similar murder rates among African-Americans and whites of similar socioeconomic status. Hence, socioeconomic class is a more important factor than race in determining murder rates.

20. Reported in Richard C. Dieter, *The Death Penalty in Black and White: Who Lives, Who Dies, Who Decides* (Washington, D.C.: Death Penalty Information Center, 1998), 11.

21. Dieter, *Death Penalty in Black and White*, 12.

22. *Death Penalty Legislation and the Racial Justice Act: Hearings Before the Subcommittee on Civil and Constitutional Rights of the Committee of the Judiciary House of Representatives, 101st Congress, Second Session, on H.R. 4618: Racial Justice Act of 1990* (Washington, D.C.: U.S. Government Printing Office, 1991), 69.

23. A 1998 study conducted by Professor Jeffrey Pokorak of St. Mary's University School of Law found that in the 38 states imposing capital punishment, 97 percent of the prosecutors who had discretionary power to seek the death penalty were white. Only 1.2 percent were African-American and 1.2 percent Hispanic. Reported in Dieter, *Death Penalty in Black and White*, 20-1.

24. *Death Penalty Legislation and the Racial Justice Act*, 156-66.

25. Cited in Deiter, *Death Penalty in Black and White*, 22.

26. Deiter, *Death Penalty in Black and White*, 22-3.

27. Deiter, *Death Penalty in Black and White*, 5-6.

28. *Callins v. Collins*, 114 S. Ct. 1127, 1135 (1994) (dissenting from denial of certiorari), cited in Dieter, *Death Penalty in Black and White*, 22.

29. *Death Penalty Legislation and the Racial Justice Act*, 115.

30. "Pat Robertson Says He'd Back Moratorium on Death Penalty," *The Idaho Statesman* (Apr. 8, 2000): 2A.

31. Jim Dwyer, Peter Neufeld, and Barry Scheck, *Actual Innocence: Five Days to Execution and Other Dispatches from the Wrongly Convicted* (New York: Doubleday, 2000), XV.

32. Death Penalty Information Center, "Innocence: Freed from Death Row," posting on DPIC website, Apr. 25, 2000.

33. Some of these stories can be found in Dwyer, *Actual Innocence*. Others appear in Michael L. Radelet, Hugo Adam Bedau, and Contance E. Putnam, *In Spite of Innocence: Erroneous Convictions in Capital Cases* (Boston: Northeastern Univ. Press, 1992). This book lists 416 wrongful convictions in twentieth-century capital cases in the United States.

34. Michael L. Radelet, Hugo Adam Bedau, and Contance E. Putnam, *In Spite of Innocence: Erroneous Convictions in Capital Cases*, listing 23 cases for which there is strong evidence of wrongful executions. Hanks, *Against the Death Penalty*, 118-22,

listing two additional wrongful executions. Because there is little reason to further investigate a case once the inmate has been executed, the number of wrongful executions listed in these sources is undoubtedly much lower than the actual number.

35. Henry Heller, "Viriginia's 21-Day Rule Shows Signs of Vulnerability," *NCADP Lifelines,* No. 83 (Jan.-Mar. 2000), 4.

36. Death Penalty Information Center, "Innocence: Freed from Death Row."

37. "Florida Makes Official Its Death Row Change [lethal injection and a speedy appeals process]," *The New York Times,* Jan. 15, 2000, A20(N), A18(L).

38. Dwyer, *Actual Innocence,* 218-9.

39. *Herrera v. Collins,* no. 91-7328, 52 Cr. L. Rpr. 3093 (1993).

40. Herbert J. Grossman, ed., *Classification in Mental Retardation* (Washington, D.C.: American Association on Mental Retardation, 1983), cited in "James W. Ellis as President of the American Association on Mental Retardation, Before the United States Senate Committee on the Judiciary, September 27, 1989."

41. James W. Ellis and Ruth W. Luckasson, "Mentally Retarded Criminal Defendants," *George Washington Law Review* 53 (1985): 414-92.

42. *Questions and Answers on the Mentally Retarded and the Death Penalty* (Washington, D.C.: National Coalition to Abolish the Death Penalty, 1990), 2; J. H. Blume, "Defending the Mentally Retarded Defendant," *The Champion* 32 (Nov. 1987): 34-8.

43. Naftali Bendavid, "Should More Money Be Devoted to Defending Death Row Inmates?" *The Idaho Statesman,* Aug. 23, 1997, 7A.

44. *About Traumatic Brain Injury* (Brooklyn, N.Y.: Brain Injury Society, 2000; cf. Brain Injury Society website).

45. Dorothy Otney Lewis et al., "Neuropsychiatric, Psychoeducational, and Family Characteristics of 14 Juveniles Condemned to Death in the United States," *American Journal of Psychiatry* 14/5 (May 1988): 584-9.

46. Fetal alcohol syndrome victims may suffer from many of the other traits of brain injury, plus aggressive sexual impulsiveness and an inability to accept responsibility for their own behavior. "Behavioral Symptoms of Adolescents with FAS/E Through the Eyes of Parents" (Lynwood, Wash.: Fetal Alcohol Syndrome Family Resource Institute, 1996; on-line: http://www.accessone.com/~delindam/index.html).

47. Otney, 587.

48. Otney, 588.

49. William A. Schabas, *The Abolition of the Death Penalty in International Law* (Cambridge, U.K.: Cambridge Univ. Press, 1997), 161-8.

50. Dieter, *International Perspectives*, 13.

51. John Laurence, *A History of Capital Punishment* (Port Washington, N.Y.: Kennikat, 1971), 18.

52. Schabas, 312.

53. Amnesty International, *International Standards*, 15.

54. Dieter, *International Perspectives*, 11.

55. Amnesty International, *Facts and Figures on the Death Penalty* (London: Amnesty International, 1999), 3.

56. Exceptions are the stories of Phinehas's killing of an Israelite man and a Midianite woman to stop a plague (Num. 25) and the killing of Achan in Joshua 7 to assure military success. Both are stories of human sacrifice to stop community catastrophes. The stories appear to be quite primitive, and they occur early in the history of the Israelites, before the courts and temple sacrifice were functional.

57. Occasionally, however, the community suffers because of the sins of its leaders. For example, in 2 Samuel 24:10-17, Israel suffers a plague because David has conducted a census. Though a census might seem to be necessary for conducting the business of the state, it showed David's lack of faith in Yahweh's ability to provide an adequate militia when needed. The plague was one of three options for the punishment. The other two were famine and temporary defeat in warfare. In the case of each punishment, the census numbers become meaningless because a large part of the population is destroyed.

58. Newport, "Support for Death Penalty Drops" (Introduction, note 1, above).

59. Mark Gillespie, "Public Opinion Supports Death Penalty" (Princeton, N.J.: The Gallup Organization, 1999; on-line).

60. Walter Wink posits that there is a "myth of redemptive violence" in which a hero must overcome a villain with super powers. To overcome the evil, the hero is nearly beaten and eventually must use the same violent methods as the villain. Wink finds this myth in the glorification of violence in American popular culture. He traces it back to the Babylonian creation myth of Marduk and Tiamat. Marduk murders the evil monster

Tiamat, whose corpse becomes the universe. Walter Wink, *Engaging the Powers: Discernment and Resistance in a World of Domination* (Minneapolis: Fortress, 1992), 13-31.

61. Based on personal knowledge of the author.

62. For a more detailed summary of arguments against deterrence, see Hanks, *Against the Death Penalty*, 70-7.

63. Hanks, *Against the Death Penalty*, 78-83.

64. In the 2000 Gallup Poll, only 8 percent of those who say they favor the death penalty say they support it because it is a deterrent to other crimes. Newport, "Support for Death Penalty Drops."

65. James W. Marquart, Sheldon Ekland-Olson, and Jonathan Sorensen, *The Rope, the Chair, and the Needle: Capital Punishment in Texas, 1923-1990* (Austin: The Univ. of Texas Press, 1994), 123-6, 182-4.

66. Quoted in Byron E. Eshelman and Frank Riley, *Death Row Chaplain* (Englewood Cliffs, N.J.: Prentice-Hall, 1962), 224-5.

67. Quoted in Richard Dieter, *Sentencing for Life: Americans Embrace Alternatives to the Death Penalty* (Washington, D.C.: The Death Penalty Information Center, 1993), 5.

68. Wink, *Engaging the Powers.*

5. The Life and Teachings of Jesus

1. Examples are Sarah (Gen. 18:1-15; 21:1-7), Rachel (Gen. 30:22-24), Hannah (1 Sam. 1:1-20), and Elizabeth (Luke 1:5-24, 57-58).

2. This is the only story in the New Testament depicting Jesus' behavior as a child. It is in contrast to stories left out of the canon. In the Infancy Gospel of Thomas, not in the New Testament but included in later, apocryphal writings, the child Jesus is portrayed as using his power to revenge himself on other children. Jesus withers a boy away for breaking up a small dam Jesus had created; another child is made to drop dead after he accidentally bumps into Jesus. These stories present a more-violent portrait of Jesus than appears in the New Testament. It is therefore reasonable to assume that the apostolic church deliberately excluded such later and violent stories from the canon, even when they depicted the power of Jesus, because they were false and did not match the Jesus known by the disciples. *The Complete Gospels: Annotated Scholars Version* (San Francisco: HarperSanFrancisco, 1994), 371-2.

3. Similar passages appear in Matthew 23:1-36 and Mark 12:38-40.

4. Walter Wink, *Engaging the Powers: Discernment and Resistance in a World of Domination* (Minneapolis: Fortress, 1992), 175-84.

5. See, e.g., Matt. 9:10-13; 11:19; Mark 2:15-17; Luke 5:27-32; 7:34; 15:1-2.

6. Under the law, an unmarried woman was considered the property of her father, and a married woman was the property of her husband. For example, the rape of an unattached woman is considered to be an offense against her father. The rapist is required to pay a fine to the father and marry the woman, whose marriage value has been sharply diminished (Deut. 22:28-29). If a pregnant woman loses her baby because she is injured when two men are fighting, it is considered an offense to the woman's husband. The fighters are required to pay a fine to him (Exod. 21:22).

7. There is evidence that the early Christians took this admonition to mean that they should not participate in the legal procedures of the government (1 Cor. 6:1-8). Also, the Christian apologist Tertullian stated that Christians could be judges only if they could avoid, among other things, "sitting in judgment on anyone's life or character" (see chap. 8).

8. Some manuscripts read "seventy times seven."

9. *Interpreter's Bible*, vol. 8 (Nashville: Abingdon, 1952), 591-3; *Layman's Bible Commentary*, vol. 19 (Richmond: John Knox, 1963), 75-6; William Barclay, *The Gospel of John*, vol. 2 (Philadelphia: Westminster, 1975), 290-2; Merrill C. Tenney, "John," *Expositor's Bible Commentary*, vol. 9 (Grand Rapids: Zondervan, 1981), 89-91; *New Interpreter's Bible*, vol. 9 (Nashville: Abingdon, 1995), 627-30; Robert W. Funk and the Jesus Seminar, *The Acts of Jesus* (San Francisco: HarperSanFrancisco, 1998), 397-9.

10. Barclay, *John*, 2:290-2; Funk, *Acts of Jesus*, 397-9; Bruce M. Metzger, *A Textual Commentary on the Greek New Testament* (New York: United Bible Societies, 1971), 219-22.

11. Barclay (2:2) suggests that another possible motive was to bring Jesus into conflict with the Romans by getting him to call for her execution. This contention is based on John 18:31, where Jewish leaders, referring to their desire to execute Jesus, tell Pilate, "We are not permitted to put people to death." Many

interpret the verse to mean that the Romans did not allow the Jews to execute any criminals. This restriction, however, is not mentioned in the synoptic Gospels, and the execution of Stephen in Acts 7:54-8:1 appears to refute this interpretation. Perhaps the leaders meant that they could not execute Jesus at that time because of the Passover restrictions; or they may have meant that they could not execute him for treason to Rome, which appears to be the reason they brought Jesus to Pilate. Hence, John 18:31 makes it more likely that the scribes and Pharisees expected Jesus to show compassion on the woman, which could be interpreted as a denial of God-given law.

12. Leviticus 20:10 and Deuteronomy 22:22 call for both the man and the woman to be executed in cases of adultery.

13. This is the only instance in the New Testament that shows Jesus writing. Barclay, *John*, 2:3 and Tenney, *Expositor's*, 9:90, suggest that Jesus was writing a list of sins of men in the crowd.

14. *New Interpreter's Bible*, 9:629: "Jesus' writing on the ground in v. 6b indicates his refusal to engage the question of vv. 4-5 as the scribes have posed it. The story gives no information about the content of what Jesus writes, because it is the act of writing itself that is important. Interpretations that attempt to supply the content of what Jesus writes miss the significance of Jesus' non-verbal response. In the Mediter-ranean world of Jesus' time, such an act of writing would have been recognized as an act of refusal and disengagement."

15. Wink, *Engaging the Powers*, 267.

16. In Matthew 12:31-32, Jesus states: "Therefore I tell you, people will be forgiven for every sin and blasphemy, but blasphemy against the Spirit will not be forgiven. Whoever speaks a word against the Son of Man will be forgiven, but whoever speaks against the Holy Spirit will not be forgiven, either in this world or the next." Commentators have many different thoughts about what blasphemy against the Holy Spirit entails. In my opinion, it is simply the continuing refusal to accept the love and forgiveness that God offers us. I do not believe that God forces himself on anyone. If we truly do not want him to be part of our lives, we can have what we want. For those of us who know what God's grace has done for us, this self-imposed separation for God can only be described as hell. However, God's offer is always open as he

continues to call his separated children and to seek their return, even if they continue to ignore him or run away from him.

17. Jacob Neusner, trans., *The Mishnah: A New Translation* (New Haven, Conn.: Yale Univ. Press, 1988), 612.

18. In the Schleitheim Confession, Michael Sattler wrote, "Now many, who do not understand Christ's will for us, ask: whether a Christian may or should use the sword against the wicked for the protection and defense of the good, and for the sake of love. The answer is unanimously revealed: Christ teaches and commands us to learn from him, for he is meek and lowly of heart and thus we shall find rest for our souls, Matthew 11:29. Now Christ says to the woman taken in adultery, John 8:11, not that she should be stoned according to the law of his Father (and yet he says, "what the Father commanded me, that I do," John 8:28) but with mercy and forgiveness and the warning to sin no more, says: "Go, sin no more." Quoted in Cornelius J. Dyck, *Spiritual Life in Anabaptism: Classic Devotional Resources* (Scottdale, Pa.: Herald Press, 1995), 109-10.

19. Lloyd R. Bailey, *Capital Punishment: What the Bible Says* (Nashville: Abingdon, 1987), 69-70.

20. Bailey, *Capital Punishment*, 70.

21. Bailey, *Capital Punishment*, 71-2.

22. Barclay, *John*, 2:2.

23. Michael Gagarin, *Early Greek Law* (Berkeley: Univ. of California Press, 1986), 133-6.

24. A. H. M. Jones, *The Criminal Courts of the Roman Republic and Principate* (Totowa, N.J.: Rowman and Littlefield, 1972), 77-8. See Jan Gorecki, *Capital Punishment: Criminal Law and Social Evolution* (New York: Columbia Univ. Press, 1983), 48.

25. St. Augustine, *The City of God* (New York: The Modern Library, 1950), 27.

26. *HarperCollins Study Bible* (New York: HarperCollins, 1993), 1987.

27. Raymond E. Brown, *The Death of the Messiah*, 2 vols. (New York: Doubleday, 1994), 1:699-700.

28. Gen. 1:27.

29. Some death-penalty proponents argue that Jesus' references to damnation and hell, along with two of his more-violent parables, show that, in fact, Jesus did support the death penalty. See, for instance, Dudley Sharp, "Death Penalty and Sentencing Information in the United States," Justice for All website (Oct. 1, 1997), "Section F: Christianity and the Death Penalty." The argument for the death penalty based on Jesus' references to eternal punishment, of course, does not recognize the difference between human judgment, limited at its best by human imperfections, and divine judgment, which is unlimited and perfect.

When humans refused to accept Yahweh's sovereignty and sought to "be like god" in making godlike judgments about what was right and wrong, they committed the first sin (Gen. 3:1-7). Thus, the story of the Fall warns people not to replace God's right to make ethical judgments about our fellow human beings with our own judgments. Hell and damnation, whatever else they might be, represent the fact that we can depend on God for ultimate and perfect justice; therefore, we do not have to seek it for ourselves. Hell may indeed be the eternal destination for those who do not wish to reside with God in his kingdom, but this is not our business to decide; it is God's.

The two parables mentioned by Sharp are found in Luke 19:11-27 and Luke 20:9-16. Luke 19:11-27 is the story of a nobleman who leaves his country to seek royal power, entrusting his servants with various sums of money. When the kingdom is given to him, he returns. The story discusses the activities of the servants, but it ends with the slaughter of the noblemen's enemies, who had opposed his receipt of the monarchy.

The parable is based on several actual events. Over the objections of Jewish leaders, Herod the Great went to Rome to receive royal authority over Judea. When he came back, he killed a number of his political opponents. A generation later, Herod's son Archelaus also traveled to Rome to receive his kingdom, again over the protests of many Jews. The Romans later deposed him for his excessive cruelty. After Jesus' death but before the writing of the Gospel of Luke, the same situation occurred a third time. Herod Antipas sought a kingship over the protests of Herod Agrippa. In this case, the protest was successful and Antipas was banished to Gaul.

Given Jesus' general attitude toward the Herods, we cannot

assume that he would have endorsed their killings of political enemies, which actually were extrajudicial murders rather than capital punishment. Unlike the similar parable in Matthew 25:14-30, this story does not focus on the activities of the servants but on the capriciousness of the nobleman. Jesus tells the parable just before entering Jerusalem, where his disciples expected him to establish a new, earthly kingdom, probably through a military revolution. Jesus uses this parable to show his opinion of the "rulers of this world," and to contrast the kingdom he will bring with the kingdoms headed by kings like the Herods (*New Interpreter's Bible*, 9:361-4).

Luke 20:9-16 is a parable told in the midst of conflicts with the chief priests and scribes. The story takes them to task for being unfaithful followers of God. It predicts both Jesus' crucifixion and the destruction of the Judean state. The leaders are compared to tenants of a vineyard who refuse to pay their landlord, and who beat up the messengers that the landlord sends to them. Their final act of treachery is the murder of the owner's beloved son. For this, it is predicted that they will be destroyed and that the vineyard will be given to someone else.

The Gospel of Luke was written after the destruction of Jerusalem in 70. This was an event so cataclysmic that it threatened the faith of the early Christians. Stories such as these were used to explain this historical event and to give it meaning within the early Christian faith. Some in the early church felt that the destruction of Jerusalem was a judgment on the Jews for not accepting Jesus as their Messiah; yet the second parable clearly leaves the judgment in God's hands (the vineyard owner, unlike the greedy nobleman, stands allegorically for God). Both parables thus recognize the need for judgment against the wicked: the first portrays the judgment of kings as tyrannical and motivated by greed; the second leaves righteous judgment to God. In neither case would these support capital punishment.

6. New Testament Executions

1. An excellent history of the church's teaching on the death penalty is James Megivern, *The Death Penalty: A Historical and Theological Survey* (New York: Paulist Press, 1997).

2. During this period of Roman history, there were two forms of legislatures. The first, called the Comitia Centuriata, controlled the military affairs of the state. In this capacity, it had

all the powers of a military commander, including the right to impose the death penalty. A second form of legislature, the Comitia Curiata or Comitia Tributa, controlled civilian life and was only allowed to impose fines as punishments. During this period of the late republic (first century B.C.), the civilian legislative body had almost exclusive control of the legislative function. Because this body did not have the right to impose the death penalty, the committees that it set up as courts to hear criminal cases also did not have the right to impose capital punishment. See Henry Sumner Maine, *Ancient Law: Its Connection with the Early History of Society and Its Relation to Modern Ideas* (1861; reprint, Newton Lower Falls, Mass.: Dorset Press, 1986), 322-3.

3. In 81 B.C. Sulla formally abolished the death penalty for murder, except in the case of parricide, and replaced it with exile. About twenty years later, Pompey removed parricide from the list of capital crimes. Jan Gorecki, *Capital Punishment: Criminal Law and Social Evolution* (New York: Columbia Univ. Press, 1983), 40-1.

4. Pilate's reluctance to crucify Jesus is reported in Matthew 27:18-23; Mark 15:9-15; Luke 23:13-25; and John 18:38—19:12. Pilate has a mixed reputation. The Jewish writer Philo, claiming to quote a letter from Herod Agrippa to the Emperor Caligula, describes Pilate's "briberies, insults, robberies, outrages, wanton injuries, constantly repeated executions without trial, ceaseless and supremely grievous cruelty." Raymond E. Brown, *The Death of the Messiah*, 2 vols. (New York: Doubleday, 1994), 1:697. In Luke 13:1-3, Jesus refers to a massacre on Pilate's orders of some Galileans who were struck down as they were offering sacrifices.

On the other hand, Pilate served for ten years (26-36) as the prefect of Judea, longer than any other prefect except Valerius Gratius, and during that period, his relationship with the high priest was remarkably stable (Brown, 1:694). In the incident of the iconic standards, Pilate was persuaded by a nonviolent protest of the Jews to forego violence and to yield to Jewish requests to remove images from his military standards when the standards were in Jerusalem (Brown, 1:698-9). All of this suggests that Pilate was a qualified colonial administrator who, like many colonial administrators, was sometimes insensitive to local customs and who probably made personal profits from his administrative duties. He was not averse to using violence when necessary, but was willing to solve problems in other ways if it was possible to do so without giving up Roman authority.

5. The official Jewish form of execution for blasphemy was stoning. The fact that Jesus was crucified shows that the Romans executed him for a crime against Rome.

6. Jeffery L. Sheller, "Why Did He Die?" *U.S. News and World Report* 128/6 (Apr. 24, 2000): 50-5.

7. The assumption that leaders of the Jewish temple were involved in the execution of Jesus does not mean that all Jews or even other Jewish leaders at that time bear the blame for Jesus' death. The argument being made here is that a few Jewish leaders at one particular point in history, primarily for political reasons that they felt to be quite legitimate, felt that Jesus was a danger to the Jewish nation. Although they conspired to have Jesus executed, it was the Roman governor Pilate who made the final decision and who must bear the ultimate responsibility.

8. See Matt. 16:21-23; 17:22-23; 20:17-19; 26:1-2; Mark 8:31; 9:31; 10:33-34; Luke 9:21-23; 9:44; 17:25; 18:31-33; John 12:27-36; 16:16-22.

9. See Matt. 16:24; 20:19; 26:1-2; Mark 10:33-34; Luke 9:23; 18:32-33; John 12:32-33.

10. Brown, *Death of the Messiah*, 1:357-63.

11. Jacob Neusner, trans., *The Mishnah: A New Translation* (New Haven, Conn.: Yale Univ. Press, 1988), 590; further Mishnah citations are from Neusner's translation.

12. Mishnah Sanhedrin 4.1: "Therefore they do not judge capital cases either on the eve of the Sabbath or the eve of the festival."

13. There is evidence that at this time in Jewish history, a Sanhedrin was merely a collection of prominent men called together by a ruler in a crisis situation. They were not required to follow formal procedures, and their primary purpose was to provide support for the status quo. Their decisions could be quite arbitrary and were not expected rigidly to follow biblical statute. Lloyd R. Bailey, *Capital Punishment: What the Bible Says* (Nashville: Abingdon, 1987), 57.

14. Brown, *Death of the Messiah*, 1:372.

15. John Howard Yoder, *The Politics of Jesus* (Grand Rapids: Eerdmans, 1972), 47.

16. See Neusner, *Mishnah*, 590. A few years later Peter was not executed soon after his arrest during Passover Week, presumably because of a prohibition on executions at that time. See Richard N. Longenecker, "Acts," *Expositor's Bible Commentary*, vol. 9 (Grand Rapids: Zondervan, 1981), 408.

17. "When someone is convicted of a crime punishable by death and is executed, and you hang him on a tree, his corpse must not remain all night upon the tree; you shall bury him that same day, for anyone hung on a tree is under God's curse" (Deut. 21:22-23). Second Samuel 21:1-14 shows the importance given to this curse in the Hebrew Scriptures. David is shamed by Rizpah because she protects the bodies of her sons left hanging after they are executed by the Gibeonites. It is only when David sees her love for her sons that he rescues and buries the bodies of Saul and Jonathan.

18. Brown, *Death of the Messiah*, 1:372.

19. *HarperCollins Study Bible* (New York: HarperCollins, 1993), 2049: "Opinions differ, but it is probable that the Romans did not permit the Jewish authorities to carry out death sentences in most cases." William Barclay, *The Gospel of John*, vol. 2 (Philadelphia: Westminster, 1975), 233, quotes the Talmud: "Forty years before the destruction of the Temple, judgment in matters of life and death was taken away from Israel." Barclay also gives evidence from Josephus that the Jewish courts did not have the right to impose the death penalty. However, Raymond E. Brown finds evidence that the Romans permitted the Jews to execute offenders for some religious crimes, and he also shows that the Jews sometimes executed offenders against the Jewish law without Roman permission. Brown, *Death of the Messiah*, 1:364-72.

20. Merrill C. Tenney, "John," *Expositor's Bible Commentary*, 9:177; *New Interpreter's Bible*, vol. 9 (Nashville: Abingdon, 1995), 820.

21. *Interpreter's Bible*, 9:448.

22. Brown, *Death of the Messiah*, 1:541.

23. Brown, *Death of the Messiah*, 1:533.

24. Jesus never stated that his followers should not pay taxes. When questioned about paying taxes, his answer is ambiguous (Matt. 22:15-22; Mark 12:18-27; Luke 20:20-26; see chap. 5, above).

25. Some commentators feel that the Evangelists tried to pla-

cate Roman animosity toward the early Christians by placing more blame on the Jews than the Romans for Jesus' execution, thus depicting Pilate as a reluctant participant in the execution. In my opinion, Pilate's reluctance may have been an attempt to get the temple leaders to share at least some of the blame for the execution, since its legality was questionable.

26. Pilate may have been the protégé of a powerful Roman noble named Sejanus, who for a time was second in command to Emperor Tiberius. Sejanus was found to be treasonous in 31 and fell from power. He died in October of that year. If Jesus' trial occurred after the fall of Sejanus, and Pilate was his protégé, an accusation of allowing an act of treason to go unpunished could have had serious, perhaps even deadly, consequences for Pilate. Brown, *Death of the Messiah,* 1:693.

27. *HarperCollins Study Bible,* 1949.

28. After describing a number of Roman amnesty traditions, Raymond E. Brown states: "The weaknesses of all these parallels are obvious, and one is left with the enduring doubt that Roman governors could ever have committed themselves to a custom that would require them to release a killer in the midst of a recent riot in a volatile province." Brown, *Death of the Messiah,* 1:817.

29. The marriage was considered incestuous, according to Leviticus 18:16; 20:21.

30. Longenecker, *Expositor's Bible Commentary,* 9:351.

31. In recent years the U.S. Supreme Court has undermined many of the protections the law has afforded defendants in capital cases by allowing evidence to be used even when it was collected by illegal means. The term they have coined for this practice is "harmless error."

32. The southern states of the United States have recorded both the most executions and the most lynchings.

33. This killing has normally been assumed to be an execution, and I will treat it as such here. However, the use of the term *machaira* in describing the killing indicates a short sword, used primarily as a symbol of authority by soldiers carrying out police duties; J. H. Yoder, *Politics of Jesus,* 206. The short sword would not have been particularly useful for beheading, the mode of execution for apostates. So it is possible that James was assassinated by Herod's soldiers, rather than executed through a judicial process. However, biblical experts believe that occa-

sionally *machaira* is used to mean a long sword, which could be the instrument of a beheading; W. Michaelis, *"Machaira,"* in *Theological Dictionary of the New Testament,* ed. G. Kittel, vol. 4 (Grand Rapids: Eerdmans, 1967), 524-7, esp. 525.

34. Longenecker, *Expositor's Bible Commentary,* 9:408. See also Mishnah Sanhedrin 9.1.

35. Longenecker, *Expositor's Bible Commentary,* 9:408.

36. William Barclay, *The Acts of the Apostles* (Philadelphia: Westminster, 1976), 94.

37. In 1992, for example, Bill Clinton, then a candidate for president, went home to Arkansas during the campaign to oversee the execution of Rickey Ray Rector, an inmate so brain damaged by a self-inflicted gunshot wound that his mental ability was that of a six-year-old child: after his execution, prison guards found that he had saved his last meal's dessert so he could eat it later. At the time Clinton was in the midst of the Jennifer Flowers scandal, so the execution allowed him to show his tough stance on crime and to divert attention from his personal problems. The Rector execution was a political boon for Clinton, who went on to be elected president. Marshall Frady, "Death in Arkansas," *The New Yorker,* Feb. 22, 1993, 105-33.

7. Atonement and the Powers

1. 1 Cor. 1:25; this passage is discussed more fully below.

2. Modern New Testament scholars generally agree that the pastoral letters were probably not directly from Paul but by others who wrote them as a continuation of the Pauline tradition. See *HarperCollins Study Bible* (New York: HarperCollins, 1993), 2229.

3. Because of our sins, we deserve to be separated from God, but through God's grace, he makes it possible for us to reconnect with him. In 1 Corinthians 6:9-11, Paul lists a number of offenses against God, some of which were capital crimes under the Mosaic Law. But then Paul shows that these are forgiven through the sacrifice of Christ. "Do you not know that wrongdoers will not inherit the kingdom of God? Do not be deceived! Fornicators, idolaters, adulterers, male prostitutes, sodomites, thieves, the greedy, drunkards, revilers, robbers—none of these will inherit the kingdom of God. And this is what some of you used to be. But you were washed, you were sanctified, you were

justified in the name of the Lord Jesus Christ and in the Spirit of our God."

4. I learned the power of Romans 5:6-11 in my work as spiritual adviser for a death-row inmate who had committed a terrible murder. At our first meeting, he asked me whether God could ever forgive him. I remembered this passage, which is one of my favorites, and we read it together. Although we had to work on this issue for several more months, I could see that the passage had made a real impact on his thinking about God's forgiveness for him.

5. See Eva Fogelman, *Conscience and Courage: Rescuers of Jews During the Holocaust* (New York, Anchor Books, 1994).

6. Walter Wink. *Engaging the Powers* (Minneapolis: Fortress, 1992), 271-7.

7. Mennonite Board of Missions, *Beyond the News: Murder Close Up*, a videotape (Harrisonburg, Va.: Mennonite Media Ministries, 1995). Cf. the title of John Paul Lederach's book *The Journey Toward Reconciliation* (Scottdale, Pa.: Herald Press, 1999).

8. The story of Bill Pelke is especially instructive in this regard. Bill's grandmother was brutally murdered by a gang of teenage girls who came to her house ostensibly for a Bible lesson, but in reality to rob her. Like other members of Bill's family, he hated the girls when he first heard of the crime and for some time afterward. But then one day at work, while he was thinking of his grandmother, he realized that because of her strong Christian faith, she would not have hated her murderers. This changed Bill's whole perspective on the crime and on capital punishment.

Bill began to correspond with one of the girls, who was in prison. He also became an internationally known spokesman against the death penalty. His story has been documented in many places, including the videotape *Murder Close Up*, but I heard it from him directly when he visited Boise, Idaho, when Keith Wells was executed on January 6, 1994.

9. One of Paul's great struggles was to free the church from its dependence on the law and the legalism caused by such dependence; see, for example, Galatians 2–3.

10. In 1 Corinthians 5:1-5, Paul advises the church at Corinth to excommunicate a member who is engaged in sexual immorality. The purpose, however, is so that "his spirit may be saved in the day of the Lord." Second Corinthians 2:5-11 may show the

aftermath of this punishment, as an unnamed sinner is taken back into the congregation, forgiven, and consoled.

11. *HarperCollins Study Bible*, 2250-1.

12. *HarperCollins Study Bible*, 2293.

13. An important early book on the subject is Hendrik Berkhof, *Christ and the Powers* (1953 in Dutch; Scottdale, Pa.: Herald Press, 1962, 1977). Walter Wink has published a trilogy, The Powers Series (1984-92), and other books on the same subject; see the bibliography. Cf. Thomas R. Yoder Neufeld, *Ephesians*, Believers Church Bible Commentary (Scottdale, Pa.: Herald Press, 2001), notes on Eph. 6:10-17, and essays on the powers.

14. Colossians 1:15-16: "He [Christ] is the image of the invisible God, the firstborn of all creation; for in him all things in heaven and on earth were created, things visible and invisible, whether thrones or dominions or rulers or powers—all things have been created through him and for him."

15. I have become acutely aware of the powers twice in my life. Once was when I tried to understand the nuclear arms race. Although virtually everyone agreed that the arms race was disastrous, none of the nations involved has been willing to give it up. I came to the conclusion that the stubborn continuation along a path known to lead to disaster was actually the work of a spirit of fear, which had completely overridden the common-sense solution of stopping and negotiating for a peaceful resolution.

The second time was when I first entered a prison. I was overwhelmed by the spirit of evil in the place—not just the evil of the criminals housed there, but the evil of a violent system designed solely to intimidate and punish, rather than to restore. In both of these cases, I came to the conclusion that simple human reason was not enough to change these institutions. They had to be changed on a much deeper spiritual level.

16. In Romans 8:38, Paul portrays the powers and principalities as impediments between humans and God, barriers that Christ overcomes: "For I am convinced that neither death, nor life, nor angels, nor rulers, nor things present, nor things to come, nor powers, nor height, nor depth, nor anything else in all creation, will be able to separate us from the love of God in Christ Jesus, our Lord." Cf. Berkhof, *Christ and the Powers*, 30-3.

17. Berkhof, *Christ and the Powers*, 37-9; cf. 1 Cor. 2:8; Col. 2:13-15.

18. Berkhof and Wink both believe that the Greek word *katargein* (1 Cor. 15:24, 26) should not be translated "destroyed," as in NRSV. Berkhof, *Christ and the Powers*, 39-43, suggests that the powers are to be "dethroned." Wink, *Engaging the Powers*, 70, 83, 349-50, expects them to be "neutralized," in "subjugation . . . under Christ's feet." *Revised English Bible* says "deposed."

19. John Howard Yoder, *The Politics of Jesus* (Grand Rapids: Eerdmans, 1972), 206. See also Everett F. Harrison, "Romans," *Expositor's Bible Commentary*, vol. 10 (Grand Rapids: Zondervan, 1984), 138-9.

20. *HarperCollins Study Bible*, 2114-5.

21. *HarperCollins Study Bible*, 2114; cf. Acts 18:2.

22. Titus 3:1 exhorts, "Remind them to be subject to rulers and authorities, to be obedient, to be ready for every good work."

23. First Peter 2:13-17 counsels, "For the Lord's sake accept the authority of every human institution, whether of the emperor as supreme, or the governors, as sent by him to punish those who do wrong and to praise those who do right. For it is God's will that by doing right you should silence the ignorance of the foolish. As servants of God, live as free people, yet do not use your freedom as a pretext for evil. Honor everyone. Love the family of believers. Fear God. Honor the emperor."

24. *HarperCollins Study Bible*, 2325.

25. *HarperCollins Study Bible*, 2325.

26. *HarperCollins Study Bible*, 2325.

27. This apparently refers to Nero. *HarperCollins Study Bible*, 2325.

28. The mark on the right hand or forehead may be a symbol of oaths likely required by the Romans for those engaging in certain kinds of commerce.

29. Harrison, *Expositor's Bible Commentary*, 10:138-9: "So it is probable that Paul is warning believers against becoming involved in activity that could be construed by the Roman government as encouraging revolution or injury to the state. In that case, he is not referring to crime in general. To engage in subversive activity would invite speedy retribution, as the word *sword* implies."

30. Neil Elliott, *Liberating Paul: The Justice of God and the Politics of the Apostle* (Maryknoll, N.Y.: Orbis Books, 1994), 217-26. Elliott makes the case that with this letter Paul was not responding to a specific event, but to a general feeling of hostility toward the Roman government coming from Jewish members of the church at Rome. If they had impulsively acted on this belligerent mood, they would have endangered the church. Hence, Paul cautions the Christians at Rome to submit to the government's authority whenever possible.

This is not a blanket endorsement of governmental deeds, however. Thus Elliott states, "That the authorities are made 'servants of God' (Rom. 13:4) no more implies divine approval of their actions than do the biblical affirmations that Assyria is 'the rod of God's anger' (Isa. 10:5), for the king of Assyria will be 'punished for his haughty pride' (10:20); or that Nebuchadnezzar of Babylon is 'God's servant' (Jer. 27:6), at least 'until the time of his own land comes' [when 'many nations . . . shall make him their slave'] (27:7)."

On these issues, see John H. Yoder, *The Christian Witness to the State* (1964; Scottdale, Pa.: Herald Press, 2001).

31. According to tradition, Paul was likely executed during Nero's reign (54-68); cf. Acts 20:22-24; 21:11, 13; 2 Tim. 4:6-8; Eusebius, *Ecclesiastical History* 3.1-2.

32. Roland H. Bainton, *Christian Attitudes Toward War and Peace* (Nashville: Abingdon, 1960), 67-8.

33. Yoder, *Politics of Jesus*, 205.

8. Early Church Fathers Interpreting the Bible

1. Michael W. Holmes, ed. and rev., *The Apostolic Fathers*, updated ed. (Grand Rapids: Baker Books, 1999), 247.

2. The Didache 1–6, in Holmes, *Apostolic Fathers.*

3. Ignatius, To the Ephesians 10, in Holmes, *Apostolic Fathers.*

4. Another letter, purported to be from Ignatius to the church at Antioch, tells believers not to murder, thus implying that they could not take part in warfare or capital punishment. This spurious letter was added to the Epistles of Ignatious in the fourth century and yet reflects teaching common in the early church. To the Antiochians 11, in *The Ante-Nicene Fathers (ANF)*, ed. A. Roberts and J. Donaldson (1885-87, 1897; reprint, Grand Rapids: Eerdmans, 1973-77), 1:111-2.

5. Justin Martyr, *The First Apology of Justin* 12, in *ANF,* 1:166.

6. Roland Bainton, *Christian Attitudes Toward War and Peace* (Nashville: Abingdon, 1960), 67-8.

7. Bainton, *Christian Attitudes,* 70-4.

8. Tatian, *Address to the Greeks* 23, in *ANF,* 2:75.

9. Theophilus, *To Autolycus* 3.15, in *ANF,* 2:115.

10. Athenagoras, *A Plea for the Christians* 11, in *ANF,* 2:134.

11. Athenagoras, *A Plea for Christians* 35, in *ANF,* 2:147.

12. Minucius Felix, *The Octavius* 25, in *ANF,* 4:188.

13. Minucius Felix, *The Octavius* 30, in *ANF,* 4:192.

14. Tertullian, *Apology* 37, in *ANF,* 3:45.

15. Tertullian, *On Idolatry* 17, in *ANF,* 3:72.

16. Tertullian, *On Idolatry* 11, in *ANF,* 3:67.

17. Tertullian, *On Idolatry* 19, in *ANF,* 3:73.

18. Tertullian, *The Chaplet* 11, in *The Fathers of the Church: A New Translation,* vol. 40, trans. R. Abresmann, Sister E. J. Daly, and E. A. Quain (Washington, D.C.: Catholic Univ. of America Press, 1959), 255-6; cf. *ANF,* 3:99.

19. Tertullian, *The Chaplet* 11, in *ANF,* 3:99-100.

20. C. John Cadoux, *The Early Christian Attitude to War: A Contribution to the History of Christian Ethics* (1919; reprint, New York: Seabury, 1982), 118-9.

21. Hippolytus, *Apostolic Tradition,* quoted in James J. Megivern, *The Death Penalty: A Historical and Theological Survey* (New York: Paulist Press, 1997), 27; this text was regarded as lost until (in 1910 and 1916) it was identified in the Latin text of the so-called Egyptian Church Order.

22. Bainton, *Christian Attitudes,* 79-80.

23. Clement of Alexandria, *The Stromata* 1.27, in *ANF,* 2:339.

24. Clement, *Stromata* 1.27, in *ANF,* 2:339.

25. The chapter begins, "Let no one, then, run down [the Mosaic] law, as if, on account of the penalty, it were not beautiful and good." Clement, *Stromata* 1.27, in *ANF,* 2:339. The immediately preceding chapters (*Stromata,* 2.25-26, in *ANF,* 2:338-9) show that Clement is referring to the Mosaic Law.

26. Clement, *Stromata* 4.8, in *ANF,* 2:420; Bainton, *Christian Attitudes,* 72-3.

27. Clement, *Stromata* 7.11, in *ANF,* 2:540.

28. Clement, *Stromata* 7.14, in *ANF,* 2:548.

29. Clement, "Maximus, Sermon 55," fragment via Antonius Melissa, in *ANF,* 2:581.

30. "Introductory Note," in *ANF,* 4:233.

31. Origen, *Against Celsus* 8.75, in *ANF,* 4:668.

32. Origen, *Against Celsus* 8.73, in *ANF,* 4:668.

33. Origen, *Against Celsus* 7.26, in *ANF,* 4:621.

34. Cyprian, "Epistle to Donatus" 6, in *The Fathers of the Church,* vol. 36: *St. Cyprian Treatises,* ed. Roy J. Deferrari (Washington, D.C.: Catholic Univ. of America Press, 1958), 12; cf. *ANF,* 5:277.

35. Cyprian, "To Donatus" 7, in *Fathers of the Church,* 36:12; cf. *ANF,* 5:277.

36. Cyprian, "Epistle (LVI.2) to Cornelius," *ANF,* 5:351; quoted in Megivern, *Death Penalty,* 24.

37. Arnobius, *Against the Heathen* 1.6, quoted in Bainton, *Christian Attitudes,* 73; cf. *ANF,* 6:415.

38. Lactantius, *The Divine Institutes* 6.20, in *ANF,* 7:187.

39. Lactantius, *Treatise on the Anger of God* 18, in *ANF,* 7:273.

40. Lactantius, *On the Anger of God* 20, in *ANF,* 7:276-7.

41. For example, as late as 295 a youth named Maximilianus was martyred for refusing to be conscripted into the military. Peter Mayer, ed., *The Pacifist Conscience* (Chicago: Henry Regnery Co., 1967), 328-9.

42. Cited by Gustave Combès, *La Doctrine politique de saint Augustin* (Paris: Librairie Plon, 1927); quoted in Megivern, *Death Penalty,* 38.

43. Letter no. 134, St. Augustine, Letters, vol. 3 (nos. 131-164), trans. Sr. W. Parsons (New York: FOTC, 1953), 10f.; quoted in Megivern, *Death Penalty,* 44.

Bibliography

About Traumatic Brain Injury. Brooklyn, N.Y.: Brain Injury Society, 2000. Cf. Brain Injury Society website.

American Friends Service Committee. *The Death Penalty: The Religious Community Calls for Abolition.* Philadelphia: American Friends Service Committee, 1998.

Amnesty International. *The Death Penalty List of Abolitionist and Retentionist Countries* (as Apr. 1, 1999). www.amnesty usa.org/abolish/abret.html.

_____. *Facts and Figures on the Death Penalty.* London: Amnesty International, 2000.

_____. *International Standards on the Death Penalty.* London: Amnesty International, 1998.

Anati, Emmanuel. *Palestine Before the Hebrews: A History, from the Earliest Arrival of Man to the Conquest of Canaan.* New York: Alfred A Knopf, 1963.

Anderson, Bernhard W. *Understanding the Old Testament.* 3d ed. Englewood Cliffs, N.J.: Prentice-Hall, 1975.

ANF. The Ante-Nicene Fathers. Ed. Alexander Roberts and James Donaldson. 10 vols. 1885-87, 1897; reprint, Grand Rapids: Eerdmans, 1973-77.

Ashby, Godfrey. *Go Out and Meet God: A Commentary on the Book of Exodus.* Grand Rapids: Eerdmans, 1998.

Athenagoras. *A Plea for the Christians.* In *ANF*, vol. 2.

Augustine. *The City of God.* New York: The Modern Library, 1950.

Bailey, Lloyd R. *Capital Punishment: What the Bible Says.* Nashville: Abingdon, 1987.

Bainton, Roland H. *Christian Attitudes Toward War and Peace*. Nashville: Abingdon, 1960.

Bainton, Roland H. *Early Christianity*. Malabar, Fla.: Robert E. Krieger Pub. Co., 1960.

Barclay, William. *The Gospel of John*. Vol. 2. Philadelphia: Westminster, 1975.

Banstra, Barry L. *Reading the Old Testament: An Introduction to the Hebrew Bible*. Belmont, Calif.: Wadsworth, Pub. Co., 1995.

"Behavioral Symptoms of Adolescents with FAS/E Through the Eyes of Parents." Lynwood, Wash.: Fetal Alcohol Syndrome Family Resource Institute, 1996. www.accessone.com/~delindam /index.html.

Berkhof, Hendrik. *Christ and the Powers*. Scottdale, Pa.: Herald Press, 1962, 2001.

Black-Michaud, Jacob. *Cohesive Force: Feud in the Mediterranean and the Middle East*. New York: St. Martin's Press, 1975.

Bendavid, Naftali. "Should More Money Be Devoted to Defending Death Row Inmates?" *The Idaho Statesman*, Aug. 23, 1997, 7A.

Blume, J. H. "Defending the Mentally Retarded Defendant." *The Champion* 32 (Nov., 1987): 34-8.

Boadt, Lawrence. *Reading the Old Testament: An Introduction*. New York: Paulist Press, 1984.

Bright, John. *A History of Israel*. 2d ed. Philadelphia: Westminster, 1972.

Bright, Stephen B. "Counsel for the Poor: The Death Sentence Not for the Worst Crime but for the Worst Lawyer." *Yale Law Journal* 103 (1994): 1835-83.

Brown, Raymond E. *The Death of the Messiah*. 2 vols. with continuous pagination. New York: Doubleday, 1994.

Cadoux, C. John. *The Early Christian Attitude to War: A Contribution to the History of Christian Ethics*. 1919. Reprint, New York: Seabury Press, 1982.

Centerwall, Brandon S. "Race, Socioeconomic Status, and Domestic Homicide." *JAMA, The Journal of the American Medical Association* 273/22 (June 14, 1995): 1755 (4).

Clement of Alexandria. *The Stromata*, or *Miscellanies*. In *ANF*, vol. 2.

"Conservatives Rethink Death Penalty." *Christianity Today* 42/4 (Apr. 6, 1998): 19.

Cyprian. "Epistle to Donatus." In *The Fathers of the Church.* Vol. 36: *St. Cyprian Treatises.* Ed. Roy J. Deferrari. Washington, D.C.: The Catholic Univ. of America Press, 1958.

Davis, Nigel. *Human Sacrifice in History and Today.* New York: William Morrow and Co., 1981.

Day, John. *Molech: A God of Human Sacrifice in the Old* Testament. New York: Cambridge Univ. Press, 1989.

Death Penalty Information Center. www.essential.org/dpic/.

_____. "Innocence: Freed from Death Row." www.essential.org/dpic/Innocentlist.html, Apr. 25, 2000.

Death Penalty Legislation and the Racial Justice Act: Hearings Before the Subcommittee on Civil and Constitutional Rights of the Committee of the Judiciary House of Representatives, 101st Congress, Second Session, on H.R. 4618: Racial Justice Act of 1990. Washington, D.C.: U.S. Government Printing Office, 1991.

"Debate over the Electric Chair," *Current Events* 99/14 (Dec 17, 1999): 3.

Didache, The. In *The Apostolic Fathers*, updated ed. Ed. and rev. Michael W. Holmes. Grand Rapids: Baker Books, 1999.

Dieter, Richard C. *The Death Penalty in Black and White: Who Lives, Who Dies, Who Decides.* Washington, D.C.: Death Penalty Information Center, 1998.

_____. *International Perspectives on the Death Penalty: A Costly Isolation for the U.S.* Washington, D.C.: Death Penalty Information Center, 1999.

_____. *Sentencing for Life: Americans Embrace Alternatives to the Death Penalty.* Washington, D.C.: The Death Penalty Information Center, 1993.

Driver, John. *Radical Faith: An Alternative History of the Christian Church.* Kitchener, Ont.: Pandora Press; and Scottdale, Pa.: Herald Press; 1999.

Dwyer, Jim, Peter Neufeld, and Barry Scheck. *Actual Innocence; Five Days to Execution and Other Dispatches from the Wrongly Convicted.* New York: Doubleday, 2000.

Dyck, Cornelius J., ed. *Spiritual Life in Anabaptism: Classic Devotional Resources.* Scottdale, Pa.: Herald Press, 1995.

Edwards, Chilperic. *The Hammurabi Code and the Sinaitic Legislation with a Complete Translation of the Great Babylonian Inscription Discovered at Susa.* 1904; reprint, Port Washington, N.Y.: Kennikat Press, 1971.

Elliott, Neil. *Liberating Paul: The Justice of God and the Politics of the Apostle.* Maryknoll, N.Y.: Orbis Books, 1994.

Ellis, James W. "James W. Ellis as President of the American Association on Mental Retardation, Before the United States Senate Committee on the Judiciary, September 27, 1989."

Ellis, James W., and Ruth W. Luckasson. "Mentally Retarded Criminal Defendants." *George Washington Law Review* 53 (1985): 414-92.

Eshelman, Byron E., and Riley, Frank. *Death Row Chaplain.* Englewood Cliffs, N.J.: Prentice-Hall, 1962.

"Florida Makes Official Its Death Row Change [lethal injection and a speedy appeals process]." *The New York Times,* Jan. 15, 2000, A20(N) A18(L).

Fogelman, Eva. *Conscience and Courage: Rescuers of Jews During the Holocaust.* New York: Anchor Books, 1994.

Frady, Marshall. "Death in Arkansas." *The New Yorker,* Feb. 22, 1993, 105-33.

Funk, Robert W., and the Jesus Seminar. *The Acts of Jesus.* San Francisco, Calif.: HarperSanFrancisco, 1998.

Gallup, George Jr. *The Gallup Poll 1991.* Wilmington, Del.: Scholarly Resources, 1992.

Gorecki, Jan. *Capital Punishment: Criminal Law and Social Evolution.* New York: Columbia Univ. Press, 1983.

Gillespie, Mark. *Public Opinion Supports Death Penalty.* Princeton, N.J.: The Gallup Organization, 1999. www.gallup.com/poll/ releases/pr990224.asp.

Ginat, Joseph. *Blood Disputes Among Bedouin and Rural Arabs in Israel: Revenge, Mediation, Outcasting and Honor.* Pittsburgh: Univ. of Pittsburgh Press, 1987.

Girard, René. *The Girard Reader.* Ed. James G. Williams. New York: Crossroad Pub. Co., 1996.

Gorecki, Jan. *Capital Punishment: Criminal Law and Social Evolution.* New York: Columbia Univ. Press, 1983.

Gray, John. *The Canaanites.* New York: Frederick A. Praeger, 1964.

Grossman, Herbert J., ed. *Classification in Mental Retardation.* Washington, D.C.: American Association on Mental Retardation, 1983.

Hamerton-Kelly, Robert. ed. *Violent Origins: Walter Burkhert, René Girard, and Jonathan Z. Smith on Ritual Killing and Cultural Formation.* Stanford, Calif.: Stanford Univ. Press, 1987.

Hanks, Gardner C. *Against the Death Penalty: Christian and Secular Arguments Against Capital Punishment.* Scottdale, Pa.: Herald Press, 1997.

HarperCollins Study Bible, The: New Revised Standard Version. New York: HarperCollins, 1993.

Harrison, Everett F. "Romans." In *The Expositor's Bible Commentary.* Vol. 10. Grand Rapids: Zondervan, 1984.

Heller, Henry. "Virginia 21-Day Rule Shows Signs of Vulnerability." *NCADP Lifelines,* no. 83 (Jan.-Mar. 2000), 4.

Herrera v. Collins. No. 91-7328, 52. Cr. L. Rpr. 3093. 1993.

Hornus, Jean-Michel. *It Is Not Lawful for Me to Fight: Early Christian Attitudes Toward War, Violence, and the State.* Scottdale, Pa.: Herald Press, 1980. Reprint, Wipf & Stock.

Ignatius. "The Second Epistle to the Ephesians." In *ANF,* vol. 1.

Ignatius, Pseudo. "To the Antiochians." In *ANF,* vol. 1.

The Interpreter's Bible. 12 vols. Nashville, Abingdon, 1952-57.

John Paul II. Mass in St. Louis, Missouri. Jan. 27, 1999.

John Paul II. *Evangelium Vitae.* Mar. 25, 1995.

Jones, A. H. M. *The Criminal Courts of the Roman Republic and Principate.* Totowa, N.J.: Rowman and Littlefield, 1972.

Jorns, Auguste. *The Quakers as Pioneers in Social Work.* Port Washington, N.Y.: Kennikat Press, 1969.

Justin Martyr. *The First Apology.* In *ANF,* vol. 1.

Kantz, Matt. "Moratorium on Executions Vetoed." *National Catholic Reporter* 35/32 (June 4, 1999): 8.

Keiser, Lincoln. *Friend by Day, Enemy by Night: Organized Violence in a Kohistani Community.* Fort Worth: Holt, Rinehart and Winston, 1991.

Lactantius. *The Divine Institutes.* In *ANF,* vol. 7.

Laurence, John. *A History of Capital Punishment.* Port Washington, N.Y.: Kennikat Press, 1971.

Layman's Bible Commentary, The. Vol. 19. Richmond: John Knox, 1963.

Lewis, Dorothy Otney, et al., "Neuropsychiatric, Psychoeducational, and Family Characteristics of 14 Juveniles Condemned to Death in the United States." *American Journal of Psychiatry* 14/5 (May 1988): 584-9.

Longenecker, Richard N. "Acts." In *The Expositor's Bible Commentary.* Vol. 9. Grand Rapids: Zondervan, 1981.

Maine, Henry Sumner. *Ancient Law: Its Connection with the Early History of Society and Its Relation to Modern Ideas.* 1861. Reprint, Newton Lower Falls, Mass.: Dorset Press, 1986.

Marquart, James W., Sheldon Ekland-Olson, and Jonathan Sorensen. *The Rope, The Chair, and the Needle: Capital Punishment in Texas, 1923-1990.* Austin: Univ. of Texas Press, 1994.

Marshall, Christopher D. *Beyond Retribution: A New Testament Vision for Justice, Crime, and Punishment.* Grand Rapids: Eerdmans, 2001.

_____. *Crowned with Glory and Honor: The Bible and Human Rights.* Telford, Pa.: Pandora Press U.S.; Scottdale, Pa.: Herald Press, 2002.

Mayer, Peter, ed. *The Pacifist Conscience.* Chicago: Henry Regnery Co., 1967.

McNeill, John T. "Asceticism Versus Militarism in the Middle Ages." *Church History* 5 (Mar. 1936): 3-28.

Megivern, James. *The Death Penalty: A Historical and Theological Survey.* New York: Paulist Press, 1997.

Melton, J. Gordon. ed. *The Churches Speak on Capital Punishment: Official Statements from Religious Bodies and Ecumenical Organizations.* Detroit: Gale Research, 1989.

Mennonite Board of Missions. *Beyond the News: Murder Close Up.* Videotape. Harrisonburg, Va.: Mennonite Media Ministries, 1995.

Minucius Felix. *The Octavius.* In *ANF,* vol. 4.

Neusner, Jacob, trans. *The Mishnah: A New Translation.* New Haven, Conn.: Yale Univ. Press, 1988.

The New Interpreter's Bible. 12 vols. Nashville: Abingdon, 1994-2002.

Newport, Frank. *Support for the Death Penalty Drops to Lowest Level in 19 Years, Although Still High at 66%.* Princeton, N.J.: Gallup News Service. www.gallup.com/releases/pr000224.asp.

Origen. *Against Celsus.* In *ANF,* vol. 4.

"Prison." *The Encyclopedia Americana.* Vol. 22. Danbury, Conn.: Grolier Inc., 1998.

"Pat Robertson Says He'd Back Moratorium on Death Penalty." *The Idaho Statesman,* Apr. 8, 2000, 2A.

Peters, Emrys. "Some Structural Aspects of the Feud Among the Camel Herding Bedouin of Cyrenaica." *Africa* 37/3 (July 1967).

Questions and Answers on the Mentally Retarded and the Death Penalty. Washington, D.C.: National Coalition to Abolish the Death Penalty, 1990.

Radelet, Michael L., Hugo Adam Bedau, and Contance E. Putnam. *In Spite of Innocence: Erroneous Convictions in Capital Cases.* Boston: Northeastern Univ. Press, 1992.

Redekop, Vernon W. *A Life for a Life? The Death Penalty on Trial.* Scottdale, Pa.: Herald Press, 1990.

Robinson, Charles Alexander. *Ancient History from Prehistoric Times to the Death of Justinian.* New York: Macmillan, 1966.

Schabas, William A. *The Abolition of the Death Penalty in International Law.* Cambridge, U.K.: Cambridge Univ. Press, 1997.

Schwager, Raymund. *Must There Be Scapegoats? Violence and Redemption in the Bible.* San Francisco: Harper & Row, 1987.

Sharp, Dudley. "Death Penalty and Sentencing Information in the United States." "Section F: Christianity and the Death Penalty." Oct. 1, 1997. www.prodeathpenalty.com/dp.html.

Sheller, Jeffery L. "Why Did He Die?" *U.S. News and World Report* 128/6 (Apr. 24, 2000): 50-5.

Starr, Chester. *A History of the Ancient World.* New York: Oxford Univ. Press, 1965.

Steinhalz, Adin. *The Essential Talmud.* Trans. Chaya Galai. New York: Basic Books, 1976.

Stephen, Andrew. "In Florida the Killing Is Just Electric!" *New Statesman* 129/4468 (Jan. 10, 2000): 20.

Swartley, Willard M., ed. *Violence Renounced: René Girard, Biblical Studies, and Peacemaking.* Telford, Pa.: Pandora Press U.S.; Scottdale, Pa.: Herald Press, 2000.

Tatian. *Address to the Greeks.* In *ANF,* vol. 2.

Taylor, Stuart, Jr. "The Death Penalty: To Err Is Human [moratorium by Gov. George Ryan of Illinois]." *National Reporter* 20/7 (Feb. 12, 2000): 450.

Tenney, Merrill C. "John." In *The Expositor's Bible Commentary.* Vol. 9. Grand Rapids: Zondervan, 1981.

Tertullian. *Apology.* In *ANF,* vol. 3.

_____. *The Chaplet,* or *De Corona.* In *ANF,* vol. 3.

_____. *The Chaplet.* In *The Fathers of the Church: A New Translation.* Vol. 40: *Disciplinary, Moral and Ascetical Works.* Trans. Rudolph Abresmann, Sister Emily Joseph Daly, and Edwin A. Quain. Washington, D.C.: Catholic Univ. of America Press, 1959.

_____. *On Idolatry.* In *ANF,* vol. 3.

Theophilus. *Theophilus to Autolycus.* In *ANF,* vol. 2.

"Tucker Death Exposes System Without Mercy." *National Catholic Reporter* 34/16 (Feb. 20, 1998): 28.

Van Braght, Thieleman J. *The Bloody Theater or Martyrs Mirror of the Defenseless Christians.* Dutch original, 1660. 3d English ed., Scottdale, Pa.: Herald Press, 1938. Reprint, 1987.

Volf, Miroslav. "Faith Matters: A Letter to Timothy." *Christian Century,* May 9, 2001, 24.

Wakefield, Walter, and Austin P. Evans. *Heresies of the High Middle Ages: Selected Sources Translated and Annotated.* New York: Columbia Univ. Press, 1969.

Walker, Sam. "ABA Vote May Be First Volley in Battle to Check Executions." *Christian Science Monitor* 89/49 (Feb. 5, 1997).

Wesely, Scott. "As Otey Executed, 'All Our Souls Are Diminished.'" *Nebraskans Against the Death Penalty Newsletter,* Sept. 1992, 1.

Westermark, Edward. *The Origin and Development of Moral Ideas.* London: Macmillan, 1906.

Wink, Walter. The Powers Series. 1: *Naming the Powers: The Language of Power in the New Testament.* 2: *Unmasking the Powers: The Invisible Forces That Determine Human Existence.* 3: *Engaging the Powers: Discernment and Resistance in a World of Domination.* Philadelphia/Minneapolis: Fortress, 1984-92.

_____. *The Powers That Be: Theology for a New Millennium.* New York, Doubleday Books, 1999.

_____. *When the Powers Fall: Reconciliation in the Healing of Nations.* Minneapolis: Fortress, 1998.

Yoder, John Howard. *Christian Attitudes to War, Peace and Revolution: A Companion to Bainton.* Elkhart, Ind., 1983. Reprint, Cokesbury Bookstore.

_____. *The Christian Witness to the State.* 1964; Scottdale, Pa.: Herald Press, 2001.

_____. *The Original Revolution.* Scottdale, Pa.: Herald Press, 1971. Reprint, Eugene, Ore.. Wipf & Stock, 1998.

_____. *The Politics of Jesus.* Grand Rapids: Eerdmans, 1972. 2d ed., 1994.

Young, Robert L. "Religious Orientation, Race and Support for the Death Penalty." *Journal for the Scientific Study of Religion* 31/1 (Mar. 1992): 76-87.

Zehr, Howard. *Changing Lenses: A New Focus for Crime and Justice.* Scottdale, Pa.: Herald Press, 1990, 1995.

General Index

(*On Bible terms and books, see also* Scripture Index.)

Scripture Index

The Author

Gardner C. Hanks was born in Chicago in 1947. He was brought up in Michigan and has lived in Illinois, Wyoming, New York, Florida, Iowa, and Minnesota. Currently he resides in Boise, Idaho, with his wife, Martha Sue, and two daughters, Karin and Kathryn. He is an active member of the Hyde Park Mennonite Fellowship in Boise.

Hanks has master's degrees in library science from the State University of New York at Albany and in adult education from Florida State University. He has worked in a number of public library systems and is currently the Continuing Education Consultant at the Idaho State Library. In 2001 the Idaho Library Association named him Idaho Librarian of the Year.

Gardner Hanks is the author of *Against the Death Penalty: Christian and Secular Arguments Against Capital Punishment* (Herald Press, 1997). He is the Amnesty International State Death Penalty Action Coordinator for Idaho, and one of the founding members of Idahoans for Alternatives to the Death Penalty. Hanks has served as spiritual adviser for two death-row inmates in Idaho. For his work against the death penalty, the Pacific Northwest Mennonite Conference gave him a Peace Cup.